M000238547

Licensed to Guide

Licensed to Guide

Susie Cazenove

First published in 2005 by Jacana Media (Pty) Ltd.
5 St Peter Road
Bellevue 2198
Johannesburg
South Africa

Hardback edition ISBN 1-77009-143-2
Softback edition ISBN 1-77009-055-X

Cover design by Triple M
Set in Hiroshige 10/17.5
Printed by Fishwicks

See a complete list of Jacana titles at www.jacana.co.za

To Dick
and my children
Heather, Jessica, Dominic and Olivia

CONTENTS

Introduction 3

The world of safari travel 4

The modern guide 4

A basement in Mayfair 5

Animal intelligence 7

Walking on the wild side 11

The difference they make 16

Sweet sixteen 16

Changing direction 17

South Africa 19

Early days in the Sabi Sands –
  getting started at Londolozi 19

Testing and training 24

Parties and high spirits 26

Lex Hes 29

Mike Myers 33

Map Ives 39

Botswana 47

Ralph Bousfield 50

Michael Lorentz 64

  Elephant-back safaris 69

  Our place on the planet 74

The story of Mothupi, a Bayei guide 76

Zambia and Zimbabwe 81

Garth Thompson 84

  Survival courses 91

  Garth in 'Indiana Jones' mode –
    his personal nightmare 95

Benson Siyawareva 100

Ivan Carter 108

  A heartbreaking episode 113

Robin Pope 116

  Along came Jo 123

  The love match 125

North Luangwa and the Zambezi Valley 127

Rod Tether 128

Grant Cummings 133

East Africa 135

A safari to Soit Orgoss in northern Tanzania . . . 142

Nigel Perks 150

  Mary Leakey and the footprints 157

  Different behaviour 160

Ron Beaton 166

Koyaki Guide School 177

Saigilu ole Looseyia (Jackson) 178

Calvin Cottar 186

  The wounded buffalo 191

  Peter Beard and the elephant drama 192

  Enter Louise 194

  Calvin's plans for the future 196

Namibia 198

Bertus and André Schoeman 199

Into the future 216

  Hope and opportunity 216

  The Buffalo-thorn 217

  What are the answers? 218

  Hand in hand 220

  Partnerships 221

  Transfrontier or Peace Parks 222

Onx and Howard 223

  Onkgaotse Manga (Onx) 223

  Howard Saunders 225

Acknowledgements 228

Canary
Islands

Cape
Verde

TUNISIA
MOROCCO
ALGERIA
LIBYA
EGYPT
MAURITANIA
MALI
NIGER
CHAD
SUDAN
ERITREA
SENEGAL
GAMBIA
DJIBOUTI
GUINEA-
BISSAU
GUINEA
BURKINA
BENIN
NIGERIA
ETHIOPIA
SIERRA
LEONE
CÔTE
D'IVOIRE
GHANA
LIBERIA
TOGO
CAMEROON
CENTRAL AFRICAN
REPUBLIC
SOMALIA
EQUATORIAL
GUINEA
GABON
CONGO
UGANDA
KENYA
DEMOCRATIC
REPUBLIC
OF THE
CONGO
RWANDA
BURUNDI
Pemba
Zanzibar
TANZANIA
Comoros
ANGOLA
MALAWI
ZAMBIA
MOÇAMBIQUE
MADAGASCAR
ZIMBABWE
NAMIBIA
BOTSWANA
SWAZILAND
SOUTH
AFRICA
LESOTHO

2

INTRODUCTION

When I left Cazenove and Loyd, the travel company that
Henrietta Loyd and I had set up to specialise in African holidays,
I realised there was one crucial ingredient to any trip
I had ever sent anyone on – the guide. He made both the safari
and its African backdrop unforgettable.

I have drawn on my own deep passion for Africa and personal observations, having travelled extensively throughout East and southern Africa during my career as a tour operator. There are many excellent professional guides with impeccable reputations, some of whom I have met but unfortunately never travelled with. My criterion for the guides I have chosen to profile is that I have been on safari with them.

Since I have enjoyed their humour and their stories, I should like to share some of the best with you, including their own tales of adventure and hardship (and sometimes a dash of love). They have helped me understand their happiness in the choices they've made, the lives they've led, their concerns, hopes and plans for the future. Wherever possible I have authenticated the family legends concerning them.

Although some of them guide all over Africa (and in some cases other parts of the world) I have divided them into their original regions, where, in most cases, their spiritual selves reside. For the reader who may never have experienced the terrain they worked in, the heat, the luxuriance or barrenness of the landscape, a small description of each area is included.

I cannot tell their stories without including some of my own, since they are so closely linked to the guide I was with at the time.

My daughter, the artist Jessica Hoffman, has drawn magnificent charcoal portraits of the twelve guides profiled, in each case capturing their personalities. The rest of the book is illustrated, with one or two exceptions, with my own photographs.

Journeys through Africa with specialist guides really can have
a significant impact on those that take them. Life is never quite the same again;
you have joined an exclusive club whose members alone truly understand
how intense and moving the African experience can be.

THE MODERN GUIDE

It's surprising how many superb safari guides there are, given the range of attributes a guide must possess. He must have detailed knowledge of the habitats, all the animals and birds and their behaviour, but must also be an excellent host, organiser, mechanic, good shot, conversationalist, paramedic and mind-reader. He must, above all, remain enthusiastic and alert all day long. I say 'he' because safari guides are mostly men. There are some women who take to the life, but by and large it is a male-dominated society. Politically incorrect it may be, but most of us do take comfort from the masculine strength of our guides.

A safari guide's guests are completely dependent on him when out in the bush – not an easy situation for people used to being in control. A boss may be used to being obeyed in his office, but he cannot be in control when walking in lion-infested terrain; he has to acknowledge the guide as his superior.

Women often find guides irresistible, which is not really surprising. When people are catapulted out of their familiar lives into an unexpectedly stimulating setting, where the earthy smells, glittering stars and most of all the underlying edge of fear creates a *frisson* of

excitement that many may not have felt for years, a strong, confident, attentive man with a sense of humour can be very appealing! This 'khaki fever', as it is known, must be handled with great discretion and tact.

Once I became involved in the safari travel business and travelled more extensively, I realised the impact of the safari guides on visitors. Good guides make the experience exceptional, not just because they open your eyes to the wildlife around you, but because they have come to terms with their own strengths and weaknesses. A mediocre guide cannot ruin the experience, because no

one can take away the beauty of the surroundings and the excitement of seeing the animals close-to in their own environment, but a good one raises the experience to another level.

A BASEMENT IN MAYFAIR

Although I now live in England I had the good fortune to have been born and raised in Africa, where my life was filled with sunshine, space and freedom. My father had a farm in the Magaliesberg, eighty kilometres from Johannesburg, where he bred trout and pedigree Ayrshire cattle. The Hartley family, who ran a rose farm nearby, were particular friends of my father and I got to know David, the eldest son, quite well. Our ways parted, but we met up again years later through mutual friends. I then discovered that he and his wife Tessa owned a lodge named Xugana in the Okavango Delta and a travel company called Okavango Explorations. In 1987, they invited me to spend a few days with them in Botswana at a time when they were contemplating taking over Tsaro, a land-based lodge that perfectly complemented the water-based Xugana.

The visit was a great success, and I found the beauty and excitement of this watery paradise completely captivating. On our last evening we were sitting under the trees at Tsaro Lodge, with the full moon shining on a hippo grazing nearby, when my thoughts suddenly crystallised and turning to David I said, "I can sell this for you in England; I know I can. I really want other people to come and experience this for themselves." Six months later Okavango Explorations (UK) opened in a basement just off Berkeley Square.

Although a complete greenhorn in the travel industry, I knew that the most important thing was to ensure that everyone we sent to Africa would see the magic and love it as I did. Of course I had to learn more about Botswana, so I revisited the two camps I had already stayed at – Tsaro, on the Khwai River in a dry area of the Moremi National Park, where game drives were taken; and Xugana, on a lagoon in the heart of the Delta, offering water activities. Map Ives, the resident guide at Tsaro, gave me my first encounter with an experienced top guide. His knowledge and enthusiasm was spellbinding and certainly set a very high standard for me to bear in mind when planning safaris and choosing guides for our clients.

Our trip ended in northern Chobe, at Chilwero Camp, then owned by Brian and Jan Graham. Here I met Henrietta Loyd whom I had spoken to in England before she left to spend six months working at Chilwero. She had spent much of her early youth running camps and lodges in Botswana and South Africa and wanted to get into the travel business in England. Brian and Jan were close friends of hers, and they were on hand with generous help and support when she and I later started our own company. Meanwhile, we were very fortunate to have her join us at Okavango Explorations in London before the end of our first year. We both enjoyed the travel business, having great fun learning how it all worked, making friends and exploring new places.

After four years with Okavango Explorations (renamed Hartley's Safaris) and craving independence, we left to start our own company, Cazenove and Loyd Safaris, which opened in January 1993.

One of the most important aspects of tour operators' lives is to research and understand the destinations to

On safari in Namibia

which they send their clients. Known as 'fam trips' or 'educationals' they can be gruelling undertakings: spending every night in a different bed; snatching time to write copious notes; and making sure films are labelled correctly – easy to confuse one bedroom with another in hindsight. Other trips were arranged to give plenty of time to understand and appreciate the various destinations. Either way they were great fun and opened many doors to interesting experiences and people.

Henrietta and I once went to Namibia together, taking nineteen days to cover about half the country. We learned a great deal about travel and thoroughly enjoyed every minute of the trip, which included the Skeleton Coast with the Schoeman family, with whom I was to do three more fly-in safaris. Our final stop was a small guest farm called Okonjima where we arrived on a most auspicious day – that of Nelson Mandela's release from prison. The generator was turned on during the morning specially for the television coverage of this great event, and Hen and I will never forget sitting with the family in their darkened living room watching those historic moments with two cheetahs and Elvis, a large male baboon.

Okonjima is now an award-winning lodge, famous for its cheetah and leopard rescue programme called Africat, run by Lise and Wayne Hanssen, but then it was still a cattle ranch with the animal-rescue operation in its infancy. The family, obviously natural animal rescuers, had cheetahs, warthogs and a baboon as pets. Elvis, who ate porridge with us at breakfast – admittedly on the floor rather than the table – and was obviously part of the family, enchanted us. In the late afternoon we took a walk along a winding path up the kopje (a rocky hill) near the house, learning about the medicinal plants the Bushmen used and how they made their snares and traps. Elvis came along too, always walking directly behind Wayne, his alpha male, and sitting quietly when Wayne stopped to talk to us. As inferior females we were not allowed pass him or look him in the eye. Wayne had brought drinks in his backpack and we sat at the top of the kopje, sipping our sundowners and gazing over a thousand square miles of Africa bathed in the evening light. Elvis drank his Coca-Cola on a rock nearby and nonchalantly tossed the empty can back to Wayne!

As the years went by and I travelled more extensively, the impact of the safari guides on the visitors became very clear. Good guides make the experience exceptional, not just because they open your eyes to the wildlife around you, but because of all the little things they think of to make your safari that extra bit special.

A graphic example of this was in the Ngorongoro Crater, where our guide had spotted a wildebeest giving birth. We spent twenty-five minutes watching entranced as she kept standing up, then lying down to push again and again, until finally the little creature dropped to the ground. It was up in a moment, wet and wobbling and seven minutes later was running with its mother. No wonder it is the most successful antelope in Africa. They all give birth at the same time of year, assuring survival of the majority in spite of the attendant predators, which gorge themselves during the calving. While we had our binoculars trained on this little miracle with our guide Nigel Perks, no less than six vehicles stopped to see what we were looking at before immediately moving on. Perhaps the guides were looking only for lions and rhinos, or racing to be on time for lunch, but whatever it was their guests had no idea what they had missed.

Not until the late 1970s and early 1980s were guides trained specifically to look after photographic safari visitors. Up to then guides were mainly hunters – great shots and extremely charming company, but few of them knew a great deal about the bush and relied mostly on their local trackers to find the animals. Gradually, realisation dawned that the guides had to know more about the world around them. Norman Carr, a legendary safari guide in Zambia, started making all his trainee guides in the early 1970s learn the names of the birds. Up to then, according to Robin Pope, the best-known guide in Zambia today, visitors generally referred to all the birds as either 'turkey buzzards or blue jays'!

In 1969, when John and David Varty inherited Londolozi, their father's farm that borders the Kruger National Park in South Africa, the general public was not deeply interested in conservation and most had never heard of ecology. The Varty brothers were already passionate about conserving their land and they soon realised that they needed to train guides to inform and entertain their guests at their budding safari lodge. This was one of the first formal training courses in this field and it did not take long for their vision to be emulated and expanded around Africa. The travelling public's thirst for knowledge was stimulated by marvellous wildlife films and books, creating a demand for interesting well-informed guides when on safari

ANIMAL INTELLIGENCE

On my first 'educational' through Botswana I visited Lloyd's Camp in Savuti. Lloyd Wilmot had a reputation for being fearless, and was known to have plucked hairs from elephants' tails. At his camp on the dried-up Savuti Channel he had put in a waterhole and placed a concrete bunker next to it with access from the riverbank above. In the dry season elephants spent hours drinking at this waterhole and people could sit inside watching them from inches away. On that first visit I sat entranced with my head pushed against one of the openings watching a

Elephant babies protected by the adults

group of old bulls drinking and jostling for position. Suddenly I felt a gentle touch on my arm as if a feather was floating down on it. I turned and there was an elephant's trunk coming through the adjacent opening inspecting me. They were obviously just as curious about us as we were of them.

On a very early visit to Zimbabwe I had my first sense of the depth of feeling experienced by elephants. With Chris van Wyk I observed a mother elephant mourning the death of her newborn baby. Chris, a tall lean man with a gentle manner and bright blue eyes, has now left the safari business but once owned a delightful bush camp called Nemba in the Linkwasha area of Hwange. He was one of the earliest guides to take guests on bush walks, but the evening I arrived we drove to the sad little

scene that was taking place not far from camp. The dead baby lay on a patch of grass, the grieving mother, who had long since been left behind by the herd, had her two older offspring nearby offering consolation. She paced back and forth, drooping in a melancholy manner as she nudged the lifeless little body. Chris had watched her for two days; on this the third and final day she would leave as thirst got the better of her and life had to go on. However, her genuine grief was very apparent.

I was astounded to learn, from Richard Leakey's book *Wildlife Wars*, that he did not know about elephant families, their consciences and their ability to communicate, until Joyce Poole introduced him to the herds that she and Cynthia Moss were studying in Amboseli in 1990. Although, as head of Kenya Wildlife Service working tirelessly with terrific results to save them from poaching, he was nevertheless bowled over by the revelation that they were creatures of high intelligence and family loyalties. I thought that everyone living and working in the bush knew this, but in reality it is a recent discovery, which has come about because people are now studying animal intelligence and communication. Much of this understanding has come from safari guides, who spend their lives observing animal habits.

Many books have been written about elephants, perhaps the most fascinating of all creatures: the more you are with them, the more you want to be with them. Their family unit is extremely close-knit; they find it hard to survive without it and will form one even in unnatural circumstances, for example at Abu's Camp in Botswana, where a disparate group of elephants brought together by Randall Moore has created a strong family bond. This is a most unusual group, because full-grown bulls live together with the cows and young. In the wild, young bull elephants are expelled from the herd once they reach maturity and form their own bachelor groups, only venturing into a breeding herd when a cow is in oestrus. Randall's elephants are a mixed bag of adults rescued from zoos, babies from culls in the Kruger National Park, problem elephants from other parks, the occasional lost wild baby and now two babies, sired by wild elephants, born to one of the females.

When I first visited these elephants I was overcome with awe (a feeling that never goes away). To touch them, walk with them, ride them and discover their personalities is a tremendous privilege. My most vivid

My moment on Abu

memory is of the first time I watched them communicate with one another. It was on a still, perfect Okavango morning that we set off to ride through the Delta. Miss B, about two years old, was the youngest elephant at that time and had bonded firmly with Bibi, an adult female recently arrived from a Sri Lankan zoo. It had been decided that Bibi, still settling in, was not to come out on the walk that morning. And Miss B was torn with indecision – should she come or should she stay? As we set off across the water I could see her darting in and out of the bushes, watching us and going back to her adopted mother, not knowing what she wanted to do. Finally the morning's excursion won and she set off on her own to join us. At first she couldn't see us or smell us and walked in a large arc through the water, her little trunk up, trying to work out which way the herd had gone. Suddenly she located us and ran through the water trumpeting, the other young elephants became very excited and ran towards her. An ecstatic noisy meeting took place; they splashed, trumpeted and generally frolicked in the shallow water. In the middle of all this confusion there came a loud low rumble from Benny, one of the adult bulls. Immediately the young ones stopped what they were doing and got into line, walking quietly and sedately with the rest of the herd. I was astounded, Michael Lorentz, an extremely perceptive guide who was leading this safari, told me later that this behaviour was quite normal; Benny had had enough of this raucous behaviour and made them stop it at once.

The lead elephant Abu was a tremendous character and film actor of note, sadly no longer living, and deeply mourned by all who knew him. Because of his gentle nature I was exceptionally honoured to have been able to sit up behind his head. He knelt, I stood on his front

knee and was given a leg up to straddle his massive neck. Once he had risen to his feet he stood still as my bare legs slipped over his neck and his ears came back gently holding them in place. The crook of his ears was soft and warm, the texture of velvet. The sheer joy I felt that afternoon will stay with me always.

Michael Lorentz worked with these elephants for nine years and they clearly respected him and listened when he spoke. His communication with and great love for them was most apparent.

WALKING ON THE WILD SIDE

A guide once said to me, "Looking at animals and the landscape from a vehicle is like seeing the movie; walking in the bush is like reading the book." In fact it's more like being in the book!

There is nothing on earth quite like the adrenaline rush of tracking a lion or walking up to an elephant

– not easy, as wild animals are generally very nervous around humans and will disappear long before you know they are there. It takes great skill on the part of the guide to get you anywhere near them.

Most guides prefer to walk with a maximum of six people; more than that is unwieldy and difficult to control. He will start with a talk on how you should behave – keep quiet, stick together close behind him and stand dead still if charged by a lion! The guide will usually choose an open space, noting the layout of the bush he is walking through. Buffalo often hide in thick bush and can be very dangerous if startled. A good guide will walk you through the bush listening for the sounds

that tell the story: the baboons' special bark when they spot a predator, a guinea fowl warning that might only be a snake but could be a leopard, although they are unlikely to be seen because of their extreme shyness. It is best to be downwind in order to get close, but when walking up to bull elephants it is preferable to be upwind, so that they know you are there. Ivan Carter describes this succinctly a little later on.

Being on foot in the bush offers so much sensual and tactile interaction that it becomes much more than just finding animals, in itself quite a challenge – one seldom gets very close because of their fear of people. What makes the experience are the countless subtle aromas; wild thyme, dry grasses, wild gardenias, the whiff of elephants or buffalo and many more smells that you long to identify. The tracks in the sand tell their own stories – a lion walked here in the night, a snake crossed there, something was dragged for a few yards along a dusty track, the delicate tracery made by porcupine quills is covered by the perfect little prints of an African wild cat – all making you aware of what a busy place this was before you came along! Guides with a hunting background are often the most confident with this because of the many hours spent tracking animals with their hunting clients. That said, many guides who have never hunted professionally have a wonderfully developed sixth sense when walking in the bush.

Matusadona National Park bordering Kariba Dam in Zimbabwe is an excellent walking area, perfect for tracking lion or black rhinoceros, the latter recently reintroduced to the park after years of devastating poaching. The 15 000-square-kilometre park was stocked mainly with the animals that were rescued during 'Operation Noah' in the early 1960s when this section of the Zambezi Valley was filling with water to form the Kariba Dam. In a race against the clock, stranded animals were plucked off trees and islands in an operation organised by Rupert Fothergill in a worldwide blaze of publicity. The land slopes down from the top of the escarpment to a low-lying area along the lakeshore. This area is heavily wooded with mopane trees giving cool shaded areas for walking; their distinctive butterfly-wing-shaped leaves are a favoured food for elephants. It is over forty years since the lake was created and the skeletal remains of drowned forests still protrude like eerie spectres from the dark depths of the lake near the shore, perfect perches for abundant varieties of water birds.

It is here in Matusadona with John Dabbs, now retired from guiding, that I first tracked a lion on foot. Early one morning we spotted fresh lion spoor (footprints) visible

In the Matusadona with John Dabbs

in the mud on the edge of a little inlet on the lake. A big male lion had been drinking not long before we arrived and we set off to track him through the bush. It was a dry October day and his spoor was clearly seen in the sand.

After a while we heard angry scrapping noises coming from a patch of dense undergrowth. Lions on a kill, snarling and growling at one another as each tried to get the choice bits! We stood quietly for a while but they got a whiff of us. There were three lionesses, not our lion, their yellow backs slipping through the dry grass, lit by sunlight as they streaked away from us a fast as possible. We peaked under the tree, a half-eaten impala carcass lay there, which must have been killed moments before.

Once again we picked up our lion spoor and walked on, zigzagging, losing then finding the tracks, when John suddenly saw a movement in front of us and dropped down low to the ground, telling me to do the same and remain behind him. We inched forward on our bottoms across the dry sandy bed of a stream. Waiting and looking. Nothing. Maybe he had moved on. We stood up in order to get a better view and at that moment the lion jumped out from behind a large fallen tree trunk and gave a spine-chilling roar. My heart stopped. I have walked many times in the bush and listened to all the instructions about standing stock still, but on this occasion without realising what I was doing I took about ten steps backwards, very quickly. John did not move. The lion stared at us for a few moments, flicked his tail and turned to walk off. We could breathe again. Moving a few paces we saw that he had walked about twenty yards and was sitting down under a tree to watch what we would do next.

"Lets go now," said John. "He is telling us that enough is enough and that this is all he is going to tolerate." Who was I to argue?

Approaching an elephant on foot is possible only with someone who truly understands them. Garth Thompson, Ivan Carter, John Stevens, Michael Lorentz and Calvin Cottar have a particularly special relationship with elephants. These men take great pleasure in walking up to them and one feels overwhelmingly excited but absolutely safe and protected in their company. Quite unlike the feeling I once had when walking alone to my tent in Botswana I found an enormous elephant standing right in the middle of my path looking at me. This time all 5'2 of me froze. My heart was pounding so hard I was sure he could hear it. This was it! However, he just looked at me for a while then turned and nonchalantly went off about his business. I felt so relieved and rather foolish for having been so flustered.

It takes a certain cockiness and self-assurance to walk up to wild elephants. Mana Pools has plenty of serene old elephant bulls that stroll through this small paradise, feeding on acacia pods, water hyacinths and mopane trees. They know the territory and feel secure. However they are still wild and caution is always the key word. Garth, John and Ivan are past masters at interacting with elephants in this park. I asked Ivan Carter to describe to me how he would approach an elephant without ending up between its toes!

"Elephants have the most amazing body language, a lot of it is quite subtle, but then, like humans, a lot of it is very obvious and vigorous. I think that the most important tones are the subtle ones, a slight lift of the head, a slight stiffness in the tail, a twitch of the tip of the trunk etc, all show that he knows you are there. Sometimes all you notice is that he stopped swinging his tail.

"You notice I always say 'he', I would not walk up to cows and babies as they are far less predictable and unless you are waiting at a waterhole or near a path, I would not by choice approach them on foot. What I do is approach the guy from two or three hundred yards with the wind straight from us to him. That is a crucial

Ivan and friend in Mana Pools National Park

point as I want to see his reaction as he gets our scent ... often as the scent gets to him his posture will change slightly and then he will relax, move on, get wary etc; this will indicate whether I can go closer or not. What I want to see is a brief moment where the tip of his trunk gets pointed to me, and then he continues like we aren't there ... that's an ideal guy to approach. Then, without hiding in the least, I try and walk slowly in towards him, as I get closer I talk, either to him or to my guests. I think that the steadiness in our voices lets them know we are there and that we are confident and that is what keeps them calm. Once I am within a hundred yards I like to try and see where he is going and position myself in his path so that it is he who chooses how close he wants to come; that way it will be of the minimum disturbance to him. Sometimes a few of the bulls I know well will actually veer off towards us and spend time feeding within a few feet of us. It's the most wonderful feeling, a feeling of great privilege and a feeling of being humbled by the great beast.

"In Mana Pools the acacia pods make up a huge portion of their daily intake at certain times of the year. I like to find a particularly laden tree and just sit under it and wait for them to come and often they end up picking up the pods literally within a couple of feet of us. It's the highlight of a day in the bush."

Having walked up to elephants with Ivan I understand exactly how he feels. As he says:

"It is very important, and not only with elephant, to be sure that you are arriving and leaving with the least impact. If you leave him stressed and ruffled out of shape, you have failed in your approach. If you leave quietly and look back to see him still doing what he was doing before you arrived, then you have achieved your objective."

People who go in for this lifestyle start with a love of the bush; they study from childhood and gain such tremendous insight into animal behaviour that it becomes only natural that they should share it with others. A guide has to have a natural rapport with people and an easy temperament otherwise he will fail very quickly. Most of them have their pet subjects – many are great ornithologists, for example – and have such a huge knowledge in that one subject as to bring people to them from all over the world. David Rattray, for example, with his knowledge of South African history, takes tourism to another plane by giving his guests at his lodge in KwaZulu-Natal a deeply emotional experience when relating the stories of the Anglo-Zulu battles that took place at Isandlwana and Rorke's Drift. The Schoeman brothers offer an equally emotional experience, only this time it concerns geology, desert life and the formation of the earth on their Skeleton Coast safaris in Namibia. Imagine the thrill of being on a horse and galloping with wild animals; it could be across a plain with giraffe or wildebeest when riding with Tristan Voorspuy across the Masai Mara. Or perhaps through the water with leaping lechwe in the wetlands of the Okavango Delta riding with PJ and Barney Besterlink or Sarah-Jane Gullick. You may on the other hand choose to canter across the roof of the world with David Foot on the Nyika plateau in Malawi. There seems to be something special for everyone, one way or another.

The specialist guides are one of the greatest drawcards of Africa, their company is congenial, I have never known the conversation to lag, laughter is paramount and the joy of being in such company and in the bush is supremely intoxicating. It is no wonder people return again and again for what was originally 'a once-in-a-lifetime holiday'.

THE DIFFERENCE THEY MAKE

Many friends and clients have come back from their safaris spilling over with enthusiasm for the things they have learned and seen and in particular the little extra-special moments created by their guide.

For many years a delightful couple called John and Jan travelled twice a year through us to Africa. They had met one another when Jan (a widow) consulted her bank manager John (a widower himself), after which he invited her to dinner. Romance blossomed and they married with the blessing of all their grown-up children and proceeded to have the time of their lives visiting Africa as frequently as they could. Every spring and every autumn we would plan new delights for them until one autumn they had to cancel the trip because John had become ill. The following summer he died and soon after the funeral Jan started to plan an October trip. I sensed correctly during our initial conversation that she wanted to take his ashes to Africa. She went on this pilgrimage alone and everywhere she was met with kindness and solicitude. Her final stop was Nxamaseri, a delightful little lodge set among trees and reeds on the Okavango River in the Pan Handle where it winds its way down from Angola to the Delta. Early on a perfectly still sunny morning she set off with her guide in a small boat, each knowing this was the moment. The boat slid gently through the water until they came upon a long white sandbank jutting out from the papyrus. African skimmers were darting and swooping over the water, a Fish eagle called in the distance as the papyrus rustled in a sudden breeze.

"I think we have found a really good spot don't you?" asked the guide. Jan agreed and he moved into the back of the boat leaving her on her own to perform her task. The tranquillity was perfect – a little prayer and John's ashes were whisked away on a puff of air, dispersing in the sunlight and across the water he had so loved. Jan sat motionless, unable to stop the tears rolling down her cheeks – the guide silently moved forward and put his arms around her and held her tight. Jan had given John his final peace in Africa.

SWEET SIXTEEN

Together with another family and their two children, we took a family safari in Botswana with David Dugmore, one of three young men who were running their own safari business, called Kalahari Kavango. David was filled with energy and enthusiasm and gave us a marvellous safari, however, he stopped guiding to make wildlife films, one of which (on Abu's Camp) recently appeared on the Discovery Channel. David now runs his own camp on the Boteti River, his brother Roger still takes mobile safaris in Botswana and the third partner, Ralph Bousfield, operates mainly in the Makgadikgadi and is featured in this book.

On our safari with David, our daughter Olivia turned sixteen in the Okavango Delta, a memorable place for a birthday in anyone's book. During dinner in the mess tent the conversation was rattling along at such a great pace that no one had noticed that David had disappeared from the table, until someone dashed in telling us to hurry, hurry, come and see! We all thought it must be the leopard whose tracks we had seen in the camp each morning. But not at all; we were taken down to the water's edge where we stood on a sandy bank watching in amazement as out on the dark water a *mokoro** lit by lanterns, was being poled gently towards the bank by David. Sitting in the boat were the two female members of his camp staff singing a haunting melody, which was then taken up by all the male staff standing on the bank. This lyrical harmony soared across the still night air as the boat gently skimmed towards us to deliver a birthday cake to Olivia. It was an unforgettable moment of goose bumps and tears and was the result of perfect planning by a thoughtful guide. The cake turned out to be a delicious sponge not the usual iced elephant turd often served up on adult birthdays!

CHANGING DIRECTION

Africa is so well known for the vastness and infinity of her landscapes, that I feel it is often this rather than the animals that brings people back again and again. To stand on a rise and see miles and miles of woodland, purple hills, desert, or towering mountains, with no more than a track that is man-made, is a breath-taking experience. Once the first excitement of seeing animals in the wild has subsided, people realise there is so much more to enjoy. The culture, the history, the cradle of both animal and geological life, is of enormous interest. Good guides help you understand Africa in its many and varied facets.

Sometimes the influence of the guide can be a life-changing experience. An example is a family with three teenage children who did a canoeing trip on the Zambezi River with Garth Thompson. Their journey was a tremendous contrast to the regulated lives that they led at school and at home in Bedfordshire. Their adventure, which provided many an adrenaline rush walking up to large bull elephants or skirting around hippo pods in canoes, and their animated discussions around the campfire with Garth altered all their previously held ideas and aspirations. After university their eldest son gave two years of his life to a charity clearing landmines. Their daughter studied travel and tourism at university, determined to get into the travel industry. Finally the youngest son, who was only twelve at the time, though not as outwardly moved as his siblings, has nevertheless been involved in Operation Raleigh and has developed a keen interest in the third world.

Journeys through Africa with specialist guides really can have a significant impact on those that take them. Life is never quite the same again; you have joined an exclusive club whose members alone truly understand how intense and moving the African experience can be.

These exciting experiences really started with the opening up of tourism in Africa in the 1970s. Hunting was going out of fashion and photographic safaris were coming into fashion in a big way. Far more people were becoming interested in wildlife and the bush. Expert guides grew out of a need to satisfy a public hunger for adventure, fun and knowledge on their safari holidays.

Chobe Game Lodge in the north-east corner of Botswana, built in 1972, a hotel rather than a bush lodge, became famous for hosting the wedding of Elizabeth Taylor and Richard Burton. This put Botswana on the map. Hunting was banned in Kenya in 1977 and while some of the hunters looked for greener pastures, others stayed at home arranging photographic safaris.

---

* *mokoro* (*pl mekoro*): a canoe made from a hollowed-out tree-trunk.

People were becoming more affluent and adventurous, and travel was becoming much easier. A great amount of attention started to turn to Africa. The die was cast, hunting was diminishing, and with easier access to Africa, photographic safaris were about to explode into the travel world.

SOUTH AFRICA

The traditional game-viewing area of South Africa is Mpumulanga
– the place where the sun rises. In the north-east corner of the country the
world-famous Kruger National Park stretches from the Zimbabwe border
nearly five hundred kilometres south to the Crocodile River,
and is approximately one hundred and sixty kilometres wide.

In the north-east corner of South Africa the world-famous Kruger National Park stretches from the Zimbabwe border nearly five hundred kilometres south to the Crocodile River, and is approximately one hundred and sixty kilometres wide. President Paul Kruger set land aside for a park in 1898 when he realised how quickly the wildlife population was diminishing. Wild animals had roamed all over South Africa in vast herds, from the Cape to the Indian Ocean. The speed at which they were being shot and killed appalled the president: his was an act of conservancy without precedence at that time.

The eastern side of the Kruger National Park borders Mozambique and on the west, farms, mines, villages and a series of private game reserves originally set up as hunting blocks, straddle the length of the park. The best known is the Sabi Sands Game Reserve, which had been divided up into private farms for many years for cattle ranching until halted by a rinderpest epidemic after which many owners turned to hunting. In 1962, the Sabi Sands Game Reserve was officially recognised as a game reserve and hunting was banned.

EARLY DAYS IN THE SABI SANDS – GETTING STARTED AT LONDOLOZI

Londolozi and Mala Mala were two of the original farms in the Sabi Sands, with Mala Mala, belonging to the Campbells, the first to open its doors to paying photographic safari guests, followed by the Vartys' farm Sparta (later Londolozi). It was the dawn of a new era. In time other private farms in the reserve became commercial safari enterprises and although all of them gave their guests an excellent experience and had good guides, it was Londolozi that gained the reputation for producing exceptional guides.

Mala Mala had been the private hunting ground of the legendary Wac Campbell, whose hunting guests included royalty, ambassadors and cabinet ministers. A descendant of the 1850 Byrne settlers, he had a powerful allegiance to the Crown. A short-wave wireless in the camp was able to pick up the BBC World Service and all guests had to sit quietly listening to the evening news, after which everyone was required to stand to attention while the Union Jack was lowered with due ceremony.

This included many visiting National Party MPs, who were not exactly pro-British!

An honorary Zulu chief, Wac was much respected by his 'subjects', who would fall to their knees when speaking to him and never turned their backs on him. When he lay ill and dying at his home in Durban two Zulu warriors appeared one day. They did not ask permission, nor did they speak to anyone, they simply stood tall and noble outside his bedroom door, being relieved by two others every eight hours until he died. More than 20 000 mourners attended his funeral. When his son Urban Campbell inherited Mala Mala he made a tentative start at bringing in paying guests, but in 1964 he sold the property to Mike Rattray, who turned it into the first really well-known safari lodge in South Africa.

When his neighbour Boyd Varty died in 1969 his sons were still in full-time education; John was at university and Dave was at school when they inherited Sparta. They had spent so much of their childhood there that their passionate commitment to the place was absolute. In spite of their youth, or maybe because of it, with time and plenty of lateral thinking they began to build a legend.

Over the past thirty years Dave and John have set a great example throughout southern and East Africa on protecting the precious few wilderness areas still remaining. When they inherited Londolozi, their first priority was the conservation of the environment. Pressure of farming and a series of bad droughts in the Eastern Transvaal (now Mpumalanga) had seriously altered the land since their grandfather had bought the farm in 1927. They were intensely concerned about reversing the damage that had been done, employing all manner of experts to help and advise. The ecologist Dr Ken Tinley was one of their major advisers, much of his

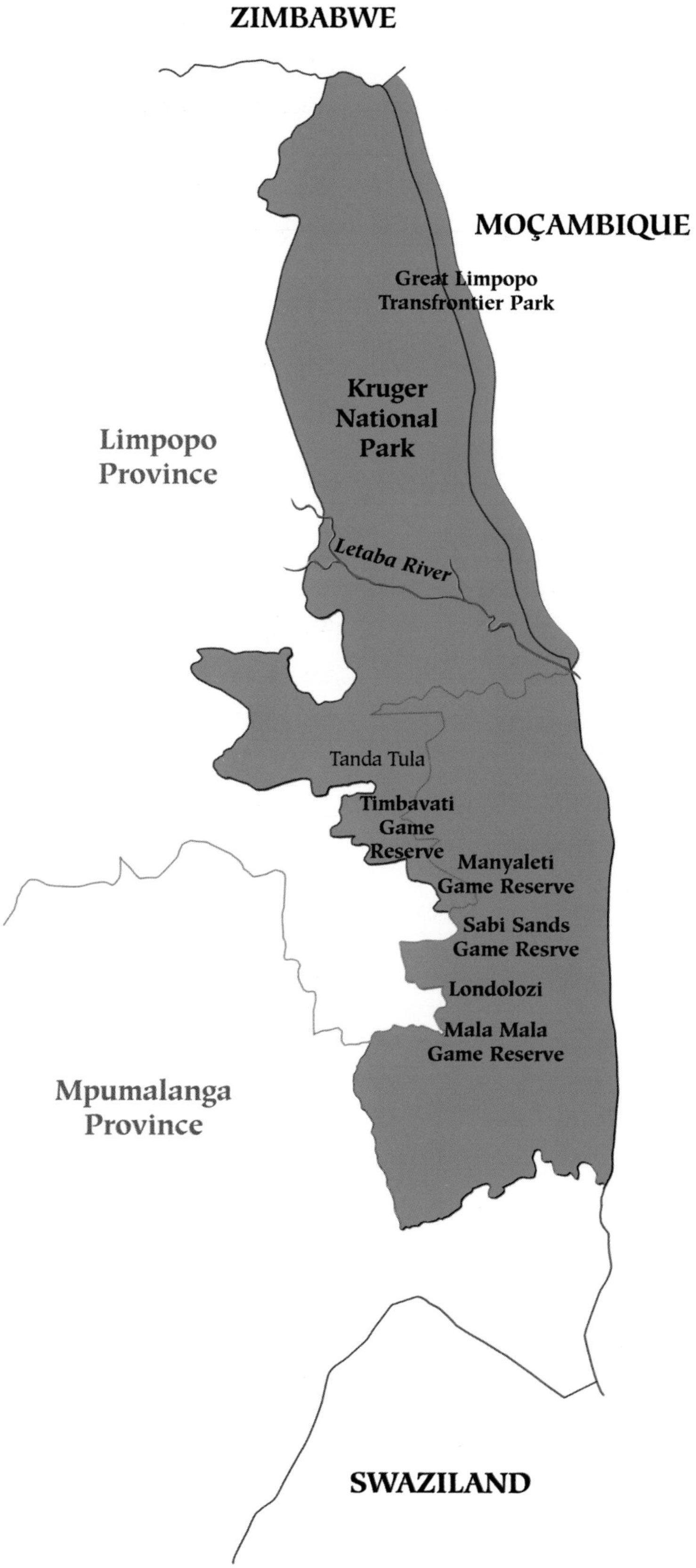

ZIMBABWE

MOÇAMBIQUE

Great Limpopo
Transfrontier Park

Kruger
National
Park

Limpopo
Province

Letaba River

Tanda Tula

Timbavati
Game
Reserve

Manyaleti
Game Reserve

Sabi Sands
Game Resrve

Londolozi

Mala Mala
Game Reserve

Mpumalanga
Province

SWAZILAND

work being aimed at repairing the land so badly damaged by cattle grazing.

Londolozi was quite primitive at first and they learned by trial and error the best way to operate. The camp was simple and a weekend in the bush had a real pioneering spirit to it. The guests were mostly the Varty's friends out for a good time. Dave and John were young and very energetic and their enthusiasm knew no bounds. They rattled their guests around in a couple of old vehicles held together with string and prayers. Dave would use one of the vehicles for the game drive, taking along a pretend radio (they had nothing as sophisticated as real two-way radios in those early days) and he meanwhile would set off on a drive knowing the vehicle would not last very long before breaking down. John would be waiting hidden along the chosen route with the spare vehicle. When the inevitable breakdown occurred Dave pretended to call John on the radio for help, pouring the drinks while 'waiting' for John to come to their aid. John, fully aware of what was happening, allowed a suitable interval before appearing, by which time they were all well into their second gin and tonic! As the popularity of Londolozi increased, John and Dave needed to spend more time running the business and decided to hire others to take the game drives and look after the guests.

They were one of the very first to initiate a guide-training programme back in the days when life was a lot more relaxed and carefree. I can only give a glimpse through the keyhole into the fun and games that went on during those early, happy-go-lucky years.

Lex Hes, a young man who was to play such a big part in the early days, arrived first. He was passionate about wildlife and photography and had badgered the Varty brothers into letting him stay and help out just for his keep. He had no role in the beginning other than counting birds and animals, but he was now roped into doing game drives while they advertised for another person to help.

In the 1970s and early 1980s Londolozi became known for its intensive guide training, many of its alumni becoming legendary characters, with legendary goings-on when they first started escorting in the bush. Clients and staff played and laughed together as one big carefree party. No one was ever harmed or injured, perhaps surprisingly, and the guides became much sought after in later years by the new safari businesses burgeoning all over southern Africa.

Mike Myers, a Zimbabwean, was in Johannesburg at this time, having left Witwatersrand University. He had just obtained his pilot's licence, but, owing to the fuel crisis and not speaking Afrikaans, was having difficulty finding a flying job. In desperation he turned to the classified columns for something – anything – to keep body and soul together, and replied to an advertisement for a Trails Officer to lead wilderness trails. The interview took place at the home of Shan Watson, then girlfriend and later wife of Dave Varty. Mike, dressed in his only smart clothes – a Wits rugby blazer and tie – walked in to meet John who was lounging around in cut-off blue jeans and no shirt. John saw a solidly built, good-looking young man with a sense of humour, energy and enthusiasm – qualities of paramount importance for the job on offer – and had the good judgement to hire Mike immediately.

John and Dave's Johannesburg friends continued to spread the word that it was the best party in South Africa. Soon many of them were flocking down to the Sabi Sands Game Reserve for their weekend's entertainment at Londolozi. Money was always in short

Mike Myers and Tutan Sithole

supply; during the week when there were no guests the staff lived on impala meat and maize meal. Their girlfriends working at Mala Mala supplemented this diet by bringing extra goodies to their weekly bush parties

Once Mike arrived both he and Lex took over the guiding, along with André Goosen, the next to join. The group consisted of the three guides, John and Dave Varty the owner/managers, Dave's girlfriend Shan, who looked after the lodge, the catering and the bookings, and the hostess, an ethereal fine-arts student who floated around looking after the guests. There was also George and Diana, the two young cheetahs they were hand-rearing. One of the great strengths of the Londolozi team was the ability, nearly always, to pick the right person for the job.

Londolozi became increasingly popular, the vehicles were replaced and more staff and guides were employed to entertain and look after the guests. Yvonne and Pete Short came in: Pete to look after guest relations and the

wine cellar and Yvonne as the catering manager. On arrival she completely reorganised the kitchen, throwing out all the old pots and pans, buying new refrigerators and generally bringing the kitchen into the twentieth century, while Dave wailed that she would bankrupt him! She was a real live wire, a bundle of energy and laughter and her arrival must have been a huge asset. After four years of working there she gave birth to twins and, like all new mothers, was up and down during the night. Her windows faced straight onto the guides' sleeping quarters, which gave her a continuous view of their clandestine meetings. They always puzzled over how she knew so much. Soon after she arrived it was decided to improve the night watch; one old man asleep over his stick was no longer good enough. So two watchmen were employed to set up the lanterns along the paths and to take them away again when everyone had gone to sleep. They were given clipboards to report what had happened during the night. Instead of noting hyenas prowling around the kitchen, or elephants eating the shrubs, their reports went something like this: the lady in No 2 went into No 4 at midnight. No 3 joined them in No 4. When the gentleman in No 2 came out and asked me where his wife was, I said she was in No 3! And so it went on.

TESTING AND TRAINING

John and Dave by now had evolved an extremely intensive and arduous five-day selection test for prospective guides and there was no shortage of suitable candidates. Personality remained a top priority; they did not necessarily choose people with degrees and previous conservation experience. They knew that if they found the right qualities the rest could be taught.

Most of the testing was to see how the applicants stood up to pressure and to see if they were quick and alert. They were given Keith Coates Palgrave's *Trees of Southern Africa*, the definitive book on African trees, and told to spend the afternoon learning the trees, their names and uses. They were tested that evening. The same applied to birds: half a day with *Newman's Birds of Southern Africa* followed by a written test at lunch time. All this was done individually, not in a group.

They had to complete various tasks devised to test them on how well they would handle themselves in the bush, alone. They were given a rock and a simple hand-drawn map of the property showing the old railway line that ran through it, one building and the extensive system of *dongas* (eroded gullies). Without guns or radios and not knowing the land at all, each prospective guide was sent out walking, carrying only the rock and the map, having been told to find a certain tree and place the rock beside it. His second mission was to find a water pump and a campsite and then to document this by placing them on the map and describing what they looked like.

Another test of character was to send them out together to sleep in the bush; they were equipped with sleeping bags but no mosquito nets and again, no guns. The next morning they were told that they were going to have to walk to breakfast, but what they thought would be a stroll was in fact a couple of hours' route march. They were tired and hungry; some had blisters, so they took off their shoes and walked barefoot. It was a hot, strenuous hike and certainly gave an indication of their stamina and character. Another similar test was conducted early in their six-week guide-training course. The staff would arrange a party in the bush one night where they would ply the new guides with drink, and once drunk become very cosy and friendly, asking

questions to see what they thought of it all so far. The following morning, hung-over and hungry, they would be handed over to someone in a no-nonsense mood and taken on another fairly long walk, only to find at the end of it the staff sitting under a tree waiting for breakfast. The guides had to cook the breakfast and it soon became apparent that there were only just enough eggs and bacon for the staff. They were not allowed to touch any remaining food until everyone else was fed and the washing-up completed.

Tony Adams, who was at one time in charge of guide training, told me that these tests truly indicated the sort of men with whom they wanted to work. It wasn't imperative that they pass every test, but their reactions indicated the types that were best for the job. It was extremely important that they should remain calm and cheerful should they came across rude or difficult guests.

Once chosen, the guides were still on probation and had some tough tasks to perform. Each of them had to go out and shoot an impala and bring it back to camp –

Lex Hes and his pet parrot Spike

on foot. One man spent six days looking for his impala, going out every day. At last he found one on the farthest border of the farm, shot it and carried it back as instructed. About five hundred metres from the lodge someone drove past him and offered him a lift, which he took, but unfortunately he was seen by John Varty and sent right back out again to a point even further away than where he had shot the original impala, to shoot another. Jackie Evans, the second female guide to join Londolozi (Tony Adams's wife Dee was the first), took a compressed-air horn along on her impala hunt. After many hours of stalking she finally sighted a small herd across the dam, but at the same moment a lioness spotted the impala and came over to investigate Jackie's presence on her hunting patch. Jackie hastily climbed a tree frantically blowing her horn at the startled lioness, which bolted in horror. Of course, the impala bolted too!

Another guide went out early one morning to shoot his impala and was back by 8:30.

> Dave Varty saw him and said, "That was quick, did you get an impala?"
>
> "Yes," he said. "It's hanging in the tannery."
>
> "Let's go and have a look at it," said Dave. "Where did you shoot it?"
>
> "Well," he said, "I shot it in the neck, then gave it another shot in the backside, just to make sure it was dead."

Needless to say, he was out, both for lying and for shooting an animal in the backside. Had he shot it in the neck to start with he would not have shot it in the backside to make sure it was dead.

PARTIES AND HIGH SPIRITS

The motto was 'work hard, play hard', and they certainly lived up to it! The fun and games for both guides and guests were renowned and once the guests were in bed they continued for the staff, with midnight parties in the bush. There was always an excuse for a party: fancy-dress affairs to welcome a new member of staff, birthdays and, of course, New Year's Eve. However, if a guide was not spruced up and on duty for the 5:30 wake-up call he was fired, or if the keys to the gun-safe went missing, the last guide to have had them was fired on the spot.

On one occasion the twenty-first birthday of one of the staff was celebrated in the middle of the bush with a *Rocky Horror Picture Show* party. After saying goodnight to all the guests they spent an hour dressing up. The party was wild and wonderful and a great effort had gone into making the costumes. Most of the staff wore fishnet stockings and all had on masses of makeup, which the guides did not realise was quite difficult to remove. They trooped back in time for the 5:30 wake-up call frantically scrubbing their faces and trying their best to look alert and fresh in spite of traces of kohl and glitter. One of the first sightings that morning, much to the amusement of the guests, was a bra found hanging from a tree, and the next day Yvonne overheard one of the guests saying to another, "That guide we had was supposed to be such a big macho man, but I swear I saw fishnet tights sticking out from under his trousers every time his boot went on the clutch!"

Dinner in the *boma* (an outdoor area fenced in for protection) would often turn into an uproarious party. The cricketer David Gower was a very popular and frequent guest, and sometimes a full-scale game of cricket would be played with the guests during dinner, which always broke the ice. Another icebreaker was John Varty's guitar playing; as the guests tucked into their dessert he would reach for a guitar and walk around the boma asking each person to name a tune. John strummed enthisiastically and, knowing the words of the songs, he managed to get everyone singing and laughing. Mike Myers an excellent guitarist produced wonderful singing sessions. Memories of singing at Londolozi crop up quite often; one of Lex's enduring memories is Tina Turner's visit, when she sat on the ground by the fire one night singing to her mesmerised audience of safari guests and guides.

Occasionally there was a small initiation ceremony, as happened when an Englishman arrived with a smart new safari hat of which he was extremely proud but which bothered his guide, Map Ives. After a day of eyeing this hat he grabbed it, tied it to a rope and dragged it behind the vehicle, even running over it now and again. Finally it was picked up, dusted off and handed back to its owner. "Now that is what I call a safari hat!" said Map.

On another occasion a very special fortieth birthday was to be celebrated by a lady coming in with a group of friends straight from Hong Kong. Yvonne rang them up to see if they would like any special arrangements. Their reply was: "What can you guys in that banana republic possibly know about putting on something special!" Naturally this was a red rag to a bull.

The group was to arrive on a commercial airline at Skukuza Airport in the Kruger Park, where the Londolozi plane would pick them up for the ten-minute flight to the lodge. Yvonne hired a gorilla suit from Johannesburg and dressed the pilot in it with only his epaulettes and cap to distinguish him from any other gorilla that might be hanging around the airport. The plane landed next to

smart, uniformed pilots from Mala Mala standing to attention and holding name boards. The Londolozi pilot swung through the trees holding a large bunch of bananas as the passengers alighted.

The other passengers dispersed while the Londolozi guests stood around bewildered, unsure who was greeting them until the gorilla bounded up to them. Scratching his armpits and grunting he herded them into his plane and as he climbed in he put his earphones over his arm and held up a book with large letters on the front: *How to Fly a Plane*, asking if any of them could

Mike Myers in a genet skin, New Year's Eve 1977

help start the plane. They realised it was a joke, but were still quite uncomfortable. Then the plane took off almost vertically, leaving them all breathless, and minutes later made a steep but safe landing at the Londolozi airstrip, to a great sigh of relief from the passengers.

An immaculate, brand-new vehicle and smartly turned-out guide were waiting to greet two passengers who were not part of the Hong Kong party and drove them back to the lodge. As it disappeared, a noisy old tractor, decked in skins and horns and towing a trailer with plastic chairs tied to it, came round the corner escorted by scouts on bicycles wearing large hats from which dangled plastic spiders. The gorilla jumped in and said, "Come with me to the Banana Republic Safari Lodge!"

That evening, in the warm glow of the setting sun, sitting on the large flat rocks in the river they sipped French champagne while being served chilled oysters and a lecture on never again calling them a 'banana republic'. They laughed and loved it.

Businesses also started using them for their promotions; one of the first being the Jaguar Car Company of Great Britain. An eighteen-page list of instructions arrived, setting out how they would like their promotional weekend to run. They wanted to be met on the airstrip with champagne and music in the background, a full choir and drums. The Land Rovers should come over the horizon in a line, the trackers sitting on the front with rifles. No problem. The first plane carrying the luggage would buzz the lodge to get the timing right. The male kitchen staff would use all the pots and pans as drums and the ladies would wrap the tablecloths round their waists so that they all looked the same. Choir and drums would be ready.

But it all started going horribly wrong when the morning game drives were late returning and the existing clients had not checked out. Time was short and the rooms couldn't be made ready while the guests were still eating breakfast. Yvonne was shouting, "Ladies and drummers, we've got to move now!" The luggage plane was circling the camp. The tablecloths where whipped from under the guests and off they went.

The planes kept circling and no one could understand why they were not landing. Yvonne, racing to see what

Map Ives 'conditioning' a safari hat

was wrong, found that a very new student guide, who had been sent to the strip to set up a table of champagne and snacks, had set it up right in the middle of the airstrip! She shouted at the lad to fetch his Land Rover and remove the table and drinks. In his panic he forgot to release the handbrake and the heat and friction set fire to the gearbox, igniting the dry grass underneath. With no water to hand the champagne had to be used to quench the fire.

Meanwhile all the staff were tumbling out of the vehicles beating their pots and pans and winding table clothes around their waists. The choir was trying to assemble and as many of them lived in the nearby village all their aunts and uncles and cousins and children had come along too. It was absolute chaos.

Back at the camp the departing guests, attended only by the guides, were trying to finish breakfast. Luckily they were all driving their own cars and, after seeing them off, the guides had to run to the airstrip with their rifles and trackers to greet the new guests and retrieve their vehicles, which had been used to transfer the staff to the airstrip. Finally everyone was sorted out and the guides were told to take the new guests on a very long game drive, pretending it was miles to the camp, so that the rooms could be prepared and some order restored. The guests, having no idea about the carefully choreographed plans, thought it was all normal and great fun. Africa, here we come!

There are many more tales in a similar vein from this decade of light-hearted freedom, but gradually this carefree attitude changed, becoming more serious and responsible as the market expanded to include overseas guests, including those quick to sue. Political correctness crept in and the fun and games were considerably toned down. No

longer are guides allowed to drink alcohol on duty, or to flirt with or even touch a client, other than to offer a helping hand. Lust, which was certainly part of those wild, fun-filled early days, has been outlawed.

As the business grew its name was changed to Conservation Corporation Africa, now known as CCAfrica, with many new lodges in southern and East Africa; some they own and others they manage. In this way they are able to spread the philosophy of conservation and good guiding that made them so well known. They have emerged as one of the most innovative in style and architecture, and run their lodges to the highest of standards. They still have extremely high-quality guide training, which now takes place at another of their lodges, Phinda in KwaZulu-Natal, where the habitat is more diverse than at Londolozi.

Although time has moved on from those early days at Londolozi and they have all grown up and taken on fresh responsibilities, the few guides that I have met who worked there in the halcyon days have certainly not lost any of their sparkle. We can follow the careers of three of them who have remained in the industry.

LEX HES

Though he was the very first guide to work at Londolozi, Lex didn't start as a guide. During his last year at school he was sent on a wilderness trail for boys who were showing potential as leaders. The trail, which took place at Londolozi and was led by John Varty, was designed to introduce them to the bush and the art of survival and to teach them to work together as a team. John's knowledge and passion so overwhelmed the entire group that they

Lex Hes in Botswana, 2003

guests came only at weekends, Lex had time to explore the bush whenever he had finished his chores. He walked alone all over the Sabi Sands, on their own property and on others, armed only with a pair of binoculars, a notebook and his pet parrot Spike, named after Spike Milligan – Lex being an ardent 'Goon Show' fan. His mother had instilled in him her own passion for birds and he compiled the first bird list for the reserve. He would return each day with plant samples to identify, noting where they grew and what ate them. He studied animal behaviour from elephants to ants. He and the Vartys learned all they could about the ecology of the bush and how each creature fitted into it. Previously the emphasis had been on simply finding the animals, but now they started to educate their guests in the workings of nature. It seems incredible today, when we take it for granted that we will learn about a whole environment rather than just the animals, that it had not been done before. Guides were generally great hosts and raconteurs, could find the animals and keep their guests amused, but did not know very much about the bush around them.

In those early days they hardly ever saw leopards, which were very wary, having been heavily hunted in the past. They saw their footprints and their kills in the trees, and heard them grunting in the night, but the animals themselves were like ghosts – invisible but for the occasional glimpse, which always caused great excitement.

Three years after Lex started at Londolozi, but while he happened to be away, one of the guides, Ken Maggs, and a tracker, Kimbian Mnisi, caught a glimpse, during a night drive, of something bright in the spotlight, high in a tree. They stopped for a better look – and there on a branch were the shining eyes of two very small leopard cubs, which ran down the tree and into a hole in the sandbank

all went away vowing they would spend their lives protecting their African heritage. This commitment never faded for Lex.

After he had finished his national service, he had six months to spare before starting university. He wrote to John Varty asking if he could use a little help for six months, as he was willing to do anything. His letter arrived as the Vartys were beginning to develop the farm and they were delighted to have help. Lex worked those six months for board and lodging and found it completely absorbing. He was nineteen, the Varty brothers were in their early twenties and together they worked and played with great intensity in an atmosphere electric with enthusiasm and joy. When the six months were up he decided not to go to university and stayed on at Londolozi for fifteen years!

Most of his time was spent helping in the camp and looking after the guests. There were four guest huts, one long-drop loo and a bucket-shower hung from a tree. As below. Ken and Kimbian waited around but saw nothing more. The next day they found the cubs basking in the early morning sunlight outside the den. They saw them again in the evening and the next day, but on the third day they had disappeared, having evidently been moved, as their mother's tracks were visible in the sand. After this very first sighting of the cubs, visitors spent many happy hours watching them. Months passed before their mother grew accustomed to the vehicles and allowed herself to be seen, but she relaxed more and more and eventually became the most celebrated leopard in Africa.

A very important project in which Lex was involved was the translocation of elephants from the Kruger National Park to the Sabi Sands, where they were kept in a stockade at Londolozi before being released into the reserve. This programme was run in conjunction with the Mammal Research Institute at Pretoria University, with which Lex was in constant contact. The institute provided a couple of radio collars, to be fitted to the elephants so he could monitor them after release. Until then no data had been collected on translocated elephants.

It was during his long discussions with these scientists that he learned about their research in Antarctica and the southern Indian Ocean. He had always longed to visit that part of the world, and through his working relationship with the people running the institute he managed to secure a place on an expedition to Marion Island, a very cold and inhospitable contrast to the African bush. The party was there for nine months – eighteen men, no women, and the only communication with home was by telex. Each man was allowed to send and receive sixty words a week.

The island's weather is harsh; snow or rain being the norm most days. Situated in the Roaring Forties, in the path of the westerly winds that blow unhindered around the globe at that latitude, the island has no trees, only low, ground-hugging vegetation. The bird population consists of Rockhopper, Macaroni, Gentoo and King penguins, Sooty and Wandering albatrosses and a huge number of petrels. There is also an abundance of Fur and Elephant seals, with Orcas (Killer whales) circling the island preying on the seals.

Lex was there to study the House mouse and its impact on the island! Mice had accompanied the early sealers and had proliferated. Someone had introduced four domestic cats to catch the mice, but naturally it was much easier for them to eat baby birds. The cat population rose to a staggering 34 000 before a programme of extermination finally eliminated them. The study of the impact of the alien mice on the ecology

'The Mother', photographed by Lex

was extremely important, and one thing it revealed was that, unlike mice in the rest of the world that eat grain and plants, these mice fed mainly on insects.

Later on he took another sabbatical to study seals on Amsterdam Island, a tiny atoll halfway between Cape Town, South Africa and Perth, Australia. This invaluable education in how to conduct scientific studies was to stand him in good stead in his future work at Londolozi.

Tracking had become a popular pastime at Londolozi; by learning from local people, who were superb trackers, the guides became very skilled at following and finding lions. It was another of the unusual activities their guests were being offered. They had never tracked leopard until that first sighting by Ken Maggs, but then, having seen the cubs, they decided to try. They followed the mother's tracks, found the new den with the cubs' footprints around it and then found each new den as the mother moved them. The cubs soon became completely accustomed to the vehicles and after a few months the mother showed herself for the first time. This was just about the time that Lex returned from his first sabbatical and he took up tracking and observing the leopard and her cubs. Cynthia Moss's book, *Portraits in the Wild*, had recently been published, setting down all that was known about the behaviour of African mammals, but the leopard section was painfully brief. Virtually nothing of their breeding biology or general behaviour was known, other than that they were very shy and secretive. Having learned on Marion Island how to produce a scientific study, Lex took this great opportunity – off his own bat – to record all he saw.

Over the next twelve years he diligently recorded all his observations while developing his interest in photography. It had been easy to photograph the creatures on the island, as they had very few natural predators and were not afraid of man. Leopards were a different story, being extremely nervous, but over time he built up a vast store of data on their lifestyle. The original female, known as 'the Mother', gave birth to nine more litters – fifteen cubs in all over the twelve-year period. He watched her offspring and their offspring have cubs in their turn. Even today, when he goes back, he sees one of her great-granddaughters, which he had watched growing up, raising her own cubs. Individual leopards are easily distinguished by the spots above their whiskers.

He gathered important information about what happens to cubs when they mature. Once they are adult the female cubs establish their territory right next to their mother's in a loose family association, though they never socialise as lions do. One of the cubs at Londolozi even gave birth herself in the lair where she was born. The mothers and daughters seldom meet, but when they do, although there is a degree of animosity, it rarely leads to a violent confrontation. The males are distributed far and wide in order to prevent inbreeding. Leopards are loners, but they do have a social order and discovering this must have been thrilling for Lex. His keen observations and conclusions have become widely recognised in scientific circles and led to the publication of his book *The Leopards of Londolozi*, containing all the information he had so faithfully recorded and illustrated with his exceptional photographs.

During his last three years at Londolozi he took up filming, learning how to operate a 16mm movie camera to record the leopards he was so diligently watching. He and John Varty set up Londolozi Productions, making wildlife films that have been shown on television throughout the world.

Lex is a tall, softly spoken man with a quick smile and an easy-going manner, who manages to get things done his way without ruffling any feathers. When I attended one of his photographic workshops I could plainly see how his courtesy and charm make him so popular, not only with his guests but also with all the camp staff, who were eager to ensure that everything ran smoothly for him.

In 1992, he married Lynn, became the father of twins and decided to leave Londolozi to live in Nelspruit, a small but up-and-coming town with good schools and amenities for family life, not too far from his beloved bush. He works independently, doing photographic projects, private guiding and, with his business partner Anton Lategan, runs a popular guide-training school in Mpumulanga. Lex now takes one or two trips a year for Wilderness Safaris clients in Botswana, along with his own private safaris, both wildlife and photographic. He is a patient and expert teacher, and his extremely popular photographic workshops started when his guests pestered him for advice on handling their cameras and taking good pictures.

MIKE MYERS

Mike lives in Johannesburg, but his spiritual home is the Okavango Delta. He was born in July 1953 in Rhodesia (now Zimbabwe), where a man named Nikodemus Sakarombe, having started as the new cook in the Myers' household when Mike was two months old, rapidly became the most important person in his early childhood. Nikodemus had come straight from the army, and his great bush sense fired the imagination of a small boy by portraying the fun and excitement of the great outdoors, which for Mike at that time comprised five acres of bush that surrounded their house on the

outskirts of Salisbury (now Harare). When he wasn't exploring the local wildlife, this small boy sat by the fire in the staff quarters while Nikodemus cooked, listening to the Africans talk and learning to speak their language.

At the age of eleven he joined the boy scouts and at the very first meeting he got the chance to go on a field trip to Mana Pools. The scoutmaster was an unfulfilled game ranger who had been pulled out of his chosen career in National Parks to help run his father's wine and spirits business. He was going to teach the boys about survival, and off they went to a campsite on the banks of the Zambezi River. Mike, a city boy who had never been in a

Mike in Botswana, 2001

Game-viewing at Mombo, Botswana

wilderness area in his life, had to sit up and keep watch the first night in camp. He was in charge of the Tilly lamps that had to be pumped every ten minutes or so, while sitting by the campfire surrounded by a trip wire with some stones attached to alert him if anything came near. He found it quite frightening with so many strange noises in the night, whooping hyena in the distance and crackling leaves nearby. But worse than the animals was his fear of the scoutmaster, whose last words before retiring were: "I will really sort out anyone who wakes me up for no good reason!"

His most vivid memory of that trip was the close proximity of about thirty elephants coming down to the river to drink in the middle of the night. He sat frozen, hugging his knees with his eyes screwed shut, as they walked down the bank only few feet away, though he couldn't resist peeping now and then out of the corner of an eye to watch them as they swayed to and fro in the water below him before moving silently away.

He continued to go on as many outings as possible with the scouts until he was eighteen. It was all about hunting, fishing, trapping and learning bushcraft. In the process he also became very keen on falconry. The die was cast, and he knew that he would work with wildlife. He went off to university in Johannesburg, but his heart was not really in it. The only non-academic in his family – his time was spent learning to fly, playing rugby and his guitar – Mike was an art student who found everything mechanical very easy. Getting his pilot's licence was not difficult, but having got it he was unable to find a flying job other than instructing, in which he had no interest.

His luck changed when he landed the job at Londolozi on nothing but enthusiasm. He found it the most wonderful place to grow; John and Dave Varty were getting into bush clearance, community projects and conservation long before any other private landowner had started thinking along those lines. Mike formed ideas and ideals at that time that have stayed with him ever since, along with his tremendous photographic skills, acquired through his friendship with Lex Hes.

When he left Londolozi he headed up to Botswana and went to work for Brian Graham at his camp in Linyanti. He spent four months there, during which time they had one guest, an American woman named Jessie Neil, and she stayed for only two days. Jessie owned a company called Desert and Delta, which had two camps, called Okavango and Moremi, both spectacular water-based camps. She had a reputation of hiring the best-looking young guides in Botswana and made them sign a contract that contained a clause forbidding them to 'copulate with the clients'! Her camps were very luxurious for their time: she was one of the first to introduce silver candelabra at table in the bush. I once had a glimpse of her bedroom at Camp Moremi when it was unoccupied, and was startled to say the least, as the walls and ceiling were completely covered with mirrored tiles, I am sure, unique in the bush.

Visitors to Botswana were rare in those days and, with only one guest for months, Brian had to make sure he got his money's worth out of Mike. This meant keeping him working all the time at everything and anything. After having him paint the barge sixteen times, service the Land Rover thirty-two times and repair the boat ninety-two times, Brian finally ran out of things for him to do.

Therefore one evening he said, "Mike, two years ago Fred Watt left a fridge for me on the corner of the Tsetse Fly Control Road and the Chobe Park Boundary Road. Tomorrow morning I want you to take Sparky [a clapped-out Land Rover] and see if you can find it for me."

"I was thrilled to have any reason to get out of camp. I, Julius the head guide and the crew shoved a few basics into the back, together with some axes, wire and a shovel, and set off at dawn. When we reached the bridge over the Savuti Channel (still filled with water in those days) we found it to be in a very ropy state. The bridges in Botswana over the shallow waterways are made from tall, straight mopane poles, cut from the Cathedral mopane forests. We set to work cutting a few logs, mended the bridge as best they could with wire and drove gingerly across, jubilant to be on the other side. Sure enough, when we reached the crossroad, there was the fridge in the middle of nowhere – a stainless-steel Electrolux standing upright and waiting to be collected. I looked inside and found it to be pretty clean; the seal was a bit loose, but all in all, it was not in bad shape, so we picked it up, loaded it onto Sparky and returned feeling very pleased with ourselves. Back at camp I cleaned the fridge, cut off the paraffin tank hangers as they were rotten and attached a spare paraffin tank that I stood on some bricks. Within four hours we had ice and Brian kept the drinks in that fridge for the next five years. However, what we had not realised was that the fridge had become a beacon for the pilots flying to Savuti from Maun. The standard instructions were to fly up the park boundary until they found the fridge then turn right. We heard that one pilot had ended up in Victoria Falls and another in the Caprivi Strip before the message reached Maun that the fridge had been reclaimed."

On leaving Linyanti, Mike started his own business guiding small groups deep into the Okavango Delta. He was a real pioneer in the northern area of Botswana around Chief's Island. One of the first people to do *mokoro* safaris along the myriad waterways of the Delta, he gave his guests an adventure they would never forget. He became friendly with the very knowledgeable local people, who had been plying these waters all their lives, and they taught him the ways of the Delta and how to behave around animals in the wild. This was essential knowledge, as not only were they without a vehicle, travelling in boats and on foot, but one cannot carry a rifle in non-hunting areas of Botswana.

Each night they slept under mosquito nets on small islands, waking to the dawn chorus of Botswana's vast variety of birds all vying to be heard in the canopies above them, punctuated by the haunting call of the Fish eagles and Swamp boubous. Poling through the papyrus-fringed channels they dodged hippos, found the secret places where sitatunga hide and came around corners to find elephants swimming in front of them while giant crocodiles slithered into the water.

One of Mike's guests whose family travelled with him when she was fifteen, and who is now married with children of her own, recalls the safari as being one of the highlights of her teenage years. She remembers the *mokoro* gliding through water lilies and seeing submerged hippos as they slid over them in the clear water. They followed a Greater honeyguide as it flitted through the woods, leading them to a beehive in a tree which Mike shinned up to extract some delicious wild honey for them all to taste.

She recalls seeing frantic creatures of all kinds swimming for their lives from a fierce bush fire. One of them was a snake that leaped into her boat; as she

instinctively flicked it back into the water she heard Mike gasp, "My God, that was a mamba!" Each evening, after dining on one of the six dishes his mother had taught him to cook, his guests would return to the glowing embers of the campfire. Mike strummed quietly on his guitar and sang and, shyly at first, she sang along with him, followed by the rest of her family. The thrill, the fear, the laughter and the beauty of that perfect paradise captivated her. She fell completely in love with Mike and is certain her little sister did too!

Mike thought the natural progression from guiding safaris would be to manage a safari company. He worked, for three difficult and very stressful years, for a company called Gametrackers, I wonder if the overwhelming misery of his final year has partly blocked out the memory of the initial fun that he had with Michael Lorentz, who joined Gametrackers soon after he did. Ultimately, he felt he was not cut out for a managerial role and was not doing what he enjoyed. He left Gametrackers and headed north to work at Chobe Game Lodge, which were much happier years for him, as he spent all his time either guiding or training Botswanan guides, most of whom are well known and still in the business.

Living in the bush as a bachelor inevitably meant life was rather lonely for Mike at Chobe Game Lodge. He wanted to base himself in Johannesburg where his friends lived. In 1995, Colin Bell of Wilderness Safaris, having just acquired a new plane, persuaded him to fly for Wilderness. Mike then proposed that he should run the private guiding division of the company, flying the guests in himself whenever possible. His proposal was accepted and life took a dramatic turn for the better.

He now had a new and fulfilling role that gave him true stability and peace of mind. He had a great job, was surrounded by friends and had never been happier. A guide can easily burn out doing the same thing for too long, but for Mike the scope for guiding has vastly enlarged. A keen angler, he fishes in the Indian Ocean at Rocktail Bay in Zululand and is particularly passionate about Bonefishing in the Seychelles and Cuba. He travels to the desert in Namibia, canoes down the Zambezi River and sets time aside for his beloved Botswana. He opens the hearts and minds of his guests, involving them in conservation issues, animal behaviour and an awareness of the wilderness that has grown from the seeds sown at Londolozi all those years ago.

Mike's theory of guiding:

> "The very top guides are the ones who work in one area all their lives and know it well. For example, Garth Thompson and John Stevens would be at their best in Mana Pools; I feel I am at my best in the Okavango Delta because I know

it so very well. I have never considered myself to be the most knowledgeable guide. I have learnt about the things that really interest me as the years have gone by applying my knowledge to the areas I am in, but I have never gained knowledge just for the sake of it. Lots of people do guide that way and are very successful at it. There is a guy called Nigel Robey in Zimbabwe to whom you would say, 'Oh Nigel, look at that African Monarch butterfly' and an hour and half later he would still be in full flight, one thing having led to another. Ken Tilney, one of the experts who helped the Varty brothers with the conservation of their land, could sit on a riverbank and write down the names of a hundred birds before breakfast just by calling them. It's wonderful to be around guys like that, but I could never do it.

"What has captivated me the most is the sheer physical beauty of the landscape and the animals as being part of it, the big picture, linked with photography. That has always been my bent. When I left Londolozi and came up to Botswana I was given this unbelievable wild paradise to head into, with no policing and complete freedom. It was what I had dreamed of all my life. I always went farther into the Delta than any of the other guides. Lloyd Wilmot knew it, as did PJ Besterlink, but none of them spent as much time up at the top of Chief's Island as I did. I had a brilliant poler as my guide. Although the Okavango looks flat, it isn't; the water does of course flow down, but not very noticeably, my guide knew which way to go by

his understanding of the way the water flows, something you know only by growing up with it. Sadly it is knowledge that is dying out, people no longer travel the Delta as they did, and there is not the same amount of water around.

"In my opinion, a great guiding experience is to approach a big herd of buffaloes on a flood plain, on foot. Crouching down and hiding behind a few palm fronds, getting as close as you can while watching them coming towards you as they feed, and finally creeping away so quietly that they never knew you were there. The last pride of lions or herd of impala that my guests see is a very different experience to their first encounter. I try to give them an understanding of the intricate way in which nature works but above all I want them to have fun, to go away with a light heart and a feeling of joy."

Mike has a rollicking sense of humour and a naughty twinkle in his eye. He has found ways to have more fun in just one month than most people find in a lifetime. But above all, he is an eloquent storyteller and no guest on any other safari will laugh quite as much as they will with Mike Myers.

He is extremely busy these days, marketing for Wilderness Safaris and concentrating on his photography. In 2004, he co-authored the book *Mombo, Okavango's Place of Plenty* (available from Russel Friedman Books), a very special area of Botswana and contains many of his brilliant photographs.

MAP IVES

One would be hard-pressed to find anyone who knows quite as much about the Okavango Delta and the ecology of Botswana as Map Ives. He grew up in Botswana and is known as a 'Delta water rat' being most at home in a *mokoro*, exploring the myriad channels, his mind brimming with ideas of how to preserve and care for this unique place. He is currently employed by Okavango Wilderness Safaris as the Environmental Manager monitoring their twenty lodges and camps, all of which are required to adhere to his 'minimum standards' and environmental auditing. In addition he monitors two large concessions, keeping accurate records of habitats, roads, fire and wildlife populations.

He supplies the Department of Wildlife and National Parks with his population figures and assists conservation groups with the collection of data on endangered species such as cheetah and several bird species. He presents papers at seminars on natural resources management, on control of fires and also on the controversial issue of the cattle fencing in the Kalahari. He is in great demand as a lecturer.

"I am more than happy to work with all wildlife decision-makers to assure the future of habitats and natural resource protection throughout Botswana. I am doing absolutely fascinating and important work; I know I am under the microscope and I love it."

Francistown, on the eastern edge of Botswana, where Map spent his childhood, had burst into life when gold was rediscovered in the area in 1866, and was named after Daniel Francis, one of the early prospectors. The discovery created a minor gold rush that petered out at about the time the rich strike was made in 1886 on the Witwatersrand in South Africa. However, the town continued to flourish, being out of the tsetse fly belt and therefore safe for the oxen that hauled the great wagons along the supply routes of Africa until the railway was built at the end of the century.

Map's father, an engineer, was employed to electrify the town, which he took from paraffin lamps to light switches in record time. Here Map grew up, one of five children, four boys and a girl, all of whom went off to boarding school when they were seven. A school in Kimberley in the Cape Province was chosen for the children, but Map and his brothers were not happy there, so they switched to Capricorn High School in Pietersburg (now Polokwane), which was very different. This government boarding school for rural children was a great success, with its many playing fields, large swimming pool and good teaching; it also had excellent rail access. School trains ran at the beginning and end of each term all over southern Africa, taking children to and from boarding schools in South Africa on journeys that could take days.

The holidays were always too short, and they spent most of their time working on their cattle ranch, dipping and de-horning the cattle and wrestling with calves. Leisure time was spent wrestling with one another, swimming in the river and bird-shooting with their airguns. They were allowed to shoot only doves and sandgrouse. Jack Bousfield, a friend of Map's father, was a strict disciplinarian with all the youngsters in Francistown, and if he heard of any boy shooting another species of bird he would seek him out and deal

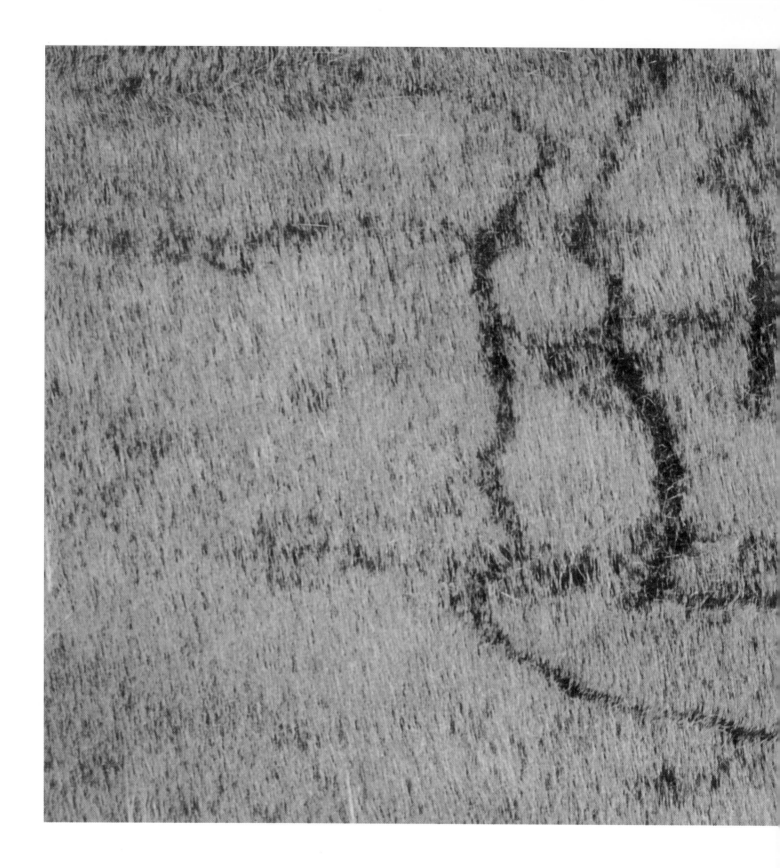

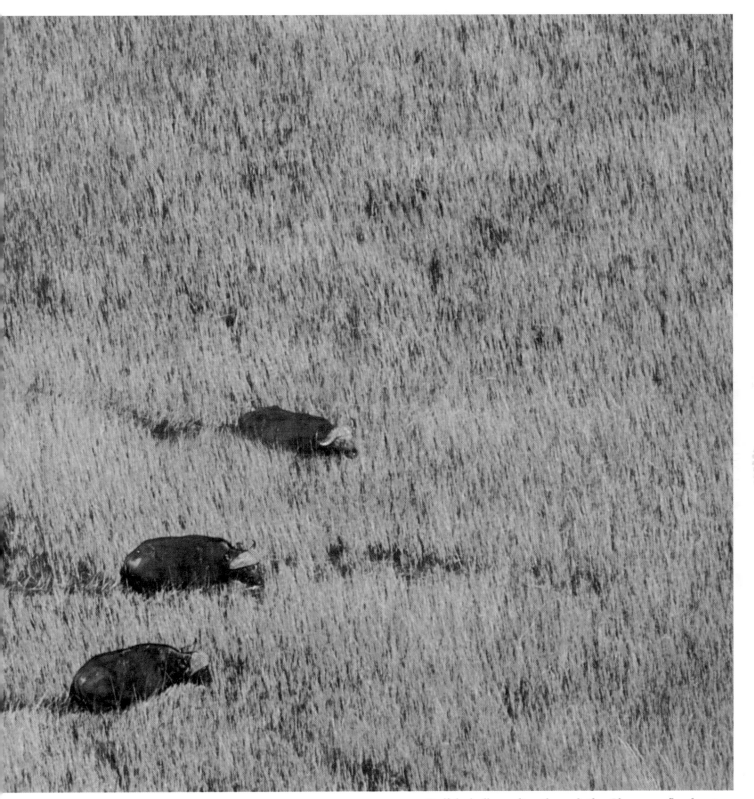

Buffalo bulls wading through the Okavango flood waters

with him very severely. Map was in awe of Jack, a larger-than-life character who disappeared into the bush for weeks on end, and whenever he visited Map's father and recounted tales of wild areas, Map would sit quietly in the corner drinking it all in, hoping not to be noticed and sent away.

In 1973, Map left school with absolutely no idea of what he would like to do with his life. His brother had joined the British South Africa Police (BSAP) in Rhodesia (Zimbabwe) but Map was unsure. He did not consider university and there was nothing happening in Botswana, no tourist industry and few prospects for a young school-leaver. At that time Rhodesia was a very successful, vibrant country, with plenty of jobs attracting many young people, so Map bought a booklet that listed opportunities, one of which was in National Parks (an idea that appealed to him much more than the BSAP) and an interview was set up. Armed with a letter from the mayor of Francistown and a few Rhodesian dollars, he bought a one-way ticket to Salisbury (Harare). After the interview they said he would make a very good ranger and that they would be delighted to employ him in the Parks Department, and invited him to join the *two-year* waiting list. Rather shocked by this latter revelation he accepted, then consulted his booklet again, deciding that the only thing to do was to join the BSAP, even though he had to sign a three-year contract.

The BSAP training centre resembled a military barracks, immaculately clean and tidy with very smart uniformed instructors to take them through the six months of basic training. Everyone knew there was a looming political problem and in time Map found himself being trained in a variety of weaponry, counter-insurgency, horse-riding, tracking and typing! His first

Map Ives, Botswana 2003

posting was to Marandellas (now Marondera), a small, sleepy town where he had to investigate cycle thefts and hand out parking tickets. Luckily it did not last long. The war was escalating; young, single policemen were being sent to the dangerous areas, and Map went to a post on the Mozambican border, where at times he slept a mere ten metres from the border fence.

He was a very strong, fit young man, no longer a policeman but a soldier in camouflage. This war was going on at the same time as the war in Vietnam, and when Map sees films of Vietnam he realises how very similar these conflicts were. It was a tough, gruelling, difficult life being part of an organised army fighting a guerrilla force; they fought hard and played hard. He knew nothing about girls and he never met any; his R&R periods being spent with other soldiers in Salisbury, drinking, playing pool and becoming addicted to the same hard rock music that blared out of the bars and dives of Saigon.

On one of his rest periods in Salisbury he enquired at the Parks Department, where his name was on the employment list, and found he was at the top. He discovered that he could transfer from the police into the Parks Department in spite of his contract, as they were both government departments, something he had not realised when signing up for the BSAP.

Very soon after he joined the Parks Department an emergency call came from Chizarira National Park, a remote park just south of Kariba Dam. While the senior staff at the research station had been away for a couple of days' Christmas shopping, guerrillas had come in, abducted the junior staff and burnt down the research building. The station staff were devastated, both by the kidnapping and by losing all their research documents and data, gathered over many years. Volunteers were called for; again young, single men, this time from the Parks Department and preferably with some military experience. This was right up Map's street. When he arrived he was bowled over by the beauty of Chizarira and took to the task of replacing the lost research with delighted enthusiasm. They all carried notebooks in which to record everything they saw, which on completion were handed into the researchers. However, they first had to build a fort to keep the staff safe. Built of adobe, with several watchtowers and surrounded by barbed wire, the fort bristled with weapons placed at strategic points, and was manned by heavily armed soldiers, who were often called out to help in skirmishes.

Map was twice involved in landmine explosions, luckily without injury, while driving armoured vehicles, but nothing could deter him from his newfound passion – scientific research.

Eventually he and his friend Charlie realised that they were not winning the war and it was time to bail out. The two long-haired, bearded men, rucksacks on their backs and not much else, boarded a bus for Johannesburg. With very little money and no contacts they checked into a seedy residential hotel in Hillbrow, an area on the edge of the city with a rather dubious reputation, but it was all they could afford. Charlie understood accounting so he rather quickly found work in a bank. Map could not find anything but a job as a waiter.

It was 1979, the year of the Lancaster House agreement. Ian Smith had capitulated, Zimbabwe was born, and there was no going back. Life in Johannesburg was a struggle, so when a telephone call came out of the blue from a man who had been a good friend on the police training course in Rhodesia, Map was thrilled. Ken Maggs had somehow followed Map's career, knew he had been working for National Parks and that he had now arrived in Johannesburg.

Map was very curious: "Where are you, Ken?" he asked.

"I'm at a place called Londolozi Game Reserve," said Ken, "and the two brothers who own it are looking for people who'd like to become guides to help them run it."

Two days later Map was driven down to Londolozi with a party of guests on their way to a weekend in the bush. His interview with the Varty brothers went well and he was offered a job, which he took without hesitation. Londolozi was the sort of place where he knew he would be in his element. Still, this was a period of adjustment for him; his life had been hard and rough and he had no experience of the civilised niceties expected in a tourist lodge, nor had he ever worked with women.

He had actually arrived to replace Mike Myers, who had gone on to set up his own fly-in safaris to Botswana. Londolozi was still a very simple place; most of the men were wearing tattered clothes, but they all had one smart shirt and a pair of shorts or trousers to wear when the guests arrived. Dave Varty encouraged them all enormously, the resident guides helped the new arrivals and Lex Hes in particular became a very good friend to Map.

Map discovered soon after his arrival that he had the ability to teach. If he knew something and believed in it he found it very easy to pass on that knowledge, an essential talent for a good guide. He was swept up in the enthusiasm of the Vartys, but their adviser, the ecologist Dr Ken Tinley, also had a profound influence on him. Dr Tinley's ideas were way ahead of his time and whenever he could, Map listened to the advice he was giving the Varty brothers. He began to understand the importance of soil, how drainage works and what causes it to change. His road to the study of geomorphology (earth sciences) began here. Most important to his lifelong commitment was learning what fun could be had in the bush.

John and Dave's philosophy of hiring the right person to be a guide is explained in a little story that Map told me about Chris Badger, a new guide who arrived after Map had been there for about a year. Map travelled with Chris to Londolozi for his interview, hitching a ride with weekend guests as Map himself had once done. They had just entered the Sabi Sands Reserve when they came upon a group of impala, prompting Chris to turn to Map and ask what they were! However, in spite of his complete ignorance of wildlife or the bush, he was taken on because he was such an engaging and entertaining fellow. He had to guarantee that he would sit on the back of a vehicle for six months, listening and learning, before he took any paying guests on a game drive. In the end he became a superb guide and a great force in the safari industry, now runs the Wilderness operation in Malawi and is married to Pam Knox, my first employee at Okavango Explorations in London.

When Map left Londolozi, because he wanted to get back to Botswana, he contacted Mike Myers, who was doing so well with his company Quest Africa that he needed another guide. Map was hired. Mike's *mokoro* trails, journeying through the heart of the Okavango Delta, perfectly suited Map, whose interest in the ecology of this beautiful wetland, which was to become his life's work, was fired on these trips. With their guide the guests explored the channels and lagoons, spending nights sleeping on islands under mosquito nets and generally having the time of their lives. Sadly, the job was not to last; Mike had a slight change of fortune and found he could no longer afford to employ Map.

Map and Mike had often passed through Xaxaba Camp, an enchanting spot on the Boteti River that was owned and run by a couple, Paul and Penny Rawson, whom he came to know quite well. The Rawsons took on Map at the time their son returned, and together Dan Rawson and Map guided and looked after the camp. The place was run on a shoestring, Map and Dan had very few possessions, they shared a tent and even their clothes – it was a case of first up, best dressed. Map was fascinated by the geomorphology of the Kalahari, the ancient lake and rivers, the fault lines whose miniscule shifts can turn a watery paradise into desert, and the plants and the creatures that survive there. While taking the guests on walks and *mokoro* trips Map made notes of all he saw in the area, endlessly following his passion for scientific research. Eventually Mike's business closed down and he joined them at Xaxaba.

It was at Xaxaba that Map met his future wife, Cathy. Penny Rawson had gone to South Africa for a few days, and at a tea party met Cathy's mother, who asked if her daughter could come up and work for her, which she did on a three-month permit. Shy, pretty and only twenty years old, she came upon three wild, hairy, rough-looking men grinning with glee at the sight of her as she walked in to the main tent on her arrival. Map has never found out what she thought of the three men that she saw sitting at the bar, but she could certainly hold her own and loved working there. It was a good two months before she and Map realised just how much they liked one another. At the end of her three months she left, but he could not get her out of his mind, so he took leave, went to Pretoria and found her. Within two months they were married and on their way back to Botswana.

Once married, Map decided to leave Xaxaba; the job and the accommodation were not suitable for a married couple. As luck would have it, Hunters Africa offered him the job of running their photographic camp on the Linyanti River in the Savuti, in a vast and extremely remote area that was mainly a hunting block. It took in part of Savuti and all of Kwando and Selinda, concessions that today have two or three camps on each of them, but in those days there was only the one six-bed tented camp to service photographic safari guests in that whole area. His guests would stay much longer in one camp than they do today, exploring a large amount of territory, especially along the Savuti Channel, which was then still full of water. On one occasion in the summer, a time of plenty, when the animals are sleek and fat and elephant families often meet on the emerald plains, he came upon over five hundred elephants massed together.

Map and Cathy spent two years in that little tented camp, where Map did everything from maintenance to guiding while Cathy did the catering and housekeeping.

Map eating wild honey at Xugana in 1986

Not having known each other very well when they married, this presented an ideal time for them to learn about one another. They were happy there but eventually Hunters Africa closed the camp down because it was too remote and did not attract enough guests.

After that they went to Maun, where David Hartley employed Map to guide at Tsaro Lodge in the Khwai area of the Moremi Reserve, which is where I first met him. He was such an extraordinary person to listen to on a game drive. Full of enthusiasm and knowledge he opened up an exciting insight into African wildlife, generating an interest that I have never lost. While at Tsaro Lodge Cathy had their first baby and, finding it very difficult to combine parenthood and lodge management, they decided to leave and set up home in Maun.

Map continued guiding on a freelance basis before starting his own company, Map Ives Safaris. With his great knowledge and experience he should have been very successful, but his marketing skills, so vital in this industry, were not well developed enough. He would sit in his little stall at the World Travel Market or at Indaba, the South African travel fair, watching a steady stream of people going to the Wilderness stand wondering why no one came to him for a meeting. He did not understand the importance of networking with agents and tour operators and was not prepared to accost people in the aisles. He did of course have some clients, people who knew him from the past and who longed to go on safari with him. By now there was a second child, a son, and simply not enough business to support his family. After four years he was ready to pack up his business when Wilderness Safaris approached him to help them with their guide-training programme. He enjoyed the training because he loves teaching, but when he heard that the position of Environmental Manager was coming up he asked to be considered. It was a job made in heaven for Map and there is no one who could have filled that post better. He could indulge his lifelong passion for research and conservation, developed at Londolozi, to his heart's content. He is strongly optimistic about the future of Botswana and the surrounding countries.

Map and Cathy live in Botswana and send their daughter to school in Nelspruit, where she is in the same year as the twin son and daughter of his old friend Lex Hes.

BOTSWANA

I have a very soft spot for Botswana. There my passion for Africa resurfaced
and the memories of that first safari linger as if it were yesterday.
I can instantly evoke the sound of splashing and grunting hippos at dusk,
the soft crunch of dry leaves on the ground as hyenas crept around my
tent in the night and the symphony of birdsong at dawn.

I have a very soft spot for Botswana. There my passion for Africa resurfaced and the memories of that first safari linger as if it were yesterday. I can instantly evoke the sound of splashing and grunting hippos at dusk, the soft crunch of dry leaves on the ground as hyenas crept around my tent in the night and the symphony of birdsong at dawn. I remember watching astounded one night as our host David Hartley plucked a small crocodile out of the water with his hands, holding it firmly so that we could all touch it and marvel at its beauty before it swam back to the bottom of the lagoon. I had no idea anyone could do that sort of thing – I was astounded.

Botswana is about the size of France with a population of 1,6 million. Most of country is flat, dry and dusty, but in the north-west corner there is a jewel beyond compare – the Okavango Delta.

Water from the mountains of Angola drains down onto the Kalahari sands, creating a unique watery paradise like no other on earth. The channels and lagoons are lined with papyrus, whose roots filter out impurities, creating crystal-clear water, home to a multitude of waterfowl, fish, crocodiles and hippos. The palm-fringed islands within the Delta and the dry areas surrounding it support a diverse multitude of animals and birds.

Besides the pleasures of the wetlands, there is the Kalahari. Visit the dry saltpans known as the Makgadikgadi to find remnants of Stone Age man and perhaps have an encounter with Bushmen, or marvel at the vast herds of elephant in the Chobe and Savuti areas of north-east Botswana

Visitors carry away with them a kaleidoscope of extraordinary visions. The annual miracle of the floodwaters from Angola creeping over parched, thirsty lands as it increases the extent of the Delta; excited flocks of birds clustered at the edge of the incoming water, gorging on grass seeds brought to the surface as it rolls over the dry sand and on trapped fish flapping in the pools when it recedes; papyrus bending towards its mirror-image in the still water adorned with water lilies and lotus flowers; the head and neck of a darter rising snakelike between the lilies while a tiny Malachite kingfisher flits like a living jewel from reed to reed.

In the hot, dry month of October this parched land has a beauty all its own, dust turns the sun scarlet as it sets and even the full moon appears red as it rises. Elephants move like spectres among the mopane trees silhouetted black against the grey, floating dust. Away from the forests the open plains stretch golden yellow under a pale blue

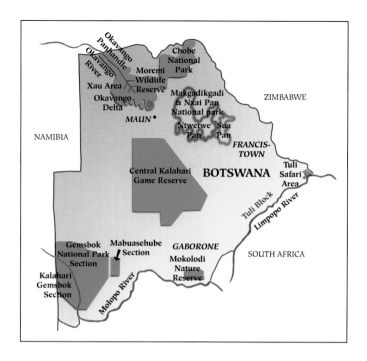

sky until the billowing clouds appear with the promise of desperately longed-for rain. Once the rain arrives the land becomes emerald green, animals are fat and sleek and the renewal of life is evident in the amount of babies in the antelope herds. Migratory birds are prolific, thousands of herons nest in the fig bushes along the lagoons and Carmine bee-eaters dig their nest-holes in high riverbanks. A memorable image for visitors is the sight of Carmine bee-eaters perching on the backs of Kori bustards in the Savuti Channel, flying off to catch the insects disturbed as the large birds walk through the grass.

Visitors to the Okavango Delta are spiritually restored by its beauty and harmony. They have spent time either in small, intimate lodges or under canvas enjoying the multitude delights of a Botswana safari and being lulled to sleep by the roar of lions, the whooping of hyenas, the grunting of hippos or the chirrup of a Scops owl.

Away from northern Botswana is the huge, dusty Kalahari 'thirstland', covered in scrub and acacia trees,

Delta Camp in the heart of the Okavango Delta in full flood

that stretches southward into South Africa, eastward into Zimbabwe and westward into Namibia. One small seismic shift and the Delta could disappear completely, as it did at Makgadikgadi. Perhaps it is this fragility that makes its beauty all the more haunting.

RALPH BOUSFIELD

Ralph is a Botswanan whose base is Jack's Camp, situated on the northern perimeter of the Makgadikgadi Pan in the heart of the Kalahari. The pans, twelve-thousand-square kilometres in extent and the largest salt pans in the wold, were once part of the bed of a great inland sea covering eighty-thousand-square kilometres, which dried up because of tectonic movements, leaving a flat, seemingly endless white surface framed with golden grass and stately Ilala palms. As you stand on the pans with the vast arc of the deep-blue sky overhead, gazing at the visible curvature of the earth, you will experience a very rare phenomenon: total silence – no birdsong, no rustle of a leaf nor the whisper of the wind.

From the camp the white, salty crust stretches to the horizon, completely flat and seemingly featureless, but when explored on quad bikes with Ralph it becomes a place full of interest. On one visit my family, friends and I, all roaring with laughter, with kikois wrapped round our heads against sun and wind making us resemble extras out of *Lawrence of Arabia*, gleefully raced the bikes over the flat surface in V formation, with Ralph at the apex. It would take most of the day going flat out to reach the other end of the pans, but in practice it takes much longer, as you stop to examine the surprising number of things that catch Ralph's eye. To explore

Makgadikgadi properly it is best to stay a couple of nights on Kubu Island, an isolated granite outcrop in Sowa Pan, about halfway between Jack's Camp and the one-hundred-and-twenty-metre Mosu Escarpment at the far end of the pans. This atmospheric place is where Wilbur Smith set his book *The Sunbird*, and it is not hard to imagine the presence of an ancient civilisation such as he describes. A simple camp awaited us on the island – a table and chairs, bedrolls laid out under the stars and a canvas shower slung over the branch of a baobab.

In the rainy season, the pans are covered with shallow water, creating a perfect breeding ground for tens of thousands of flamingos. In the dry season the remains of flamingo nests are seen, often with the chicks that did not survive, mummified by heat and salt. On our journey across the pans we came upon a Monitor lizard lost in the middle of nowhere, blind and nearly dead from heat, thirst and exhaustion. A little water dripped into his mouth helped revive him before Ralph zipped him into his canvas bag. Christened Larry the Lizard by our children he was taken to the Bousfield Animal Orphanage in Francistown, where he lived another five years, blind but content and well fed.

The pans abound in ancient history, both human and geological. We marvelled at dinosaur footprints in the bedrock, found fossilised dung-beetle balls and dislodged stone arrowheads and handaxes from the sand with the toes of our shoes. Beads and pottery shards, relics of ancient settlements, lay scattered on Kubu Island and on top of the Mosu Escarpment.

This rocky precipice, rising unexpectedly from the flat surface, marks the shore of the ancient lake, whose depth may be clearly seen almost halfway up the cliff, where the smooth, water-sculpted rock abruptly

Ralph Bousfield

The Makgadikgadi Pans

becomes rough and jagged. At its base lies a forest of unusually stunted, orange-coloured baobabs. Ostrich, Brown hyena and aardvark are among the few animals that survive in this harsh climate during the dry months. We wondered what nourishment could possibly be available for the string of thin, bony cattle that wandered through the sparse tufts of dry grass on their way to drink at a government-funded borehole.

As the afternoon drew on, Ralph, after looking anxiously at the sky to judge the length of daylight left, hurried everyone back onto the quad bikes. Once again he was at the apex as we headed towards the setting sun as fast as the bikes would go. The approach to Kubu was spectacular. First a tiny black bump appeared on the horizon, then the mysterious island seemed to rise from the earth, looming larger and larger against the blood-red sky as we moved like the wind across the flat pan, our machines pushed to their limit, until the spiky baobabs and rounded boulders welcomed us back. This exhilarating ride created a vivid and lasting impression on our minds. All guides have a great sense of theatre and Ralph is a master at using his backdrop to the greatest effect with his guests.

From the moment Ralph's piercing blue eyes lock onto yours you are completely swept up and enthralled by his extensive knowledge of the natural world. He is a captivating Pied Piper, who draws you into an enchanted world of discoveries. His particular area of expertise is Botswana and the Kalahari, but his interests are wide-ranging. You will be mesmerised by his tales of the desert, the Bushmen, ancient settlements, wildlife, archaeological finds, early explorers and a host of other topics.

He is extremely well read and has a remarkably enquiring mind, of boundless curiosity, questioning

everything. Once in my garden in England he tasted every single berry; naturally it ended with a dreadful stomach-ache, but there was no stopping him. He has a dazzling array of artefacts and memorabilia, enough to open a good-sized museum. His house in Francistown is crammed with his treasures. They are not all to everyone's taste, unless you are a devotee of the weird and wonderful. Many samples are displayed in glass-fronted cabinets at Jack's Camp, where intricately beaded Bushman handbags and aprons lie alongside the anal gland of a Brown hyena, an ostrich penis and the skull of a Sabretoothed cat. On another shelf lies a skull-cast of 'Mrs Ples',* burial pots of the Zhizo,** a petrified

Ralph in desert mode

---

* 'she' is Australopithecus africanus, 2,8 million years old, found at Sterkfontein, South Africa.
** the first Iron-age Bantu people to arrive in southern Africa in the 7th century AD.

porcupine, preserved in salt with its stomach contents visible, and all sorts of ancient stone tools found in the area. Tucked away at home are traditional medicines, stuffed animals, the largest stone tools ever found in Africa, animal skulls, shrapnel from his grandfather's war wounds, medals, a crossbow with traces of 'angel dust' (hallucinogen) used by his father for trapping baboons, and a German general's sword from World War One.

Ralph's childhood in Francistown was filled with action and adventure, and his head with accounts of daring exploits. His parents entertained streams of visitors, mostly family, whose life stories and tales of derring–do captured his imagination. Ralph's family has an intriguing background in Africa on both parents' sides; exploring, guiding, hunting and civic duty have been strong forces in their genes. One ancestor was a Member of Parliament in South Africa and Auditor-General of the Transvaal, another was Johannes Myers, thought by some to be one of the people after whom Johannesburg was named.

The tale of his uncle, Peter Whitehead, was to have a profound influence on him. The son of a tea planter in China, Peter having seen his father beheaded by the invading Japanese, escaped to Australia with his mother and became a jackaroo (sheep drover) before studying veterinary medicine. However, his dream was of Africa and its wild animals and he joined the Northern Rhodesia Wildlife Department as a stepping-stone to Kenya, where ultimately he became General Manager of the Ker and Downey Safari Company. But his real flair was with animals and Ralph was fascinated by his stories of training the lions for the film *Born Free* and a Hollywood film *Africa Texas Style*, a forerunner to a television series *Cowboy in Africa* where the actors had to lasso buffalo and wildebeest! It was Peter who rescued a few of the remaining Arabian oryx, creating a successful breeding project for them, which resulted in their reintroduction into their natural habitat. Another uncle, Gerald Swynnerton, senior game warden of Tanganyika (Tanzania), came from a family of renowned scientists in East Africa, having various species named after them, for example Swynnerton's francolin and Swynnerton's robin.

Ralph's great-grandfather, Major Richard Granville Nicholson, was one of the leaders of the famous Pioneer Column into Rhodesia and a friend of Jan Smuts. Condemned as a traitor for fighting for the Boers, he was due to be imprisoned on St Helena Island, but luckily was pardoned during the peace process. Twelve years later, in the First World War, he captured a German general who had disembarked with a force of two thousand men in South West Africa (Namibia). Leaving his own two hundred men hidden in the dunes, he approached the general, holding his rifle high with his white handkerchief fluttering from the barrel. He convinced the general that he was completely surrounded and should surrender in order to save lives. This the general did, and the sword he handed over is in Ralph's museum.

Ralph's paternal grandfather joined the South African Army and arrived on the Somme in 1916 where he was badly injured by shrapnel and his lungs damaged by mustard gas. He spent the rest of the war in hospital in England, being nursed by a young woman named Nora. Once recovered and back home he wrote proposing marriage to Nora, who accepted and booked her passage to Africa. Just before she departed, however, her father died, leaving his mother, his wife and Nora's two sisters

The bucket shower on Kubu Island

with no man other than Nora's fiancé to look after them. Nothing daunted, they all packed up and left for Africa with Nora. The major, waiting on the quayside for his bride, must have been astonished when five ladies trotted down the gangplank to greet him. They all lived happily together in Francistown, a dusty mining town in Bechuanaland and a very long way from the soft green fields of Surrey!

In the 1930s, Ralph's grandfather moved his family to Tanganyika, the journey to Lake Rukwa, where they settled, took six months in a Chevrolet and a Model-T Ford. A loyal British subject, he resented his children being taught in Afrikaans in spite of living in a British protectorate. He planned to mine gold and grow coffee, but ended up crocodile hunting, a business his son Jack took over after World War Two, selling a record fifty-three thousand crocodile skins to just one dealer in Paris.

After independence in 1964, everything in Tanzania was being nationalised, making it increasingly difficult for the Bousfield family to live there. Ralph was still a baby when Jack moved his family back to Botswana and became involved in trapping animals and birds to sell to foreign zoos.

Ralph grew up in a 'Boy's Own' world, inspired by the remarkable accounts of his family history, exploring, trapping and hunting with his father from a very early age. He was the youngest of five children and closest to his father, who had an enormous influence on him. Jack was a colourful and legendary character throughout Africa, but especially in Botswana, and it is due to years of training by Jack that Ralph has his wide knowledge and incredible sixth sense in the bush.

He was only six years old when Jack sent him out on his own with Samweli, his trusted right-hand man (who is still with Ralph today). Samweli's strong sense of propriety meant that Ralph had to sleep by himself in a tent set apart from the staff, removed from the fireside chat for which he yearned. He begged to have his tent moved, but Samweli was adamant that this was not correct. On the fun-packed expeditions with his father, however, Ralph shared his father's tent.

Inevitably, schooling loomed, and Ralph was sent to St Alban's School in Pretoria, an excellent choice, for they had an incredibly flexible attitude to this boy from the wilds, allowing him to keep animals, even building an animal house for the jackals, snakes and Monitor lizards under his care. Afternoons were spent at the Transvaal Museum's Zoological Department, helping with preserving and labelling. Each holiday the professional staff gave him a project of collecting certain specimens for the museum. He was mainly asked for snakes and reptiles that burrow in the sands of the Makgadikgadi, as these were rare and hard to come by. Once he brought them a Quill Snouted snake, only the second specimen ever to be found.

School holidays were spent in the bush accompanying Jack on his expeditions, always with the second agenda of finding specimens for the Transvaal Museum. Ralph had a multitude of adventures while participating in his father's business. He tells of one frightening night when he was fourteen years old, going out on an ostrich-trapping mission with two of his father's employees:

"During one of my Christmas school holidays I was employed by my father to earn pocket money to catch ostrich for his farm. On this particular trip, I headed out with two fleet-footed assistants, Joseph and Milton, both not much older than me. We set out in my father's old Land Cruiser, Geisha Girl, for a week's trapping expedition. We headed up the old trek route from Bushmen Pits through to Sleeping Baobabs and beyond, one of the best areas for trapping. It was very flat with few holes so we could race at high speed after our quarry without danger of damaging our vehicle. By day six we had managed to trap about a dozen or so birds and decided to head back to my father's camp.

"The old Land Cruiser that we were driving had a set of enormous eighteen-ply tyres, which an American client had given my father. Being wide, and so very heavy, they never ever suffered a puncture. The downside of this was that they were too heavy for the vehicle. While driving along in the middle of the afternoon, I noticed a wheel overtaking me. Immediately the vehicle lurched to a stop, as the result of the side shaft having sheared off.

"I had been out of radio contact with my father all that day, so we decided that one of us should stay with the vehicle and the ostrich and the other two should walk to the main road. There we hoped they would get a lift back to my father's camp before he got worried and therefore angry. The walk was a distance of about forty kilometres to the main road, which could quite easily be covered in a night. It was decided that Milton and Joseph would do the walk and I would stay behind to look after the birds.

"After divvying up the remains of our food supplies, Milton and Joseph set off in the late afternoon. They took the majority of the food as well as all the water that they could carry and left me a can of baked beans and bully beef.

"The rains had been good and there was a pan not far from where we had broken down. In the early evening, I wandered over to get water to cook with and found it full of enormous bullfrogs. I managed to catch three of those to supplement dinner. As there were no trees in sight I had little wood to keep a fire going so I was in bed soon after sunset.

"It was a very clear bright moonlit night and I had thrown my bedroll down at the front wheel of the car, foolishly not setting up a mosquito net. My father always insisted upon us using a white mosquito net as he was convinced that no predator would ever take anyone from under a white mosquito net.

"Late at night, I have no idea when, it must have been at least midnight or one o' clock in the morning, I woke up, confused and not quite sure what was going on. I was aware of the most terrible smell and it took me a moment to come to. All I could see was a dark patch in front of me, surrounded by a halo of light. Then, to my horror, I realised what it was. An enormous head of a lioness blocked out the moon and the awful smell was her breath as she sniffed at my face. Fortunately, it was a hot night and I was just covered with a light blanket not zipped up in my canvas bedroll. As one does in a nightmare, when confronted with something incredibly frightening, one tries to sound authoritative. I swore at the top of my voice, hopefully sounding very aggressive but which probably came out as a squeak, and threw my blanket at the lion. This sham seemed to work and she reeled back leaving me absolutely starkers and lily-white in the moonlight. Fortunately, I was right next to the door of the car, and it worked ... I managed to rip it open and dive in.

"Once back in the safety of the cab, I realised there was not just one but six lions, the other five waiting in the slips for me to make a dash for it. There was no way that I would have been able to escape ... at least that is what I felt at the time. In retrospect, they were probably just being inquisitive.

"The lions hung around the car until the first light of dawn, by which stage I was absolutely freezing but not cold enough to be tempted to fetch my blanket! I did try once to open the door to grab it but that made them jump to attention. To my great relief my father arrived early the next morning. Being worried about not hearing from us on the radio he had left to come and find us and had met Joseph and Milton along the way and all was well."

His first task on leaving school was to learn to fly, which he did in Pretoria and became an excellent pilot.

Meerkat family at Jack's Camp

However, on his first solo journey home to Botswana in his single-engined Cessna, he inadvertently flew over Pelindaba, the nuclear research station, and within seconds was surrounded by menacing fighter jets, which forced him to land and explain himself. Flying is an excellent way of getting about in Botswana, where the distances are vast and roads rough, and it was to play an important role in both his thesis work and his explorations and bird trapping with his father. Along with Jack's quad bike on the Makgadikgadi it gave them greater access to a vast area.

Once school was over Ralph went to the University of Pretoria to study Conservation along with Botany and Zoology. He continued his higher education in the United States with the Endangered Wildlife Trust and wrote his thesis on the Wattled crane under the auspices of the Crane Foundation in Wisconsin. Part of this thesis involved pioneer work for George Archibald, the man responsible for rescuing the American Whooping crane from extinction through captive breeding and innovative vocalisation techniques. Cranes throughout the world act as a barometer for the ecology in which they live and the Crane Foundation continues its work to help restore habitats world-wide to the benefit of all.

Back from America he met a Zimbabwean man who had come to Francistown to buy a diesel Land Cruiser and was looking into hunting in Mozambique. War was still raging in Mozambique but Ralph, encouraged by his mother, thought it would be an excellent idea to go with him to trap birds. With his cousin Colin and the ever-faithful Samweli he headed east with his new hunting friend. The officials at the border post thought they were quite mad, as everyone was trying to leave Mozambique, not enter. They travelled in three vehicles. The first one had to go well ahead in case it was blown up. This was bandit territory. Their trick was to blow up the first vehicle, forcing the second to stop so that the guerrilla soldiers could kill the occupants and steal the vehicle and contents. If the next vehicle was far enough behind and the occupants saw the blazing lead vehicle it gave them a chance to turn around and escape. Happily they avoided such incidents and all got back in one piece, with a few new bird specimens.

Ralph had to get a job and continue his work on his thesis, and it was essential for him to be employed in an area inhabited by Wattled crane while doing his research. Luckily Jessie Neal had spotted him; she employed him in her Moremi Camp, home to Wattled crane. It was here that he realised that research and tourism could work well together. The researchers had always dismissed this idea, convinced that tourists disrupted and ruined their work, but he found that the guests at Camp Okavango were also extremely interested in his findings, which added an extra dimension to their safaris.

The thesis completed, he left his job at Camp Okavango and, together with his friends David and Roger Dugmore, hatched a plan to create a mobile safari company to operate around the Delta and the Makgadikgadi. David was put in charge of the marketing, while Ralph, along with Roger, continued to help his father in the trapping business to earn the money to support their mobile company, named Kalahari Kavango. A few agents supported them and Ralph led the safaris for the first two years, with either David or Roger helping until they obtained their own licences. They did fairly well but never earned enough money to support all three of them. They took their guests into the Moremi Wildlife Reserve and to the Makgadikgadi, where Jack had a base and quad bikes to

guide their guests on the pans. Their next plan was to have a camp in the Delta which they would use to form a circuit, giving their guests experience of water, big game and desert in the same safari, something no one else was doing at that time. This was before concessions were granted; if you were a Botswana citizen you could simply choose a place, get permission and build a camp.

They were all extremely excited about the glorious plan; with their youth and energy they knew they could conquer the world! Ralph meanwhile had fallen in love with the beautiful Catherine Raphaely who was spending more and more of her time in Botswana with him. Together with Jack they took off to inspect a site in the heart of the western Delta that they thought would be perfect, flying to the nearest airstrip, Pom Pom. But fate was about to deal them a terrible blow. After their inspection of the proposed site, their plane had hardly cleared the trees on take-off when it lost power and fell to the ground. Ralph and Catherine managed to escape, but just as they got out the plane burst into flames, trapping Jack in the back seat. Ralph braved the inferno to pull his father out, but in the process was himself horrifically burned. Both Jack and Ralph were flown to

Jack's Camp

the Burns Unit at Baragwanath Hospital in Soweto, South Africa, where, sadly, Jack died the next day.

Ralph was in what was, because of the dreadful atrocities prevalent at that time in Soweto, the most experienced burns unit in Africa, and he remained there for a gruelling six months, having countless skin grafts with Catherine at his side. The 1990 referendum was imminent, and the doctors, worried that if the vote went the wrong way Soweto might erupt in violent outrage, released Ralph a month early. They were afraid that he, being the only white patient in the hospital, might become a target.

Once recovered and back in Botswana, Ralph found himself in charge of his father's businesses, one of which was an ostrich farm opened in 1973 on the Boteti River. Ostrich farms are now quite common and very successful but Jack's was the first ever to open in Botswana and was not profitable. The following year, for the first time in living memory, the Boteti River ceased to flow, so he closed down the farm and sold the land. He also wanted to close the bird-trapping business, but as it was their only source of income it was not possible.

Kalahari Kavango needed to support all three of them (Ralph, David and Roger) full-time, so they planned a high-profile marketing strategy. They stuck to the mobile safari plan. No longer having Jack they were unable to get a Delta camp on their own. They made themselves known to as many agents and tour operators as they could, pooling all their resources for an overseas trip. In 1994, these three attractive young men, with long curly hair and boundless energy, took the travel industry in England by storm on their first visit to the World Travel Market, the industry's annual trade fair in London. Like three musketeers they cut a swathe through the African section, where everyone was talking about them and wanted to meet them. Their safaris, always being led by one of the three, became hugely popular.

Ralph had a passion for the Makgadikgadi Pans and longed to set up a permanent camp on his father's favourite site. Returning to Botswana after Jack's death he opened up a locked shed filled with teak crates, unopened since the family's arrival from Tanzania, and found them meticulously packed with a brand-new, full safari outfit. Jack had completely refurbished his equipment in 1959 in Tanzania before their unexpected exodus to Botswana and had not touched it since. Everything Ralph needed was there: tents, lanterns, basins, silver and china, jugs and glasses, beds, chairs, bucket showers – all beautifully made in the style of the 1950s. Kalahari Kavango, though extremely popular, had never been able to support three people. This discovery of Jack's new outfit gave him the impetus to stop the bird trapping, build his own camp and start making a living out of the safari business. The Makgadikgadi, which he knew so well, was the natural place for him, and Jack's Camp came into being on his original campsite, in the elegant style of a bygone era.

He knew the Pans area intimately, having explored it thoroughly with his father and he knew it was a natural extension to a safari in the Okavango Delta. He and Catherine, his partner, have worked extremely hard to make this one of the most sought-after destinations in Botswana. Ralph delights his guests with the wonders of the desert, conjuring up one surprise after another and creating memorable experiences.

A very stylish couple, Ralph and Catherine have put a great deal of thought into all their tents and equipment. When time made refurbishing necessary, they preserved the original ambience, always designing tents that were

elegant and welcoming. Today their original camp, Jack's, is twenty minutes' drive from a seasonal simpler camp called San – whose white tents grace the edge of the Makgadikgadi like historical campaign pavilions. Their mobile unit, for adventures in the Delta and further afield, was also designed with the elegance of a more spacious age in mind.

Saying hello to a member of the habituated meerkats

Making this destination popular has not been easy. That the unique attractions retain the interest of the guests without the Delta's daily parade of big game is due entirely to Ralph's approach. His knowledge, charisma and enthusiasm, as well as his ability to instil the same passion for the area into the guides he trains, keeps the excitement happily on the boil every day. Because this area is unique, Ralph runs specialist guide-training courses for zoology graduates carrying out research in the Kalahari – an idea he formed when doing his crane research at Camp Okavango. This research also benefits the guests, with frequent sightings of the solitary Brown hyena, especially at den-sites not far from the camp. The other special thrill is walking with meerkats (suricates). A local troop has been habituated and is most charming at dawn, when its members keep popping out of their burrow to warm themselves in the early sun. They are quite unafraid of people, tumbling and playing around the guests, but always have an eye on the sky for eagles.

But most exceptional are Ralph's visits to the Bushmen. He has fought long and hard to gain recognition for Bushmen in Botswana, and has become a pioneer of cultural safaris. He has formed a deep friendship with a small Bushman family, with whom he works very closely and who take him and his guests for a few days into the world of our hunter-gatherer ancestors. On such a visit you can walk with the men as they track and hunt, go with the women to collect herbs, roots and medicinal plants and, if really fortunate, you may witness a trance dance. This is truly the experience of a lifetime.

Ralph is a mixture of sophisticated worldliness and artless charm. The breadth and diversity of his knowledge seems endless, and his deep interest in everything around him will keep you spellbound every minute you spend with him.

MICHAEL LORENTZ

Water rippled along my legs as the elephant sank slowly into the lagoon with Michael, the mahout and me on its back. We were in the heart of the Okavango Delta and there I was, swimming with African elephants! It was my first encounter with Abu.

Michael turned to me and said, "What we are doing right now is unique; you can guarantee no one else on the planet is doing the same thing as we are right now."

There aren't many experiences about which you can say that. It was extraordinary. Michael's experience with elephants is vast, intimate and all encompassing, and his ability to share them with his guests is exceptional.

Michael is the only guide in this book that I did not meet through my life in the travel business, having had a close association with his family for most of my life. My earliest memory of him is in his grey school uniform, short pants just a little too big and no front teeth. He has grown into a man with an extraordinarily deep understanding of animals, feeling strongly that he has as much right to walk through the bush, to be there, as an impala, baboon, lion or elephant. No more and no less.

His first awareness that he really cared for animals came when he was about six years old and acquired a white rat called Blanche, whom he loved dearly. By the age of eleven he had decorated his room in the family home in Johannesburg with a large poster of a *mokoro* being poled through the Okavango Delta, depicting his dream of faraway places. He spent hours identifying birds or watching ants hurrying in and out of their nest going about their daily business. He found it all fascinating, but had to wait until he was fourteen, when his father took him on a walking safari in the Kruger Park, to be exposed to the real bush. The die was cast; Michael knew exactly where he wanted to be.

However, his conventional upbringing had him enrolling at Witwatersrand University to study law – clearly the wrong thing for him, as he lasted only a year. In 1984, by sheer good luck, he landed a job as a guide at Tanda Tula in the Timbavati Game Reserve, adjacent to the Kruger National Park. He was to take over from Bruce Measer, who stayed to help him get started and became his earliest mentor. Bruce had spent a nine years

Michael Lorentz

My dive off Abu

as a mounted scout in Zimbabwe during the war, only ever riding one horse, and was the first person Michael met who had that feeling of belonging, along with all other creatures, in the bush. He shared the position of hero and role model with Jack Mathebula, a Shangaan tracker with an incredible sixth sense about lions.

Jack gained fame as the tracker who found the white lions of Timbavati, made famous by Chris McBride's book of the same name. He had been away in Botswana, tracking lions in Savuti for seven years and Michael met him on his first day back at Timbavati. He realised what a gem he had for a tutor on the very first meeting when Bruce told him to go out with Michael. Quite soon they came upon some lion spoor at a river crossing. Michael said he knew which pride this was and was sure they were lying up in a wooded area to the north. "Hmmm," said Jack. "Maybe, but I think that they are lying at the crossing of Piggy Dam and the Rhino Loop." Something made Michael head Jack's way and sure enough, there they were, exactly as Jack had said. He had not been

back for seven years, he hadn't met these lions and was not tracking. He just knew. Jack and Bruce were phenomenal teachers, who set Michael on the right track for life.

Jack would only work for Michael. He was a stubborn chap and did as he pleased. If asked to track for another guide he would just sit on the vehicle in stony silence finding nothing. He was the most superb lion man Michael was ever to meet, but he didn't like anything else. He would look at leopards under sufferance, was terrified of elephants, loathed snakes and was uninterested in all small creatures. When Michael was carefully pointing out say, a mongoose or a dik-dik or an interesting spider to his guests, Jack would pipe up in Shangaan: "Mike, stop this, people haven't paid good money to see this rubbish, they only came to see the lions!"

In 1986, Michael left Tanda Tula and went up to Botswana to work for Gametrackers, a company with a collection of four (later six) safari camps. He was to take over managing and guiding at Santawani after three months' orientation at all the camps. He drove from Johannesburg with a couple of Gametracker managers who were transporting a new vehicle and a drum of paint to Maun for Mike Myers, the newly appointed General Manager. They stopped overnight at Francistown, leaving before dawn the next day so as to reach Maun in daylight. At 4 pm, after eleven hours' drive, they arrived exhausted, but quite pleased that they had made it. The roads were diabolical – thick sand and potholes most of the way. During one ghastly lurch the drum of paint fell and spilled its contents all over the floor. Mike Myers took one look at his brand-new vehicle, covered in inches of dust and spilled paint, and, according to Michael, went ballistic! He tore a strip off everyone and sent Michael packing for Santawani that afternoon. Exhausted and not knowing where to go, he headed off in more or less the right direction. Luckily he found that all roads led to his destination; there was nowhere else to go. When he first arrived at Santawani, it took his breath away. Here was the Garden of Eden; lush, fertile and packed with game – even better than Mombo is today. Extraordinarily, the poster he had hung in his room as a child was an advertisement for Santawani.

For the next three months he visited all the camps, spending a little time at each, doing transfers, guiding, transporting supplies, learning how the Gametrackers business ran and getting to know the area well. Eventually he settled down to run Santawani with two Botswanan guides, Buxton and Motuphi. Together they did some of the mapping for Ken Newman's *Birds of Botswana* and translated all the names into Setswana and Seyei (the language of the Bayei hunter-gatherers, Mothupi's tribe).

The guests came in by private charter from Gaborone or Johannesburg (there was no Air Botswana then) bringing fresh vegetables and fruit with them as the little grocery shop in Maun was only sparsely stocked. They had a wonderful time; game was so abundant it was not uncommon to see cheetah, leopard and lion on the same game-drive. Michael remembers a herd of eight hundred elephant passing through, along with large herds of eland and sable antelope. Today the Santawani area has dried up, sagebrush and acacia scrub have encroached and the game has all but disappeared. The lodge is no longer used on a commercial basis.

After their unfortunate start, Michael and Mike Myers became firm friends and had a glorious time together for the first couple of years. After managing Santawani,

Michael was made assistant manager to Mike, who was based in Maun. They would fly in a Cessna 210 checking on each camp in turn and helping out with the guiding. Once on a night-drive when guiding together, with three travel agents whom they wanted to impress, they caught sight of a springhare in the tracker's spotlight. Slightly over-enthusiastically they chased after it on foot, trying to catch it in order to show it to the agents. As Michael ran ahead it veered back, connecting hard with Mike's boot. Scooping it up, he held it firmly and took it to the car, showing the agents the teeth, the ears, the eyes, etc with a straight face, all the time trying to make sure it did not look limp in his hands. Turning to put it down they prayed the tracker would take the spotlight off it, but he kept it relentlessly lit while they placed it in a warthog burrow, assuring the agents that it was just a little disoriented and would soon come round in the safety of the hole.

These were the halcyon days; Maun was a wild, frontier town where life revolved around the Duck Inn opposite the airport and everyone knew Bernadette, the owner. She would not acknowledge the existence of newcomers for a year, they would have to earn their stripes and prove they would be sticking around before winning her approval and friendship. The Duck Inn was going strong when I first went to Botswana, it certainly had a Wild West atmosphere, with wooden tables dotted about, packed with locals and visitors; jolly photographic safari operators and their clients at one end and dour-looking hunters at the other.

Things started to go wrong at Gametrackers in 1990, four years into Michael's employment. Everyone had rather grandiose ideas on how it should be run and life at managerial level became very complicated. Michael could see clearly that he and Mike Myers were being led up the garden path. Mike had the responsibility for running the operation, but not the authority. At this point Michael decided it was time to have a year away from the bush and took off for London, leaving Mike Myers to face the music in Botswana.

Michael was a fish out of water in London, dressed in a suit and tie and working for an insurance company. Homesick and miserable away from the bush, he would watch Gametracker promotional videos, but they really didn't cheer him up. He fell in love, got engaged, fell out of love, got disengaged and was glad to return to Botswana, having finally accepted that city life was not for him. Gametrackers was being taken over by Orient Express and he helped out where needed at their camps for a few months before starting his own company with Katie Evans, training guides and providing relief management at various safari camps. Randall Moore and his elephants had recently arrived and he employed Michael for six weeks at Elephant Back Safaris to help him get the camp up and running.

His next phase was eight months with Hartley's Safaris where, along with Stephie Whitcombe, he did marketing and helped set up the private safari side. It was the first time he had led safaris by himself and he very much enjoyed it. Some of them were quite spectacular, for example, the private safari a German company gave their chairman as a farewell present. Hartley's sent Michael and Stephie to plan it, and they came up with wonderful ideas, all of which were taken on board and agreed to. Michael was the guide and Stephie went along as the hostess. A helicopter stood by every day to take them to different areas of the Delta to explore on foot and by *mokoro*. Not one meal was eaten in the same place; they had different locations for breakfast and lunch. Each night

they would leave camp for a bush dinner, again always in a different spot. Michael and Stephie both received an album full of photographs from the grateful clients, who had had the time of their lives.

Sitting with Michael while he talks to the elephants

Michael left Hartley's Safaris when Randall Moore invited him to manage and guide full time for Elephant Back Safaris. Stephie went with him for the first year, to be succeeded by Caro Henley, Daniela Bleattler and Sandor Carter. Those were the glory years; they had wonderful clients and wonderful safaris, all of which were five-nights long, the amount of time that they felt was needed to get to know and understand the elephants. Randall was in partnership with Ker and Downey (an established safari operator in Botswana but not part of the company of the same name in Kenya) and the original camp, though simple, had very comfortable tents with bucket showers and long-drop loos. Later, when

Randall acquired his own concession, the partnership with Ker and Downey ceased and he built a more luxurious camp on the current site.

Michael managed and worked with these elephants for nine years. He knows them intimately and part of his soul belongs to them. He didn't own the business, he was a bright, intelligent employee who eventually wanted to move on in life. He does not talk of the elephants very often but once he starts reminiscing on the 'glory days' his face lights up as the years melt away.

Elephant-back safaris

"The difficulty I have in talking about Elephant Back Safaris is that what has happened in recent years, with the direction it has taken with the development and management of the herd, is such that it has rather consumed my good memories. It has really made me question whether we ever did things right – and I'm sure we did, but I find it hard to reconcile the present with the past."

Michael's comments were made prior to the sale of EBS and in no way refers to the current management.

I have already written about the elephants and how I loved them, and how privileged so many of us were to have known them. The experience was created purely by Randall's innovative idea and his hard work, but for many of my friends and clients, and for me, the enjoyment was purely because of Michael. He made our safaris so special – for some it was life-altering, but everyone has exceptional memories of their experiences at Abu's Camp.*

Many of Michael's good times were had while filming with the herd. Once, when making a film for a French company, the site chosen was the lagoon on which the current camp is situated, but then it was twenty-six kilometres as the crow flies from their camp. As Abu had to walk there for the four days' filming, Michael and David, one of the mahouts, took him. For Michael it was the strangest, most magical journey. They left camp in the soft light of dawn, two men and an elephant, the three of them part of the bush, at one with the world in which they travelled, straight across the Delta. David rode Abu there and Michael rode him back. Hot and tired after the five-hour walk, Michael jumped up to join David on Abu's back as they plunged into the water to cool themselves and wash off the dust.

To walk with an elephant is quite extraordinary, you become like an elephant, part of the big scene; other animals usually see only the elephants and tend not to even smell humans.

I was walking with Michael when we came upon three lions on a buffalo kill, not twenty yards from us. The elephants stopped, their riders silent, as we tucked ourselves under Abu's tusks and waited. The three male lions looked up, one stood and turned towards us, staring at the elephants but not reacting to us at all, then, completely unperturbed, he flopped down with his companions, doing what lions like best; dozing with their fat tummies full of meat. Had we been walking without the elephants we would never have seen the lions, they would have scented us and run off long gone before we got anywhere near the kill. It was a tiny glimpse of that sense of belonging that is so important to Michael.

These outings were not always without incident. One cold winter's morning they were tracking lions, which had been seen in the distance; all the guests were riding and Michael was the only person walking. Following them

---

The dry season in Savuti

involved crossing some shallow, muddy water and, not wanting to get cold and wet, he decided to wait where he was for them to come back once they had seen the lions. Leaning his rifle against the trunk of a large tree, he sat down and lit a cigarette, quite relaxed and at peace with the world as the herd headed off after the lions. After a while, he cannot say why, something made him turn around and look through a fairly thick bush growing next to the tree, and there behind it was a large lion, trotting through the grass, looking over his shoulder at the elephants, which were coming along behind him. When the lion was five yards away and still completely unaware of him, Michael, with his heart pounding and his stomach churning, opened his mouth and shouted as loud as he could "BAH!" The terrified lion turned and fled. Everyone on the elephants saw the lion run off and heard the strange noise, but didn't realise that Michael was behind the bush until he jumped out and waved at them. They had followed the lion in a full circle back to his tree.

Michael has many entertaining stories of his time with the elephants, but I rather liked his tale of walking with three city slickers on their first visit to Africa:

> "Quite early on, about a year after I had started guiding with the elephants, three Americans arrived from New York, two men and a woman. They had never been to Africa before and were rather precious; I don't think the sun had seen their legs since they were four years old! On their first morning they turned up in their brand-new Ralph Lauren safari kit and decided to walk with me rather than ride the elephants. All the other guests were riding and only the four of us were on foot. Suddenly we saw lions in a palm

thicket, the herd was manoeuvred so that all on board could get a better view and we too had a great view as they ran out from under one palm thicket into another with the cubs following, not ten yards from us. I started hearing loud shouting from the outskirts of the herd, one of the mahouts was calling and instantly I realised that a wild elephant was approaching. It was without doubt the worst experience I had ever had with a wild elephant near the herd. There was one other guide with a rifle, on a young elephant at the back of the herd, who probably shot into the air far too soon. A young bull, in his twenties, was approaching and was definitely intent on getting into the herd.

> "I clapped loudly but he took no notice. I had guests on the elephants, the baby elephants all milling around, lions with cubs no more than ten yards away and three Americans on foot. I turned to the mahouts and told them to get out of here now, quickly, and to the Americans I said, 'stay within two feet of Cathy [the calm matriarch of the herd] all the way, Joseph is in charge and he will look after you. Now go!'

> "I had a dreadful ten minutes, this elephant did not want to be stopped. I fired three shots above his head, he kept trying to get around me to the herd, charging me as I dashed back and forth trying to cut him off. Finally he realised he wasn't going to make it, but it was a terrifying ten minutes.

> "When I returned to the herd, which had gone about five hundred yards, I found the Americans had taken me at my word! They had glued

themselves to Cathy, who had gone straight through Ilala palm scrub, which is covered in hooked thorns. Their clothes were ripped to pieces and blood was streaming down their legs. But the grins on their faces stretched from ear to ear; they had had one of the most exhilarating experiences of their lives. But they would not walk again on that safari. They rode the elephants on every outing, saying that although they enjoyed walking, nothing could surpass the walk they had on the first day."

Michael had an extraordinary and moving experience with a wild elephant that altered his perspective on life, on communication and on who we are. He felt it was truly a link between two souls. In his own words:

"The most significant moment I have ever had in the bush was one afternoon when driving from the Abu main camp to my tent on the other side of the lagoon. I saw a big old bull elephant in his forties or fifties standing thirty yards from the road, eating and just chilling out, calm and relaxed. It was a hot, still afternoon and the flies were bothering him, buzzing around the moisture in his eyes, so he was picking up a little dust from the ground in his trunk and puffing it on the flies. As I stopped he looked at me and shook his head. I watched him for about ten minutes, talking to him all the while as I do with our elephants, when he started to walk away. I called out 'Hey! Don't go, come here!'

"He turned and walked straight up to me, stopping about five feet from the car. My first reaction was to picture that big leader of the herd of elephants in *The Jungle Book*! Looking down on me was a very big boy and I was looking up at him feeling somewhat intimidated. His body language was not threatening, his trunk was quite relaxed, the end lying on the ground. It was as if he was saying, well, you called me, now what do you want? I kept talking while we just looked at each other, connecting, the most incredible energy passing between us, two different species were actually communicating. He was letting me know that he knew I belonged there, I was not an occasional visitor, but part of his world. It felt like hours but was only a few minutes before he turned and walked away. I was so elated, I felt I had won the lottery and drove home with a big grin stuck on my face.

"The next day I saw him again, not in the same place but it was the same elephant. I stopped and once again I called out, 'Hey come here,' and once again he did. I kept talking and again we had this great buzz between us; it was a moment of such emotional intensity that I find it hard to describe. I told Daniela about it, she being the one person who would really understand, as she had an exceptional rapport with our elephants. We went out together to look for him, found him, but this time he would not come up to the car. He just walked on.

"It was an experience of great revelation, I knew, right then that I had equal rights, not just with elephants but with all the species, it started to change fundamentally the way I looked at life."

Michael at Linyanti

Eventually the time came for Michael to move on. He had been in Botswana for many years and felt it was time to return to South Africa. Along with Mike Kurkinis he has now set up his own safari business, Passage to Africa. They are much sought after as consultants to safari companies and lodges and, along with taking his own safaris, Michael is kept extremely busy.

Many people who knew him at Abu's have chosen to travel with him again. His bush walks are recognised as being extra special; having walked on equal terms with all creatures in the bush, he feels a great empathy with them, and those who walk with him recognise that the animals return the compliment. He knows Botswana extremely well, but also loves to take his guests to explore South Africa, where he has a few little-known gems, way off the much-trodden tourist tracks, in the Karoo, parts of KwaZulu-Natal and Limpopo Province.

When he lived in Botswana he was married, and later divorced. The marriage produced his beloved daughter

Tagatha, whom he sees as often as he possibly can. He has now married Katie McGhee and feels that his life is at last complete and utterly happy. Katie has just completed a degree in Zoology and Botany, which, combined with his knowledge, gives them both an even deeper understanding of the bush.

Our place on the planet

Michael explains his unusual philosophy of walking in the bush, a feeling that grew from that hot, still afternoon when he made contact with the large wild bull elephant:

"Reading the map of the wilderness is the first step in personal evolution on a walking safari. As you find your own pace and clear your mind of its daily baggage – leaving it strewn to blow away in the morning breeze, the world around you comes to inhabit gently the space so made.

"We have this Judeo-Christian ethic of dominion over the planet and all its inhabitants, which is just utter nonsense. We could learn so much about humility and our role on earth from an animal like an elephant. With its communication skills, emotional intelligence, lifespan, the caring, the depth and the social bonds, it's impossible to think of ourselves as better – you really can't.

"Think of a female elephant: she will spend in her life of sixty-odd years, all of it, no more than maybe one hundred and fifty metres from one of her relatives. Think of it in your terms, being born into a herd or clan, with the matriarch and the whole family structure and all that that involves.

The bonds you create day in and day out, going through the good times, the bad times, the droughts, the fruiting, the matings, the first child, expelling your sons from the herd and the deaths. Think of the intelligence required to maintain those bonds over sixty years with very little aggression or animosity – there is a little – some don't get on, some are a bit difficult, all those little things, but on the whole they manage extremely well and could teach us so much.

"I am, as we all are, fundamentally an animal – we have the same senses and we all have our strengths and our weaknesses. We are very weak of body, but we are very strong of eyesight, we are very inventive and can consequentialise quickly and effectively. If we walk into a situation we can assess it at once, which gives us a lot of advantages. Each animal has to learn how to deal with the situations that arise. An Impala has its advantages; a lion has too; if you learn to play to them and understand them, then you are not an intruder. Everyone going on safari thinks they are an intruder; they are not, at least not on foot, in a vehicle you are, undoubtedly. On foot you are reacting to each other, all animals react to each other one way or another.

"An example of subtle inter-species communications is the way impalas react to baboons. Half the time they just sit together relaxed in each other's company; baboons are quick to give a warning bark when danger is near, but sometimes one of the big male baboons may take a young impala, they love the curdled milk in the stomach. Impalas understand this and are on guard with their young, always aware of what the baboons are doing. Hanging out with the elephants taught me to recognise these subtleties – seeing them happening all around me in their natural environment, camouflaged by the elephants. I learned how to walk on my own, without the elephants, knowing the animals were aware of human intrusion, but without influencing them or their reacting unfavourably to me.

"I have an unconventional attitude to walking in the bush; I feel we have a right to be there. It's all about territory; drop me into the Elephant Back concession and I walk as if I own the place, because I did, for nine years, but when you walk on someone else's land, you are the stranger and must be polite and respectful. I try to always have a gun-bearer when walking with clients, preferring not to carry the rifle myself. It is best to walk as if you don't have a rifle, relying on animal body language instead.

"People, like animals, also have personalities and it is up to me to learn to understand each of my guests, which ones really want to walk, which only want a short stroll and which really don't want to leave the vehicle. I try with all my heart to make them understand that they too, are only a part of nature and that we have to strive to live together in harmony in the ever-decreasing space on this small planet of ours."

Michael would never have understood the Okavango Delta as he does without the influence of Mothupi when he first started guiding at Santawani. They remain friends to this day and I spent an enchanted afternoon talking to Mothupi at Khwai Lodge on the edge of the Moremi Reserve.

THE STORY OF MOTHUPI, A BAYEI GUIDE

The Bayei people have lived in northern Botswana for over two hundred years, where they have traditionally plied the waterways on the Okavango Delta in *mekoro* that they fashioned from tree trunks. The tribe had moved down from the north and shared the area already occupied by the River Bushmen, or San, whose existence stretches back into the mists of time. The Bayei led a semi-nomadic life; during the dry months they lived, hunted and fished throughout the Delta, but once the rains came they returned to their villages in the dry land on the edge of the Delta, rebuilt their grass huts and grew crops.

Mothupi's family hunted the Xakanaxa area in the eastern Delta long before it became part of the Moremi Wildlife Reserve; it was their place and all that they knew. There Mothupi was born, in one of the most exquisite places in that special wetland, where immense, luminous lagoons melt into the distance, giving a sense of space lacking in the more common narrow channels and waterways. With prolific game, including plenty of hippo (the Bayei's favourite meat), it was a veritable paradise for Mothupi's father Sinokora Morutha and his family.

Mothupi is now an arthritic old man, who walks with difficulty but conceals any sign of pain with a beaming smile that shines among the folds of his face. A natural raconteur, he tells the stories of the life of Bayei hunters before the advent of tourism with humour, wisdom and wit. On a sunny afternoon, while sitting on the banks of he Khwai River, Mothupi told me how it was in the beginning:

"It was at Santawani that I started in safaris. Santawani was my hunting ground and I was there hunting – but I heard a rumour that someone was coming to put up a camp, a safari lodge. So I waited, making my palm wine, hunting and fishing until eventually somebody came. There were not many people around, just

Mothupi Morutha

me and my friends – these new people needed somebody to help them to put up the camp, so I came with my friends. We were casual temporary workers – we made the camp stand, then I was supposed to go away. But the guides came from South Africa, it was 1969 and they don't know this area, there were no roads, nothing, so I had to go with them to show them which way to go. Then the people had to go in a *mokoro* and none of these white guides could take a *mokoro,* they asked me if I could take the *mokoro* and I told them that poling the *mekoro* is what I do.

"I was born in Xakanaxa in 1940; it was my father's hunting area; he had to move away from the village and go there to hunt because there were no animals around the village and he took my mother with him when she was pregnant. In the hunting area we sleep on the islands away from the lions under a tree, sometimes with a little wooden fence around us for protection. We wore skins and hunted with snares and spears. We did not have wire snares, now you can find wire everywhere but in my time there was not wire, you had to find the plants to make the rope for the snares. The animal would step in the trap, which would catch him on the foot and then we would run to kill him with the spear.

"We would stay there for all the dry season, which maybe would start from May just as we finish harvesting our small crops. We didn't abandon the crops, we would dig a hole in the ground and put the ash in to protect the grain then cover it up. No one stayed in the village – everyone, all the children and the old people went to the hunting areas. We would stay there until December when the rainy season starts – if it starts early we make a very small grass shelter to keep us dry, just big enough to lie in. Then we would move back home and start to plough. Our houses at our village are also temporary houses; we make them each year. We always use *mekoro* to move – sometimes we kill the big animals and we take the skins in the *mekoro* too. If we want to go by *mokoro* to Maun with our skins it is a very long way. There is a big land in between Xakanaxa and the river that goes to Maun. It is Chief's Island and we have to go all the way up, practically to the Panhandle, before we can turn down the other side. This is why we keep some *mekoro* the other side because we can walk there and pick them up, making the journey to Maun much quicker. We had plenty *mekoro,* we kill the hippos, the leopards, the lions, all the animals and we take the skins to Maun to sell them – but today the river is too dry, you can't go to Maun by *mokoro* any more.

"We came back every year to hunt the same area, until 1962; that was the last year for me, my father came in 1963 but I didn't go with him, I was working then for Tsetse Fly Control. That year they told my father he had to stop hunting his area because it was going to be adopted into the Moremi Reserve. They gave him two weeks' notice to take everything away from there and move to a new bit of land outside the reserve. It was a good area but he was not really familiar with it; everybody was unhappy, they didn't understand what game reserve means, they are not educated people. I think about my *mokoro*; I have not seen this *mokoro* since 1962 when I put it under the water by the island with a small Marula tree. I wrote the date on the Marula tree, August 1962, one day I will go back and fetch it.

"I never went to school, my father taught me to read and write. A long time before I was born my father ran away from his parents in the Panhandle to find a job in Maun. The only job he could find was to herd cattle. Maun was just mud huts and a trading store. He was employed by the man with the trading store; that man was a white man. He would buy some cattle from the local people and hire some boys to drive the cattle all the way to Rhodesia, crossing the river at Kazungula to sell the cattle. When he got there he didn't want to come back, he found a job with a very kind man who put him in school otherwise he would never learn to write. There was nothing here, only bush and no one to teach. But his parents missed him and his brother was homesick for him. His father was a chief in that area and he organised some guys to go with his eldest son to Rhodesia to find him and bring him back because he can't go alone. He was very worried when he heard people were looking for him, he thought maybe he would go to jail, but when he saw his brother he decided to go home. He took with him his two books, the Bible and a book that tells me how far it is to the moon from the earth.

"He started to teach me in 1953 when I was thirteen years, he taught me from the Bible which was in Setswana, the other book taught me how far the moon is, but it was in English and too difficult for me. In those days everybody learned from the Bible, that was the only book. First I want to learn how to read then I want to try to do writing, but beyond that if I could only find a place where I could go to school, where I could try the English, I would be glad.

"Then in 1958 I went to South Africa to work in the mines. I went because I wanted to see what it was, I had heard a lot of stories and I wanted to go to school. And there was no work in Botswana. I went to Maun to sign up, I was wearing my skins so they gave me trousers, shoes and a shirt, then they flew me to Francistown to take a train to Johannesburg. I went with somebody who was older, he had been before, and he was the one guiding me. He helped me even with the language; you speak another language on the mines: *fanagalo*. [This is a simple language developed for the mines so that people from different tribes could communicate at a basic level.] So in my spare time I went to the night school. I worked for fourteen months in the mines, then I went home and hunted, then later I took out another contract to work in the mines again. I did that for five times until 1968 when I stopped mining.

"They looked after us very well at the mines, the work was very, very hard, but the night school was good and the food was very, very good. There was not shortage of food, you don't have to store the food, you just eat and when you have had enough you throw it away. I had never seen that before. I worked for Anglo American in some very deep mines, City Deep Mine, Western Area and Western Deep. Sometimes we were two or three kilometres underground, with no room to move under the low rock, where we would break up the rocks and put them onto a little belt that would ship them up to the top. We worked from four o'clock in the morning until four o'clock in the afternoon. Sometimes you would finish your work early but you had to wait in a queue to get in the cage to go up. It was a very strange place for a Bayei, especially at that time, because I knew nothing, except about the animals, I just went there like a lechwe or an impala, I had never seen a train and I never got up into the aeroplane. The pay was not very good, three shillings and four pence per day; things were cheaper in those days, but it was not a lot of money. My people don't really save money because we could not keep domestic animals as our land was covered in tsetse flies, so what I did with my money was to buy clothing and weapons for hunting and a big trap for catching lions and leopards. My father had one gun so I had to buy another gun for when the two of us go hunting. It is better to have a second gun, then we can help each other if one of us is attacked; the spear is not good enough.

"In 1968, I finished in the mine. 1969 is when I started that camp. George Bates is the man that started the camp but he died in an aircraft crash. It was called Mekoro Trails but in 1973 they sold it to Gametrackers and it was called Santawani. My job was to tell the South African guides where to go. Now there are roads everywhere but then there was nothing, it was only the third lodge, first Khwai then Xugana then Santawani. We never had visitors from overseas; they all came from the neighbouring countries. I didn't know any birds, the South Africans taught me all the birds, my job was to do the *mokoro* and they were very knowledgeable about the birds, they made me stop for every one and this is how I learned their names. And beyond that I took the other guides to teach them where to go with the *mokoro*.

"For twelve years I did the *mokoro* until Mike Myers came in and they decided to train me as the guide driving. In 1982, they took me to Khwai to learn to eat at the table, they trained me how to use the knife and fork and I was the only black man eating with the guests. Even I believe I was the first or maybe second black man to get my guide's licence. I have worked all these years for the same company; other people have bought it but it is the same lodges. Now Santawani is not used, the water has gone away and so have the animals. But in the beginning it was very, very lovely.

"It was in 1969 that I found my wife, Njahe. She lived in the area and we were related, we would marry maybe the third or fourth generation, not closer than that, it was because there were not many people. It is not like the old days; nowadays we choose who we will marry. Girls would marry after fifteen years, after they start to be a lady. In our culture when a girl turns to be a lady she is hidden in the bush for one year, only the mother and other ladies see her. No men can see her. Men are told not to go on this side; you have to go the other way to start hunting. She has a hood over her head and the exposed parts of her body, her legs and arms and her face are covered in clay from a termite mound.

"I had the time to approach her because her family had come to hunt in the area where I was working, I knew the family but had never seen her. She came out of hiding and I think, that is the one for me. She was dressed in nice beads, and all her skin and the skins she wore was covered in ochre. We are engaged together from 1970 and we have two daughters and one son. Ten years ago we got officially married because the rules say you must have a legal wife. I did have another wife before Njahe, she was very pretty but she was always complaining so I left her.

"Now I live at Khwai and my wife lives at Shirobe on the road to Maun. I work like everybody, three months on and one month off. My first daughter got married on the 29th August 2003, and I have taken her and her husband in a powerboat I hired to see the Xakanaxa area where I grew up. Even though I asked permission from the Parks Department if I could go and find my *mokoro*, I did not find it because we did not have the time to get there. One day I will be going back to get it."

Mothupi is a fount of information on the Beyei culture – their medicines, methods of hunting, superstitions and legends – and can talk about them for hours. The Gametracker lodges where he spent his whole professional life are now owned by Orient-Express Safaris and Mothupi, the living treasure they inherited, is employed at Khwai Lodge as their resident storyteller.

ZAMBIA AND ZIMBABWE

The great Zambezi River divides these two fascinating countries,
each unique in its own way. The river rises in Zambia
and flows south before turning east on
its journey to the Indian Ocean.

The great Zambezi River divides these two fascinating countries, each unique in its own way. The river rises in Zambia and flows south before turning east on its journey to the Indian Ocean. Along the way it is joined by the Chobe River, tumbles over the Victoria Falls, broadens into Lake Kariba, surges through narrow gorges and widens out to flow more slowly between the wildlife areas of Mana Pools National Park in Zimbabwe and the Lower Zambezi National Park in Zambia, areas of great beauty and tranquillity. From Zambia both the Kafue and the Luangwa rivers flow in as it surges into Mozambique through the Cahora Bassa dam. The crystal-clear waters of Lake Malawi flow down the Shire River entering the Zambezi beyond the dam before it finally spills over white sands onto the coral reefs of the Indian Ocean. These rivers have been the lifeline into central Africa for centuries and early explorers would have been overwhelmed by the huge herds of wildlife they came upon from the mouth to the sources.

The Luangwa River meanders through a vast, fertile valley that is home to a large variety of birds and animals. The continuation of the Great Rift Valley; its escarpments reveal primitive fossils and hot springs occur on the valley floor. Some of the best walking safaris in Africa are on offer here, where walking with professional guides has always been encouraged in the national parks, particularly in the Luangwa Valley.

The Busanga Plain in the northern area of Kafue National Park is a birder's paradise. From June, when the floodwaters begin to recede, until the end of October, visitors might be forgiven for thinking they had entered an aviary inhabited not only by a multitude of birds but thousands of puku and lechwe antelope and their predators. Zambia is not a place of mass tourism but has a pioneering spirit where it is still possible for a safari guide to take his guests to some of the least visited places in Africa.

Of all the countries specialising in safaris, Zimbabwe has the most diverse scenery and remarkable places, whether reached in a vehicle, on foot or in a canoe. Its most famous landmark, the Victoria Falls, never ceases to astound visitors with its power and beauty. This is a country that has produced excellent safari guides, the first to introduce formal training and stiff exams. Wherever you go the guiding will enhance your experience. In the north and the west are the main wildlife areas, where huge baobabs, mahogany and acacia trees shelter immense herds of buffalo and elephant; in the eastern highlands, the rolling hills and morning mist rising over trout streams is reminiscent of

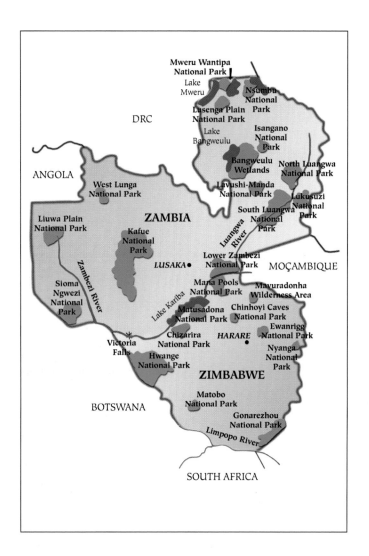

Scotland. South of the heat and dust of Hwange National Park near Bulawayo rise the atmospheric, bush-fringed granite boulders of the Matobo Hills, steeped in history and magic. This ancient place was once home to the San people, who left behind countless cave paintings thousands of years old; an epitaph to the enigma of their past.

The border runs through the middle of the Zambezi

GARTH THOMPSON

Garth is a Zimbabwean, based in Harare, but is happiest as far from cities as possible. His favourite place on earth is Mana Pools on the northern border of his country, where many of his guests meet him on a red earth airstrip surrounded by thick thorn bushes a few miles from the Zambezi River. The energy he radiates is contagious, filling his guests with excited anticipation from the moment they meet. Without doubt Garth would have spotted something special on the way to collect them, making sure their game-viewing began before they were halfway through the cold drinks provided as they clambered aboard his vehicle.

Game-viewing is of paramount importance to Garth; he believes this is what his guests have come to Africa for and not a moment should be wasted. His speciality is canoeing down the Zambezi River, where he makes every minute of the day count. All experienced guides are adept at creating memorable and special moments, knowing that the pictures in your head will long outlast any scene you have ever photographed, and Garth Thompson is a true expert at 'stage productions' in his beloved Zambezi Valley. He chivvies everyone out of bed and into the canoes before sunrise. And how right he is – all the moans and groans about the early rise are forgotten in one moment, as that spectacular red ball eases up over the horizon, painting the river with pink, then golden light. Feelings of joy and exhilaration overtake us as the canoes slide peacefully over the smooth water. Roosting cormorants stretch their wings to catch the first warmth of the sun and herons glide silently by on their way to their favourite fishing grounds. Ten minutes longer in bed and we would have missed it all.

Like all good guides he has an exceptional knowledge of wildlife, but on the lower Zambezi it seems to go deeper. This is his spiritual home, where he has personal knowledge of individual animals, especially hippos and elephants. He certainly knows where the bad-tempered lone hippo bulls hang out, giving them a wide berth in the canoes. He also knows many of the bull elephants, so prominent in Mana Pools, which have adopted that stretch of the Zambezi as their personal property. Some of the best game-viewing may be had in the heat of the day, when thirsty animals flock to the water. Garth is adamant that an hour or two spent sitting in the shade of a tree near a water hole is a lot more rewarding than a siesta in a zipped-up tent! He really loves listening to the natural sounds of the bush, which is why he prefers canoeing, walking and riding, as opposed to vehicles and noisy motorboats. However, as a good photographer himself, he does understand the necessity for a vehicle when one needs to get up close and in getting a good position for a photograph.

Once when walking with Garth he saw a little group of elephants heading for the river. We were close to the river so he took us over the edge and into a small dip, where we were all instructed firmly to crouch down and keep dead still. These wonderful beasts appeared just above us and trundled down to the water's edge only a yard or two away. Hearts pounding, we watched as they drank and swam. Their stomachs rumbled (were they acknowledging us?) as they strolled into the beds of water hyacinth for their morning snack, and we could relax and let out our breath at last!

Garth knows how to make a Zambezi canoe trip a most rewarding experience. His famous 'leg over' on the river (canoes all held together by legs over the next canoe) allows everyone to keep still while watching a baby

Garth Thompson

elephant frolic with its mother at the water's edge, or a timid impala coming down to drink. Breakfast is sometimes served in the middle of the river on a sandbank in shallow water, the table and stools pushed into the sand, everyone calmly eating homemade muesli and drinking hot coffee while knee-deep in the Zambezi (apparently crocodiles like only deep dark water). Being on that river is a thrilling experience, but being there with Garth lifts the experience into another realm.

He comes from tough pioneer stock. His Huguenot ancestors arrived at the Cape in 1688 and his great-grandparents were among the very first settlers to arrive in Rhodesia two hundred years later, farming cattle, fruit and maize near Fort Victoria (now Masvingo), the first town to be pioneered in what became Southern Rhodesia. When Garth was born his parents lived on the outskirts of Salisbury (Harare) by then a bustling city. His father was involved on a part-time basis in 'problem animal control' in farming areas, where elephants were breaking fences and destroying maize crops and lions were killing the livestock. Farmers regarded these wild animals as a major hindrance to their livelihood.

Garth's outdoor life began at the tender age of three when he was considered old enough to go out with his father on some of these expeditions. Although he was not allowed to go on the hunt, remaining with the camp staff under the bucksail – a canvas tarpaulin put up for shade and shelter – until his father's return, he still managed to sense the adventure. During these early days the seed of excitement and appreciation of the great outdoors began to grow. By the age of nine he had become obsessed with the wild areas around his home and spent many hours devising interesting trails on which he took his mother's guests at the weekend. The landscape included a river,

waterfalls, rocks and jungle areas, all of which provided a surprise at every turn – the germination of his guiding style today. He loves to create surprises.

His deep interest in nature remained with him all through his teens; in fact his girlfriends were persuaded to explore the trails with him, rather than spending time waterskiing and dancing the night away in the local discothèque. During his A' levels he was employed by Goldfields, a South African mining company, to assist a geologist in the south-eastern corner of Rhodesia, adjacent to the Gonarezhou National Park. He had little interest in the rocks and soil that he awoke each morning at four to help collect, but after nine, when the geologist was examining his finds, Garth's services were no longer required and he had the freedom to explore this vast and fascinating area for the rest of the day.

After military service (he spent four years in the army, three on active service) he had planned to join National Parks, but by a twist of fate his future was sealed during a squash game. His squash partner that day was a particularly pretty girl who had definitely caught the eye of one of the men playing on the adjacent court. One ball went astray, then another. The second time this happened Garth went to borrow a ball from the men on the next court. The man who could not takes his eyes off Garth's friend said that he would only lend him one if he could have a game with his pretty partner! While the two of them played squash, Garth sat talking to the other player, who turned out to be the personnel manager of Southern Sun Hotels, owners of the only three safari lodges in Rhodesia at that time. By the end of the game Garth had landed himself a job. Three weeks later he arrived at Hwange Safari Lodge, situated on a twenty-six-thousand-hectare concession bordering the Hwange

National Park. The plane he had arrived in was shot down by guerrillas on its return journey, killing all fifty-two passengers on board. The tourist industry, almost non-existent at that time, had suffered another blow and ten days after this incident the lodge was closed.

Garth in his office on the Zambezi River

However, Garth remained in the camp, training a militia force to protect both the animals and the lodge, building and repairing roads, firebreaks and boreholes, and heading up the anti-poaching team on the reserve. He took this opportunity to really study the wildlife and learn all he could from the experience. He would ask the local people for the names of the trees in Ndebele and then find them in the *Rhodesian Botanical Dictionary* to get the Latin names before looking them up in Keith Coates Palgrave's *Trees of Southern Africa*. He noted what the animals ate, picking up their droppings to examine them; he learned of the intelligent behaviour of elephants, the breeding habits of the birds and generally how the whole ecology linked together like a jigsaw.

Once the lodge reopened in 1980, the company changed from Southern Sun Hotels to Zimbabwe Sun Hotels. Garth was apprenticed to Dave Rushworth, the newly appointed resident guide, and began studying for his guide's licence. Dave Rushworth had a huge influence on Garth because of his knowledge not only of wildlife but also of tourists – there had been so few that most young guides were ignorant of their requirements. The Hwange Safari Lodge had only one 1964 Land Rover station-wagon to do the game-drives on the estate bordering the game reserve. The vehicle had a viewing hatch above the seats behind the guide, and could comfortably seat four guests and the guide.

Dave and Garth always went together, whether it was one guest or fourteen! This latter number sounds incredible, but one could squeeze into the front with Dave, three behind him, four facing one another on the back bench-seats, Garth would be on the roof along with six other guests, three in the front and four behind the game viewing hatch in the back. In those days the game-drive cost Zim$4 per person. Although $4 was worth a lot more then than it is today it was still excellent value. The drive started at four pm, returning at five to nine to be ready to take out the night drive at nine o'clock. The night drive was scheduled to return at eleven, but often they stayed out until one am. The $4 included all alcoholic and soft drinks.

Today, game drives at Hwange Safari Lodge cost a lot more, depart at four pm, only include soft drinks and return bang on half past six.

"Dave Rushmore had absolutely no need of money. He was oblivious to time and did not succumb to stress or pressure. He was equally

Above the Victoria Falls

at home with the rich, the poor, old and young alike. He treated everyone as equals and gave 110 per cent of himself to everyone, all of the time! He gave the guests what they had come on safari for – a genuine wildlife experience and to really feel wanted." Garth Thompson: *A Guide's Guide to Guiding.*

When Garth gained his licence in 1983 he was one of only eight licensed guides in Zimbabwe, of whom he and John Stevens are the only two still in active guiding. When Dave left to run a wildlife park for the King of Swaziland, Garth was made the Wildlife Manager of Hwange Safari Lodge and later the manager of all Zimbabwe Sun properties. At the time these included Bumi Hills Safari Lodge and Water Wilderness.

Garth, always a keen photographer, created a number of slide shows to share his knowledge with the guests at Hwange. Garth's forte was elephant behaviour, having spent six years with what was called the Presidential herd, which roamed in the large concession area adjacent to the Hwange Safari Lodge. It was a time when much more was being learned about the behaviour of elephants and their remarkable intelligence. It was from these many hours of observations that he first witnessed what was then a new discovery about African elephants: that mature bulls come into musth once a year; a secretion appears from their temporal glands and they dribble urine down their back legs – the condition known as the green penis syndrome. I have seen a large male elephant in full musth, he holds his head up high as he swaggers, radiating power and arrogance; you can almost hear him saying, "I am the greatest!" as smaller bulls and those not in musth back off and keep out of his way. In normal circumstances, full musth is achieved only when bulls are in their thirties and it is most likely that such a bull will be the one to mate with females that are in full oestrus.

When North American guests travelling with zoo groups saw the slide shows, they invited Garth to go to America and Canada to present his shows at various zoos. He travelled all over both countries explaining animal behaviour to a variety of audiences, with the largest being seven hundred in Calgary. On his first trip to England the World Wildlife Fund arranged for him to do a show in Godalming, Surrey. It was so successful that it brought a summons to Buckingham Palace for Prince Philip to see the slides. This was for an audience of two!

At about this time he was invited to invest in Rukomechi Lodge in the Mana Pools National Park, which meant leaving Zimbabwe Suns and running the lodge himself. He made his way to the banks of the lower Zambezi, where his love affair with the river began.

Mana Pools is a most delightful national park – an enchanted place. It is situated on the lower Zambezi River in north-eastern Zimbabwe, overlooking the mountains that are the continuation of the Great Rift Valley in Zambia. It is a gentle landscape of majestic trees with sweet-scented flowers, long vistas and hazy pastel hues that change hourly from a soft golden glow in the morning, through silvery blue at midday, to violet and pink in the evening. In the dry season it is packed with animals; wherever you look, there they are, moving quietly as if in slow motion – eland, kudu, impala, buffalo, baboons and a constant stream of small groups of elephant families. In the latter part of the dry season the acacia (*Faidherbia albida*) seedpods are the food of the gods to the elephants, which spend many hours shaking the trees and scuffling in the dry leaves to pick them up. A few of these intelligent giants have even learned to stand on their hind legs to reach them. This is a superb safari area and Garth's favourite. Although he guides all over Africa it is to Mana Pools that he keeps returning.

His love affair with Mel had started a few years earlier and now, married and expecting a baby, they arrived in Mana Pools to run Rukomechi Lodge together. Mel went to Harare for the birth of their son, David, returning with him to visit the lodge when he was six weeks old, but waiting until he was three months to move back permanently. Their home was a converted water tower; the bedroom was on the top, surrounded by wooden planks and consisting of their bed, a cot and a flush loo. Underneath there was a camp table, two folding chairs and a cold shower. Youth and innocence made this brave move work, the baby just had to fit in with their plans; the alternative – being apart – was not an option. Luckily David was a very easy, good baby and their guests hardly knew he was there. He was seldom ill except for one or two ear infections, which involved consulting a doctor by radio, then waiting anxiously for the next plane to land with new guests – and the antibiotics. Happily, problems of this kind were few and far between. Malaria is always a worry, but with prophylactic syrup for babies and his little canvas cot tightly covered with a mosquito net, he was kept free of this dreaded disease.

The real problems started when David began to crawl; his safety was, of course, paramount, so a cage was erected outside the kitchen to keep the animals out and him in a safe place. Here he happily played all day, a favourite toy being the brightly coloured rattling acacia seedpods. It was not possible to have a female nanny; as all the staff at Rukomechi were male, it would have made life far too difficult for her. Instead, an eighteen-year-old boy was employed, whose only duty was to watch over David all day.

They had one rather uncomfortable experience when returning to camp with a supply of frozen meat. On board the truck were Garth, his right-hand man Johannes, Mel and the baby. They were running a little late and were far from any habitation when the vehicle got stuck in the mud, right up to its axle. Try as they might, they could not get it moving and had to spend the night in the truck. Luckily they had brought some baby food and the canvas cot so David, oblivious of the drama, slept peacefully all night. The rest of them had only a bottle of brandy, so they passed the night taking turns to sip from the metal screw cap. Mel spent a sleepless night, convinced that the lions roaring nearby could smell the meat slowly thawing in the back of the vehicle and would appear to investigate at any moment. Luckily the night passed without further incident and help appeared at dawn in the form of a search party from the camp. It took five hours to dig out the vehicle.

That Garth and Mel managed so well with that tiny baby, while spending eighteen hours a day looking after guests, is almost miraculous, but finally, when David was about thirty months old, they decided it was time to get him back to civilisation and commute to and from the lodge. Ever since then Garth has continued to commute to the bush from their lovely house in Harare. David is now in his late teens and has two sisters. They have horses and dogs and are surrounded by all the trappings of a happy family life. Garth's deep love of the bush and animals has manifested itself in Danny, his eldest daughter, who occasionally helps him with his safaris during school holidays.

In 1987, the family decided to live in Harare for David's education, so Garth forsook lodge management and all that went with it: the storerooms, rubbish pits, workshops and staff problems; the endless repairs to generators, water pumps and all things mechanical, and took to the canoes. And there he has primarily remained, taking ecstatic guests on magical mystery tours of the Zambezi River, skirting hippos, walking in forests, sleeping under the stars and having many close encounters with elephants.

He created two companies: Natureways for his canoe and walking safaris and Safari Consultants to handle lodge bookings and transport. He has high principles and would send his clients only to those camps and lodges that lived up to his expectations, no matter what commission they offered. Unless they were up to scratch he would not use them, and Safari Consultants became one of the most respected tour operations in Zimbabwe. His annual detailed reports on all the safari lodges and camps became a bible to the overseas operators who used him as a ground handler.

Survival courses

During the first ten years, Garth's Natureways river safaris flourished, with guests coming from all over the world, but during this time he also ran ten-day survival courses for children between the ages of ten and fifteen. It was not only the Scout movement that ran survival courses in Mana Pools. Over one thousand children passed through Garth's hands on these outward-bound holidays where they were taught to track and live off the land:

"The survival courses were to instruct young people on the most important principle in life, survival; to be able to compete and survive against your peers at school, at work, in sport and in love. The most important tool in survival is a positive attitude; if you have this you can do almost anything. There we taught them how to find water and food, build shelters, track each other and animals, how to make fire without matches, direction finding, stars, frogs, basic birds, plants and their uses, and mammals and their behaviour.

"Usually on the fourth day of the course while out tracking, Johannes would drive to our canoes and take everything out of them except for my medics bag, fishing rods and worms. We would come back to find the canoes empty no clothes, food or bedding. I would explain that we were now shipwrecked and I was dead and they had to choose a leader. The younger kids, ten to twelve, always chose wisely, the thirteen- to fifteen-year-olds normally chose the loud-mouth bully boy who was mostly a bag of hot air and quite useless as a leader.

"Although I was 'dead', I followed them around closely to make sure no harm would come to them, bearing in mind there were lion, buffalo, elephant, crocodiles and hippo in close proximity. They would put into practice the various things that they had been taught; collecting edible plants, various spinaches and fruit, some would catch fish and others would collect firewood. That night we would all sit around the fire and they would eat what they had collected. Some were only wearing a pair of shorts, which is what they had been tracking in. When your ship sinks you can't ask for your suitcase.

"I would set them initiative tests, like offering them coffee if they could boil water in a plastic mug; obviously they couldn't put it in the fire as it would melt. They would put river pebbles in the fire and once they were glowing red, they would take them out with a pair of sticks and place these incredibly hot stones into the plastic mug of cold water, which would soon come to the boil. If there weren't stones around they would submerge the glowing ends of hardwood sticks that had made up part of the fire. They then strained the water through a hat to separate the ash from the water and make it cleaner.

"The following day they were split into groups of two, each little group given a match, the side of a matchbox and an egg. They had to use their own ingenuity to cook the eggs in as many ways as possible, boiled, poached, fried or baked. By now they were all quite hungry from small amounts of food the day and night before, so they were keen to cook the eggs. There were no man-made containers of any sort, no pots or pans etc. Those who cooked their eggs successfully could eat them while those who didn't had to wear them on their heads, i.e. they were cracked over their heads. If cooked, into the mouth they went, if soggy, then on the head they stayed! The most difficult thing was to collect good tinder and wood to make the fire with one match. I knew a few ways to cook an egg, but learnt many

more from their fertile minds, here are some of the ways they would cook an egg:

- Dig a shallow hole in the sand, place the eggs in there, cover up the hole and build a fire on top, the heat would bake them.
- Pack the egg with a generous quantity of mud and place the mud-enclosed egg in the fire until it baked.
- Wrap leaves around the egg; tie them with creepers and place the leaf wrapped egg next to the fire, turning it every few minutes until they thought it was baked.
- Place a flat rock in the center of the fire to heat up, temperature was gauged by the spit test, i.e. when spit evaporated quickly it was hot enough to break the egg which would fry on the hot rock.
- A youngster once asked me if he could have an orange to poach his egg in. I always kept a few oranges for the kid who became weak from the lack of food. He sliced the orange in half and ate the fruit (a bonus for his ingenious idea) he then broke his egg into the empty half orange, placed the orange on the coals, the egg bubbled away in its tough orange skin and poached well. Once it was cooked he ate a perfectly poached egg with the added taste of a slight orange flavour.
- Some kids would take the large woody fruit from a baobab, the cream of tarter tree, cut off the top third of the pod, some large pods could hold at least a pint of water. They filled the pod three quarters with water and placed their glowing stones in it until it

boiled. Once boiling, took out the stones and added one last glowing red rock to keep it boiling and then in went the egg, timed for three or four minutes and then tested with the egg test on the head!

• Amazingly if you just place an egg close to the fire and keep turning it, it eventually cooks itself, making sure not to have it too close or it will burst.

"They were given all sorts of other initiative tests, but these would fill a book on their own. In brief, once we were doing a twenty-five-kilometre walk after the night on Survival Island, after six kilometres they were tired and whining. I told them if they could stop a tourist vehicle and tie up its occupants they could drive the rest of the way in the abducted car. They decided to pretend a snake had bitten me (I was lying in the ditch moaning and groaning). The youngest most angelic-looking boy stopped the car. When the driver bent over to see how I was they attacked him and tied him up. They bundled him into the back of the car, I couldn't drive because I was 'dead' so one of the fourteen-year-olds drove and off we went!"

As time went by and the river became busy, there were quite a few hippo incidents: boats were bumped or knocked out of the water and when one man lost his leg Garth felt it was time to put a stop to the children's survival courses (even though no hippo incident ever occurred on a Natureways safari). Undoubtedly there are many young men and women who feel very privileged to have had this experience.

Ralph Bousfield reading Garth's book

Garth ran Safari Consultants and Natureways for fifteen years before selling them both in order to guide full time on a freelance basis. He continues to weave his magic on this special river to the lucky few who manage to book a safari with him.

His interests not being confined to Africa, Garth has explored many parts of the world. His passion for riding, taken up quite late in life, is huge. As well as joining horse safaris and local events, he has hunted enthusiastically with some of the best English and Irish foxhounds. He has climbed Mount Kilimanjaro, enjoys scuba diving and skiing. Besides energetic outdoor activities, he enjoys the theatre and writing. His curiosity has led him to explore most of the United Kingdom, Tuscany, not to mention parts of Canada, the United States, South America and Antarctica but his heart is in the African bush, where every day is filled with the delight of new discoveries and the comfort of the familiar.

He has written an extremely practical and amusing book called *The Guide's Guide to Guiding* (available from

The baobab – Chief Chikwenya's grave

94

Russel Friedman Books) – an absolute must for every safari operator.

Although close to his father, Garth only ever received one letter from him during his time at boarding school. It was in reply to a letter he had written complaining about an unjust punishment he had received. His father wrote back as follows: 'There were two prisoners locked in a cell peering out between the bars on the window, one could only see the muddy derelict yard, the other looked up to the stars. Which one is you, my son?'

Garth not only looks up to the stars but lives under a lucky one. He often tests fate by going where he ought not to go. Sitting alone by a busy waterhole in 2002 he survived a severe attack by an elephant, defying all medical prognosis by walking without even a limp within three months of the accident. Another of his adventures is the story that follows, a good example of his courage and luck, this time in Mana Pools.

Garth in 'Indiana Jones' mode – his personal nightmare:

"I thought you would be interested in a little bedtime story to ensure sweet dreams!

"It was at the end of my last safari for this season; we spent a night at Rukomechi, three nights canoeing and then the last night at Chikwenya. Brilliant elephant experiences, crowned by nearly an hour with an old cow elephant that lives on Chikwenya Island, possibly the biggest female tusker in Africa, she has a single tusk, dead straight and reaching to the ground if she doesn't hold her head up, some six feet from the lip.

"Yesterday morning, our flight was due to leave for Harare from the Chikwenya airstrip at 07:30. We left camp at 06:45 as I wanted to show the group of Wilderness Safari directors Chief Chikwenya's grave in the huge baobab not far from the lodge. What happened was without doubt the closest shave I have ever had in the Zambezi Valley.

"When baobabs get old (over a thousand years) they rot naturally from the inside and form massive smooth caverns within, which have been used in the past as stores, toilets, jails, armories, bus shelters and, in this case, a grave. The tree is about seventeen hundred years old. Chief Chikwenya was laid in her in the 1930s with his bow, arrows, spears and a large clay pot. During the Rhodesian bush war the grave was pillaged by the army, all memorabilia being taken other than the clay pot. I have taken a number of people into the tree tomb over the years. It is quite difficult to get in, as the hole is only about eighteen inches wide and as high. The hole is three and a half feet above the ground on the outside of the tree; one worms one's way through the entrance and then down into a handstand in the base of the tree, which is a five-foot drop. From the handstand you drop down very ungracefully and can then enjoy the coolness of this massive hollowed tree that could stand about ten people. I have not taken people in for a number of years because of a beehive that became active within the tomb. It takes about a minute to scramble and squeeze oneself out of the tree, which could prove fatal if attacked by the swarm. I have called the bees the custodians of the grave.

"When I looked in yesterday I had a torch with me and noticed that the honeycomb had been abandoned. Because the group was so enthusiastic I knew they would appreciate the inside of this exciting tree. I wormed my way in, did my handstand next to the pot and flopped over into a standing position. Everyone was excited and keen to join me. I shone the light up at the comb, definitely nothing there and then down at the pot. I began to play the light around the tree, I hadn't panned more than two feet from the pot when there in the beam was a seven-foot Black mamba rearing up, with its black mouth wide open and swaying its head from left to right!

"Well, let me tell you, I didn't want to be in there with this new custodian of the grave, but I couldn't get out as he was about three feet from the hole that I had to climb up to exit the tomb (about five feet above the floor) and who goes clambering a metre from a seven-foot Black mamba? I realised that my handstand had been less than three feet from the coiled snake; I had nowhere to run to and no stick to defend myself. All the other unpleasant situations that I have been in have been with my trusty old Mauser rifle in open space and with a mammal that is semi-predictable! So many thoughts went through my mind; here I was in the hollowed tree with Africa's most poisonous and aggressive snake, the world's fastest snake and nowhere to run. Enough to spoil my breakfast. I told the guys outside my predicament and they went to fetch a stick, during this time the snake continued to rear and weave, threatening me with its wide black gape. There are a few fifteen-foot-long, thin poles in the tomb, possibly rafters from the chief's hut. I tried to climb up them but they were old and rotten and snapped, breaking towards the snake and making it even angrier. I was less than pleased with my predicament. By now a stick to do battle with the snake, should the occasion arise, was passed through the entrance, it was less than three feet long and thin, not quite the weapon I had hoped for.

"I quote from the handbook *Snakes of Zimbabwe*: 'Black mambas inhabit termite mounds, hollow trees and rock crevices. Unlike the cobras the mambas hunt by day. When disturbed it will rear up and spread a narrow hood at the same time opening the mouth wide to show the black interior, any sudden movement will provoke a strike, which is likely to be inflicted on the upper body or face of a human intruder. This snake has a very potent and dangerous venom of the neurotoxic type, bites usually occur on the mid-trunk, hands, arms or head. Initially a variable burning pain is felt, cold clammy pale skin, faintness, nausea and vomiting. There is a tightening of the muscles across the throat and chest, partial paralysis of the lower jaw and tongue, drooping jaw, profuse salivation and slurred speech. The victim has difficulty swallowing, the eyelids start to droop, the pupils become fixed and do not contract in response to light, the eyeball is immobilised in the socket, producing a 'staring' effect. Muscle twitches and spasms occur, the victim shows abnormal sensitivity and pain to even a light touch on the body. Respiration and movement of the ribs becomes progressively more difficult and painful and as generalised paralysis sets in with spasmodic convulsions, breathing stops followed shortly by the heart!' Charming stuff!

"The last minute had been a stand-off; the snake continued to weave as did my thoughts, including the possibility of him streaking forward and striking with lightning speed and attaching himself to my left cheek or neck with those long fangs. The mamba, that I am sure was also feeling quite uncomfortable (thank goodness), then found a hole at the base of the tree and his long and slender body began to disappear into it. What absolute relief! It continued to disappear into the base, I was informing my anxious friends on the outside of the tree of the positive developments. There was still eighteen inches of tail left when lo and behold the coffin-shaped head pops out of a crack in the bark (still inside the tree) about twelve inches from the hole where I had entered the tomb and was hoping to evacuate through as soon as an opportunity arose. Well this really put a dampener on things, I thought of future tourists coming to the grave with various guides to visit Chief Chikwenya's grave and that of some fool guide called Thompson who didn't make it out of the dusky cavern. The

snake surveyed the scene, I felt trapped and helpless. After no more than a few seconds, its head disappeared and down it came to its original position and began to sway in an upright position and display the black open gape of a little under 180 degrees. I thought my only way out was to kill the snake, I didn't really feel that this was a good conservation ethic in

Garth at the entrance

front of all the Wilderness directors who stood outside giving me encouragement and moral support. I also thought that if I did do battle with the mamba, there was a good chance that I could sustain a bite along the way, which was at the bottom of my life's priorities.

"At this point I decided to try and lift myself up on a strong stick (about seven feet long) that was leaning against the inner wall. I found a good hand-grip on the inside of the bottle-necked tree cave, told the guys I was attempting an escape, legs first. I found some incredible strength from somewhere and levered my bulk up like an Olympic gymnast, pushed my feet into the hole, with that the guys latched onto my ankles and pulled me through the tight hole like a rifle cleaner coming out of a barrel. Well, there was much gusto and relief from us all, not the least of all, myself.

"After every walking and canoeing safari I breathe a long sigh of relied that no man or beast was hurt. I had so enjoyed this trip with such enthusiastic and like-minded new friends and to think I was in this predicament on the way to the airstrip, having taken a ten-minute diversion. How quickly the events of life can change.

"What a very unpleasant experience, certainly one of life's worse. As I exited we heard our aircraft circle overhead and prepare to land. What a pleasure to be going home in one piece.

"I vow never to disturb the grave of Chief Chikwenya and its custodians again. I can only thank God it all turned out as it did. Sweet dreams!"

Susie checking the cavity

A safari with Garth is without doubt one of the most exciting and exhilarating experiences you will ever have. Your journey with him will create everlasting memories and a strong desire to return, to live through the enjoyment again.

Dick, Olivia, Hetti Jackson-Stops and Garth on our family safari

BENSON SIYAWAREVA

I first met Benson when he was managing and guiding at Little Makalolo, a camp in a game-rich private area of Hwange National Park that is open only to guests at lodges within the area. Benson's charming six-bed tented camp is tucked into a grove of trees that looks out on the water hole set in a wide grassy plain edged with thickets of trees. It is one of the few waterholes in the area and a vital lifeline to animals in the dry season. Benson had designed a superb hide on the edge of the waterhole; it is constructed of dead trees piled together to hide a shallow concrete pit, in which people can stand, unnoticed behind the branches, and watch the animals drinking and interacting with one another in the water. This particular style of hide is his own and very successful invention.

Benson is an exceptional man, calmly assured, pragmatic and in control. His passion is his country and its wildlife. One of the first black Zimbabwean guides not involved with the National Parks to obtain a professional guide licence, he has risen through the ranks, developing great managerial and leadership qualities, a fact recognised by Wilderness Safaris, by whom he has been recently employed

His first brush with nature was at his birth. His mother started her walk to hospital to have her baby a little too late; he arrived when she was only halfway there and, with the help of a companion, she gave birth to Benson in a gully by the side of the road. He is certain that this must have had an impact on his choice of career! He had a happy, carefree childhood in a loving and close-knit family living in a rural area not far from the Great Zimbabwe Ruins. His father was the headman of their village in charge of about fifty families. His home was a traditional thatched hut with no electricity, and water being drawn from a nearby river. As the last-born child his responsibilities with the animals and household chores kept him at home longer than normal – he was seven before he went to school. He remembers those early school days with all the other children laughing and having fun while walking the seven kilometres to and from school each day. English was the language used in all schools; difficult for him to start with, as it was not spoken at home. However, he was a quick learner and soon became the most proficient in the class.

Benson's childhood was in the late 1970s, during the Rhodesian war (the *chimurenga* – 'the war of liberation'), and his two elder brothers were involved with the Rhodesian forces. His eldest brother was in the army and the next eldest in the police force. As the war intensified it became difficult to continue their rural existence; they were threatened by the liberation forces and eventually had to leave their home. Having a brother in the army meant there was someone in a position to look after them and he arranged for them to rent a house in Fort Victoria (Masvingo) near the barracks. Moving into a house was very strange for them all. Having light at the flick of a switch and water at the turn of a tap was astonishing in itself, but the strangest new custom of all was having to go to the loo in the house. This was something completely alien to a boy who had always been taught that this was done as far away from the living quarters as possible, out in the bush. The first time he looked into the lavatory bowl he thought it was a well to collect the water.

Benson's soldier brother, whom he hero-worshiped, was very eager that he and his family should get on in life, so

Benson Siyawareva

he encouraged Benson to work hard and achieve good grades. All the children in Rhodesia who had relatives in the army were given free education, with the condition that when the education was complete they would be inducted into the army. The education continued along lines that would prepare them for this. They joined the Boy Scout movement, which taught them self-sufficiency and leadership and gave them practical experience in the bush. Most weekends were spent camping in the small park outside the town, where they were taught to ride horses among the game, to put up tents, cook and generally look after themselves out in the bush. Benson flourished in these surroundings; it was the beginning of the love of wildlife and the bush that was to become his life's passion.

His brother was now responsible for not only his own wife and children but also his parents and siblings. When not on military duty he would take Benson into the bush to do a little hunting; it was really poaching, but it was necessary to help feed his extended family. He taught Benson the art of silently stalking animals, keeping downwind from them in order to kill duikers and hares or guineafowl and doves – whatever they could find for the pot.

Fortunately for Benson the war ended as he finished his seven years' schooling and he did not have to join the army but could continue into higher education. With the ending of the war his brother wanted to get away to start a new life as quickly as possible. This was not so easy as the new government needed to incorporate the freedom fighters into the established army and prepare them for the civil war starting in Mozambique. This was the very last thing he wanted to do but they required the help of experienced soldiers. In the end he obtained his discharge from the army to join some of his white military friends who, knowing how skilled he was

with weapons, invited him to join them in their hunting company. His new career was to have a great influence on Benson, who would go up into the hunting area each weekend to help around the camp, learning all the while about tracking and camp life. He enjoyed it all but found the killing and the bloodshed difficult to cope with, bringing the awareness that his future path was more likely to be concerned with conservation.

Just when he had passed his O' levels his plans took a serious knock. Much to his and his father's dismay, his girlfriend became pregnant. The family disapproval was severe; both his brother and his father told him he could not go back to take A' levels, as he would have to find work to support his child. He was so miserable that he locked himself in the house and cried, day after day. He just could not believe what a mess he had made of everything. Finally a friend of the family persuaded his brother and his father that it would be in all their best interests if he could complete school. He was truly delighted and once he had his A' levels he desperately wanted to go to university. This was too much for them to accept, so he had to buckle down and care for his own family. His only choice was to take a job teaching for a year while he decided what to do.

His brother, who had by now left hunting to join a photographic safari company, came down to see Benson. He felt that the poor, ill-equipped school where he was teaching was doing nothing to help him get on in life and tried to get him to leave and come to his camp. Benson would not go, in fact he would not allow anyone to help him. It was a low moment in his life, but he knew he had made a mess of things and wanted to work it out for himself, without being beholden to anyone else.

The change came when his brother asked him to escort his children on a visit to their father at the camp where he was working. After their long hot dusty journey on foot and in overcrowded buses from Masvingo, it is not difficult to imagine what a joy the sparkling blue expanse of water at Lake Kariba must have been to those travel-weary eyes. None of them had ever seen such a vast amount of water and here it was, bathed in sunshine, Fish eagles calling from the trees and pleasure boats buzzing about in the water. Over on the Zambian side the hills were barely visible through the haze, but where he stood the steep rocky slopes, dotted with baobabs, rose from the green floodplain that edged the lake, on which huge herds of buffalo, zebra and antelope grazed contentedly. The shallow waters near the shore were spiked with stark-white leadwood trees, long since killed by the rising waters but too tough to rot down. Clusters of cormorants perched on bare branches while elephants

An evening drink at the Makalolo waterhole

Benson at the Little Makalolo waterhole

bathed beneath. Fothergill Island is just off the shore in the Matusadona National Park and had become a popular tourist lodge; it was here that Benson arrived by boat with his brother's children. This brief visit had a profound impact on him and he returned to his school with a heavy heart, realising how different life could be. A few months later his brother decided to take the initiative and sent his headmaster a telegram saying that Benson was to leave immediately as his brother needed him right away. He left and never went back to teaching..

His life had taken the right turn, but it was not all plain sailing. Fothergill employed him, but he could not do any safari guiding, as he couldn't drive and was, in fact, completely untrained to do any job other than teaching. He was the camp gofer for a few weeks, then they sent him to Chikwenya Lodge on the lower Zambezi, which was short-staffed. Again he was no real use and was sent back to Fothergill where he was now on his own, his brother having decided to move on. He knew he had to pull himself together and find something to do in order to remain at Fothergill. He learned how to drive a boat and acquired a boat licence, and this was his first step to his main ambition of becoming a safari guide. The competition was fierce. Many young white school-leavers were coming up to Fothergill to train as guides; most would not last the course, but Benson hung on.

Noting his obvious desire to succeed, the management decided to make him a test case. They felt sure a black Zimbabwean could learn to be a guide and look after foreign tourists. He had to start from scratch. With his boat licence under his belt, he studied bird books while taking guests out for boat rides until he knew all of the species indigenous to the area. He then learned to drive a vehicle, took his courier licence and could then drive tourists. In 1991, he was granted a professional guiding learner licence and could legitimately take game-drives, finally attaining his professional guide licence in 1992. It was a very proud day for all his family. He had worked extremely hard to reach that level of proficiency, and the examinations in Zimbabwe are particularly tough. Having stayed at Fothergill for his entire training and becoming head guide, he decided in 1993 to move on. He joined a government-owned camp called Detema where he was made the estate manager responsible for all the vehicles, the guides, their training, the gardens and looking after the concession ... and he had his own company car. He stayed for three years until a new manager arrived, a woman who apparently did not like men at all, especially those in authority. He hated the conflict it caused and moved on to the Landela Safari Company as manager and guide, first at Sanyati, their beautiful lakeside lodge, and then at Gache Gache. He never felt he was qualified as a manager, as all his qualifications were to guide, but the experience and necessity had made him quite capable of managing the camps.

While still at Fothergill he helped with a project to reintroduce cheetah into the Matusadona National Park. His duties included rising at five each morning to shoot an impala, then taking it to be disembowelled before feeding it to the cheetahs that were still in a *boma* waiting to be released into the wild. He lived in a tree house near the *boma* in order to keep an eye on the cheetahs. He thought it would be fun to suspend some of the old impala carcasses from his tree house to attract lions. That night he awoke to a dreadful commotion; the lions, which had discovered this little prize but couldn't reach it, were climbing up the steps to his room for a better chance to grab the carcass, only to flee in fright when Benson appeared clapping and shouting at the top of the steps.

He tells of what a wild young man he was, always trying to be macho and daring, particularly with lions, which he found tremendously exciting. Having been saddled with family responsibilities so young, he had never really had time to let go, to be a bit wild, to hang out with the guys and have fun. Although he took his responsibilities seriously, and had put his whole heart into getting his qualifications, he did in those days, have a wild, slightly reckless side. One of his favourite tricks was to chase lions to impress his guests, making the lions run and snarl at him; it was all fun and games with no thought for the animals. He remembers this unfortunate stage of his life with regret. A couple of incidents had a very sobering effect on him. It took only a few very frightening moments to knock this recklessness out of him and make him the top professional guide he is today. Benson relates the first one himself:

"One of the incidents that altered my outlook happened when taking a group of young Australians on a game-drive. They taunted me with the fact that so far they had seen no lions on their holiday and did not believe there were any. They wanted to walk and were all rather puffed up and cocky. They got out of the vehicle and after about five minutes I found lion tracks and told them all to stay tightly together behind me, to keep quiet and on no account to run. The tracks showed the lions had small cubs. We had followed the tracks for a short while when suddenly a lioness rushed out of the grass, straight at me. I stood my ground and told everyone to inch back very, very slowly, but the lion kept roaring and pawing the ground and was soon joined by another. My heart was pounding as I gently retreated while talking softly to my guests, not realising that no one was behind me – they had all fled and tried to climb trees and this is what had so upset the lionesses. Oh my God, I thought, not only have I upset a pride of lions but also I have lost all my guests, how on earth do I go back to the lodge and tell them this? I searched and found the first lady crouched under a bush with her head in her hands, the others soon appeared from behind bushes and down trees. Shaking and terrified they wanted to rush straight back into the vehicle, but as the lions were sitting on the road between the vehicle and us, there was nothing for it but to take a long walk through the bush, circling around them to get back to the car."

The other incident, although equally frightening, was not his fault. With a vehicle of seven people out on an afternoon drive in February, when the grass was very high, he inadvertently drove into a herd of elephants. The car stalled and the elephants went mad. One large cow charged the car and broke the door but luckily her tusks went under the chassis rather than through the door. She lifted the left side of the vehicle trying to push it over, but it teetered on its right front wheel while being dragged across the road. Benson was frantically banging on the bonnet while trying to restart the car. Suddenly it did start, and she took fright, dropped the vehicle and made off. The other elephants gathered in fury, trumpeting and mock-charging to the abject terror of the guests. It transpired that the baby elephants had crossed the road ahead of the main herd, becoming separated from them by the vehicle. Strange as it may seem, these particular guests regard that incident as one of the high points of their lives, and have returned many times to go on safari with Benson! This underlines my conviction that many people go on safari in order to experience and conquer fear.

Coming close to death has a profound impact. It certainly made Benson regard the animals in a different light. He now realises that mutual respect makes game-viewing a much deeper experience, engendering knowledge and understanding of our fellow creatures, and has become adept at judging how close one can get and still be safe. We had a wonderful evening together at his waterhole at Little Makalolo, where, instead of going into the bunker, we sat on a branch quite near the water but out of reach of elephants. As the warm glow of twilight washed over the land the elephant families came down for their evening drink, each family taking turns to approach the waterhole. They came very close, raising their trunks to sniff us, but never being aggressive, only curious. More and more arrived in the next hour, until about one hundred and fifty were in the water or nearby.

One family included a rather mischievous young bull, too young to leave the herd but clearly wanting to; his mother and aunts were constantly chivvying him to stay with the family group, but he kept wandering off, doing exactly as he pleased. When he saw us he came to shake the branches we were sitting on but not with malice. We bumped into them while out driving the next day, and knew it was the same family because we recognised the young male, still being naughty and wandering off. It was fun to see elephants trying to deal with an errant teenager with about the same amount of success as human beings!

Benson had been running Gache Gache Lodge with a Scottish-born woman called Melissa Gilchrist, who lived in Zimbabwe with her mother. He was very fond of Melissa and they worked very well together, so when she went back with her mother to live in Scotland, he decided sadly that he too would leave Gache Gache. Uncertain where to go next, he was contacted by Wilderness Safaris, who were investing in lodges in Zimbabwe and looking for good people to run them, and Melissa had recommended him. They flew him to Victoria Falls for an interview and immediately offered him a job at Makalolo in Hwange National Park. Benson became involved in the project of rebuilding the old Makalolo Camp – the first time he had been on a building site – and he found it very stimulating.

Benson and Noreen at Savuti Camp

Wilderness Safaris' intention, once Makalolo was up and running, was that Benson should start his own venture, which was to build and run a small tented bush camp. In May 1997, the directors began flying all over the area, trying to locate the best spot, but Benson told them to get out of the plane to drive and walk with him; it had to be found on the ground, not from the air. While walking they came upon an area with a couple of small pans in which buffalo were lying while elephants strolled by. This was the perfect spot. The four sites for the tents were carefully chosen and the drilling machines came in to dig

a borehole. Fortunately they found the water in one day, as the camp had been sited before the water had been found – it is usually the other way around. Little Makalolo Camp opened in July 1997 and became Benson's life and his home for four years.

In 2002, Wilderness Safaris sent him to the Linyanti area of Botswana, where, together with his second wife Noreen, he manages and guides at Savuti Camp. A large waterhole in front of the camp is an important feature and once again Benson has excelled himself by building a hide there in the same style as the one at Little Makalolo. This is arguably the finest hide at any water hole in Botswana, where guests can see spectacular parades of animals all day long from the hide and above from their own rooms.

He has a house in Masvingo where his first wife and children live. His first son is at his old school in Masvingo, studying for his A' levels. He and his wife Noreen were the joint managers of Savuti Camp and kept a rented house in Victoria Falls His greatest wish is that all his children get a good education and he works hard to achieve this.

Benson told me he was uncertain about his future and waits to see where the wind blows him. Well, a warm wind has blown him a sponsor. He has been able to set up his own private guiding company, which he calls Ngoko Safaris, *ngoko* being the Shona word for dung beetle and his boyhood nickname. He is now available for private safaris which I know will prove popular.

Although it is highly unlikely, with his great love of guiding and the outdoors, that he would ever take a desk job, one cannot help thinking that with his common sense, vision and superior intelligence, he would be the greatest asset to Zimbabwe in their tourism and wildlife departments.

IVAN CARTER

Ivan, yet another Zimbabwean, is the youngest of the twelve guides I have profiled in this book. His youthful zest for life and vibrant energy are contagious and heart-warming. When on safari with him I was convinced I could do anything, stalk a buffalo, climb a tree, walk up to elephants and count the stars. For a quick beat of time, I felt nothing was beyond me. Mana Pools is his spiritual home but he takes enormous pleasure in visiting all safari areas in Africa, particularly little visited places, spurred on by his insatiable curiosity of the unknown. He sees all aspects of life at a slightly different angle and as a lateral thinker he comes up with alternative slants on most accepted beliefs and convictions.

On our first day at Mana Pools we were sitting on a sandy bank of the Zambezi River at sunset. The air was still and the purple evening light lay softly on the mountains rising steeply across the river in Zambia and the sky was streaked with wisps of orange clouds reflected in the still, dark water. A crocodile silently raised his eyes out of the smooth surface of the river with hardly a ripple, noted our position and sank back. We moved a few feet back from the edge. Ivan turned to me and said, "When you took your shower this afternoon did you reflect on the fact that the last time one of those drops of water landed on a living creature it could have been a dinosaur?"

The constant recycling of water is only one of quite a few unusual observations that Ivan comes up with while exploring the 'big picture' and wondering about the universe. This wonder boy of the new generation of safari guides seems to soak up knowledge like a thirsty sponge. His questioning and probing make for lively conversations around the campfire.

Born in 1970 to farming parents he grew up, in common with most other safari guides, exploring the bush and learning with interest all that went on around him. His earliest letters home from boarding school aged seven or eight were all about the birds he had seen and what eggs he had found. However, also in common with most other safari guides, school was not his preferred place – being shut in a classroom, learning things that had no relevance to his life, was a bore. Homework was ignored and exams were failed. During his last two years of school, his A' level years, he practically skipped classes altogether. He learned how to work the system by not turning up for classes right from the first day, so that the teacher thought it was a mistake that he was on the list. It seems extraordinary that he got away with it, but he did. Falconry was his great passion and as the school had a falconry club he could keep his bird at school. He managed to persuade one of the masters to let him keep his dog at school too. The master looked after the dog, but insisted that if anything went wrong it would be sent home immediately. Ivan obviously has always had tremendous persuasive powers; even getting me to try to climb inside a hollow baobab tree packed with bats. Luckily I couldn't squeeze through the hole in the trunk!

Every morning, straight after breakfast, he went into the fields surrounding the school with his dog and his falcon, always returning in time for roll-call or meals, usually at a sprint. No one knew he had been missing, though he was once very nearly caught out. He joined the athletics meeting one afternoon and ran a race that he won more than comfortably. He was promptly put on the school

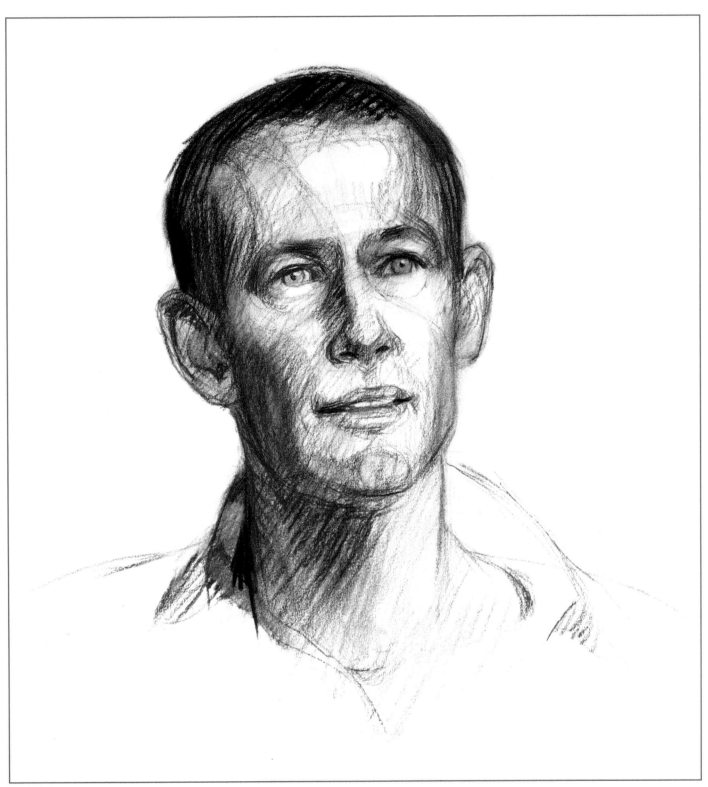

Ivan Carter

team and, afraid he would come to the notice of the school hierarchy, he had to make sure he never won again, even in practice, so that he was soon thrown off the team. He managed to survive two whole years doing this, naturally with abysmal academic results. Ironically, a few years later, some of his erstwhile schoolmasters came asking for work in his safari business.

Ivan's ambition was to work with animals, originally as a vet. At about the age of eleven, he spent his school holidays at the little rustic tented camp belonging to Hwange Safari Lodge when it was run by Garth Thompson, and Garth's enthusiasm planted the seed of his love for wildlife. However, with his A' level results the study of veterinary science was clearly out of the question. Instead he got a job working in an animal orphanage in Bulawayo. It was not really a zoo, as all the animals needed to be there, but it was open to the public and Ivan had the job of showing people around and helping to care for the animals.

A man from the Bulawayo Zoo, who visited the orphanage frequently, suggested that Ivan might like a career as a safari guide and introduced him to Hans Strydom, who ran Sanyati Lodge, a most attractive establishment on a hillside overlooking Kariba Dam. It was 1988, a busy time in Zimbabwe, and Hans, needing another pair of hands, took a chance and gave Ivan the job.

Hans did not have a professional guide's licence, so very little training came from that quarter. Ivan was just thrown in at the deep end. He had never run a boat in his life, so on the day he arrived, Hans spent half an hour showing him how to do it and sent him out on the lake with clients that evening. He had tremendous fun working at Sanyati and always feels that he learned a huge amount there by simply having to learn the hard way. One memorable weekend a group of Johannesburg businessmen, cut loose from the conventional constraints of life, arrived at the lodge with some good-time girls, all determined to live it up in the bush. While the men went on a serious fishing expedition, Ivan was told to take the girls out for a spin in the boat and they, seeing this callow youth, decided to have some fun with him. The minute the boat took off, they all stripped naked, posing around the boat for the duration of their sundowner cruise and teasing Ivan to his obvious embarrassment. It must have been quite a feat, steering through the forest of skeletal leadwood trees that rise out of the water near the shoreline without hitting a single one – especially as one of the girls sat crossed-legged on the bow, right in front of the steering wheel smiling sweetly at him all the while.

His next step was to apply for a guide licence and then find someone to whom he could be apprenticed. He asked John Stevens, one of the best-known and most highly respected guides in Zimbabwe, but John would take him on only if he had a canoe licence. This he proceeded to get by working flat-out wherever he was needed, with a variety of companies, until he had it. John then asked Ivan to help run his Ruwesi Canoe Trails, taking clients down the Zambezi River in the canoes, camping each night on the riverbank and enjoying the abundant wildlife that is seen along the river, and it was while doing this that he became entranced by Mana Pools.

A few years later he was lucky enough to get permission to run his own seasonal camp, Vundu, on the banks of the river within the park. He had his professional licence eighteen months after first taking the job at Sanyati – quite an achievement, as it can take two or three years to pass the exams. He then took and

Elephants on the banks of the Zambezi River

passed his hunting licence and was invited to examine candidates for guide licences for the next two years. He now had a canoe licence, a professional guide's licence and a hunting licence, which gave him great flexibility.

He then proceeded to get as much experience as he possibly could by working for as many different companies as possible as a freelance guide, which allowed him to learn about all the different areas in Zimbabwe.

He was very keen to start up his own mobile safari company but could not find the finance. His big break came when Neil Hewlett, a businessman with a game farm and a vision, asked Ivan to come and work for him. Neil planned to turn his incredibly beautiful game farm into a nature reserve, which, to his mind, would be an excellent tourist attraction. The only problem was that the land was short of big game and that, after all, was why the tourists came.

Ivan knew the nature reserve would not work and discussed an alternative idea with Neil. They came to an agreement that Neil would finance Ivan's mobile safaris if Ivan promised to spend half his time at the lodge. The mobiles became more and more popular and he was less and less at the lodge, which, because of the lack of animals, was not being booked.

Although this was not very satisfactory for Neil, he released Ivan from his obligation to run the lodge and continued to fund his mobile operation. It was a difficult time for Ivan; borrowing money in his part of the Third World at that time came with thirty per cent interest rates.

He wrote a business plan for himself and asked a safari client – a Scottish financial adviser – if he would take a look at it. This man was so impressed with the forty-page handwritten document, which had come right from the heart, that he decided on a hunch to back him. With this new backing, Ivan bought out Neil Hewlett, allowing him to concentrate on growing his own safari operation, but is eternally grateful to Neil for opening the door for him. He could now kick-start the company, which grew very rapidly. Within two years he had equipment for three safaris to be out at the same time, eleven Toyota Land Cruisers, two Bedford trucks, two boats and his clients provided passengers for a charter company with three small aircraft carrying his guests between camps. He was also responsible for thirty-five members of staff, camp hands, drivers, boat drivers, guides and office staff, along with three or four freelance guides at any one time. Ivan was just twenty-five years old, and the owner of the most successful mobile safari company in Zimbabwe.

His was the first company to attach the showers and loos to the backs of the tents. The safaris were personalised to such an extent that if the guests were there at Easter, as clients of mine had been, they all received Easter eggs with their names written on them in icing – a much-appreciated personal touch. The safaris travelled between Hwange Game Reserve, Matusadona Game Park (Kariba) and Mana Pools, and were immensely popular.

As they grew so did the responsibilities and Ivan found he was spending more and more of his time on

Ivan at the end of the day

administration rather than on safari. Logistics occupy more time than practically anything else in the safari business. His mother Claire managed the bookings, the boats and vehicles supplying Matusadona and Mana Pools were based in Kariba and the Hwange Camp was supplied from Victoria Falls.

It's funny how often one small incident crystallises what you had been thinking all along. Ivan remembers well the day he heard that the guide taking a safari in Matusadona had left behind in Kariba a case of Coca-Cola, which had been particularly requested by the guests. A boat was sent back to Kariba to fetch it, the three-hour journey making those Cokes more expensive than a case of Moët et Chandon. The Coca-Cola incident was the trigger – the moment he decided to close down the company and work for himself as a private safari guide.

It had not been easy for him. Administration was getting him down and he longed to spend more time guiding. It was also the year of a tragic accident in one of his camps, when a young man employed by the company was killed by lions, which had an enormous effect on all concerned (see below). Closing down took great courage: first there was the sadness of putting so many people out of work; Secondly, all the tour operators had to be informed and, finally, a crippling debt to pay off, because all the money they had made had been ploughed back into the business to improve facilities. However, Ivan does not lack courage.

A heartbreaking episode

In 2000, a dreadful tragedy occurred when lions killed a young Englishman working for Ivan Carter Safaris. It had a huge impact on Ivan's life, because the man was not only an employee but also a friend. The following are Ivan's own words on dealing with tragedy in the bush:

"The way I can describe it is that out here when you are in the bush you are at any moment in danger of becoming part of the big picture. That is one of the attractions on being out here, the slight element of danger is what brings people back, possibly the element of danger is why everyone wants to see cats, people think that every lion wants to eat you at any moment. Everybody knows somebody who knows somebody who has been either killed or injured out here in Africa.

"Then all of a sudden it happens to you and the only way to deal with it is to face it absolutely head on. It is very easy to hide behind all kinds of excuses, all sorts of make-believe logistics, all kinds of reasons – but there is no hiding. You have just got to face it, as with any tragedy; you have to think, what is the best way for me personally to deal with this. Having said that, it is very important to deal with the people involved as sensitively as possible; this of course is the hardest part of all.

"When the accident happened in one of my camps I cancelled all my safaris to be there to help the people involved in the best way that I knew how. The boy's mother came to Zimbabwe and I took her personally to the spot where the accident had happened and talked her through it. I then went to the UK for ten days, spending time with the family and they paid me the utmost compliment in that they put me in a situation which I could never have backed out of and hope I did it justice. They got me to write and read the eulogy at the funeral, truly the hardest thing I have ever done. But I am really glad to have been able to do that. It was the most horrible and difficult thing I have ever done in my life but it helped me too. When I recently visited them I saw they had put a quote from the eulogy on the gravestone – which I felt was a great honour. No matter what you do, you feel a huge responsibility. It would have been all too easy to hide; lots do.

"Time is a great thing from many perspectives, but one thing is definite; whenever an accident happens one day the blame is going to swing around to you; you are never going to be blameless. While time may heal the overall problem someone is going to say, 'I wonder if Ivan was careful enough, I wonder if this guy did enough or that guy did enough.' I think we are all on the brink of something like that happening to us out here. Dreadful accidents can happen, a client can fall off the roof of a vehicle in the Ngorongoro Crater, hyenas can crawl into half-closed tents, somebody can get stomped on by an elephant or an elephant can fall onto someone having been shot by a guide; that has happened. Hippos bite canoes and crocodiles jump out of the water. But when it does happen it is so horrifying – suddenly it's happening to me. Help! I am now part of the story and so many people are quick to point fingers, quick to try and reconstruct it in their own minds what

happened, to condemn you, but on the other hand there are more people who know you and will support you. Provided you have done the right thing.

"I think a lot of accidents are the result of guide error, but also, they are just one of those things. It is a huge learning curve dealing with the human element afterwards; I hope I never have to go through it again, but if I did, I don't think I would do it any differently.

"The hardest part of the whole thing was having to answer for another guide. I wasn't there and with any profession you wish deep down that you were there – it probably wouldn't have been any different but you can't help thinking it might have been. I have wished from the absolute centre of my soul that I had been there, just because to go and answer for myself rather than someone else would have been so much better. It is something you have to deal with and get through; it's everyone's horror to have something happen to a client on safari. It stays with you always.

"It is incredible that there are not more accidents, there are lots of non-professional guides out on safari and just the thought of walking in big game areas unarmed does not appeal to me at all. I have seen people do the most stupid things and they get away with it. I think nature is very forgiving, but it can be completely ruthless."

At this low point in Ivan's life he gained comfort from his empathy with nature and his high degree of bush knowledge; as he says, if you walk for six to eight hours a day stalking a buffalo or an elephant you have to be very aware of all that goes on around you. Animals are so different in the hunting areas, much more aggressive. He believes that if you guide only in photographic areas you get a false sense of security, especially with the extremely relaxed, big bull elephants in Mana Pools. It would be easy to forget that this is not natural. His hunting safaris help to pay off his loan and as he is one of the best most ethical hunters in Africa, the amount of clients he has for both hunting and photographic safaris keeps him working most of the year. However, it is my own belief that elephants become aggressive only when threatened and national parks contain little to threaten them.

Ivan has always enjoyed photography – his ability to see unique angles on familiar subjects produces fascinating images – and is now a professional photographer. He has had extremely successful exhibitions in Edinburgh and London, with exhibitions in America to follow soon. He takes time to help his guests with their photography, making them catch a bit of the spirit of what is going on Instead of just taking an animal portrait he tries to help them bring out the atmosphere of the habitat around the animal. Many of them go away, take photography lessons and return.

His skills as a guide are remarkable. He has a large following of clients asking him to guide them wherever they go in Africa. He enjoys seeing new areas through the eyes of resident experts as he travels in Botswana, Zimbabwe, Zambia, Namibia, Kenya, Tanzania, Uganda, Rwanda, South Africa and Madagascar, and is the first guide to have taken groups into the newly formed Niassa Game Reserve in Mozambique. He likes to stay in one place as long as possible, so that his guests can truly learn an area. He walks as much as he can to allow them to experience the closeness of nature with the quiver of apprehension one gets from the unknown. His idea of sitting beside an active water hole is to be there all afternoon, if not all day, getting a feel of the cycle of life and the daily pattern surrounding it.

He is fast becoming one of the best-known guides in Africa, creating an exhilarating, thought-provoking safari for people of all ages. He tries to plant a seed of inquisitiveness, to make his guests think about the natural world and to keep on wondering and dreaming about all these things when they get home.

ROBIN POPE

Robin is a born naturalist with wide interests and many talents: all creatures appear to one in a new light as he concentrates on even the most familiar. It may be appreciating the subtle and exquisite colours in the feathers of a dove, understanding the size of a lion from studying its spoor on a dusty road, or discovering that mongoose climb trees! We spent an enthralling two hours following a young leopard that had recently left her mother but not her mother's territory – he explained how she was skirting the perimeter, weighing up when and where to make the break. Most of Robin's adult life has been spent in the Luangwa Valley in Zambia and his observations of the changes over the years are fascinating. The Luangwa River meanders through a wide valley in large sweeping curves, flowing serenely when the water is low, but becoming a roaring torrent in summer that constantly alters the landscape as it swirls around the bends, eating away the banks and toppling colossal ancient trees like puny saplings. Changes to the course of the river leave oxbow lakes – tranquil pools that are home to hippos and a multitude of birds for a time and eventually dry up to become grazing land for plains game. The process takes many years, but slowly new trees take root on this fertile ground: first the acacias, then the hardwoods, until one day hardly a sign is left of that curve of the great Luangwa River.

Robin is a softly spoken, gentle man with a disarming smile that lights up his face, drawing you into his world with a feeling of warmth and comfort. He communicates his understanding and enthusiasm in a quiet, intimate manner, so that each of his guests absorbs his unique insight into the way the natural world fits together. A naturally shy and reticent man, he has overcome this by being superbly confident in the knowledge he has acquired over the past thirty years. He is most definitely a guide for the connoisseur. With his encyclopaedic knowledge of birds, it can be a black dot against the bright sky, a flash of wings in a bush or a call in the background of at least ten other calls, he recognises it immediately, revealing an understanding of rare depth. On safari in the Luangwa Valley, not only was there nothing he couldn't identify; I was astounded at how quick he was, never making a mistake (everything could be verified in a book of species). In this department, he outshone every other guide I have ever met.

One morning we left in the dark, wrapped up in blankets against the chilly pre-dawn air, to drive the long stretch from Tena Tena, Robin's base camp, to the salt pans. Not salt pans as in the Makgadikgadi, which is flat, white and dry, but an expanse of hot water boiling up from underground and filled with minerals that, when dry, create a white, salty crust along the edge of the pools. There was much to see along the way, starting with a sighting of the rare Bat hawk, streaking silently in front of us on a pre-dawn hunt, to numerous herds of Blue wildebeest, eland and Burchell's zebra. The incredible dawn chorus of the Cape turtle doves occurs as the sun rises and although we had left camp long before dawn, with the many distractions along the way we were only just in time to hear them. Through the dark trees on the edge of the wide plain the blood-red ball of the sun rose, while thousands of doves performed their morning ritual. We are all accustomed to hearing lone turtle doves giving their *work HARder, work HARder* call, but few know that thousands calling in unison makes the air vibrate like a squadron of jet fighters revving their engines in preparation for a dawn flight.

Robin Pope

Now Robin's diversity of skills once again came into play; a dab hand with the frying pan, he cooked a most delicious bush breakfast of eggs, bacon, sausages and tomatoes for a group of ravenous people.

His maternal grandfather, Cuthbert Jenkins, was educated at Trinity College, Dublin. He was an officer in the Royal Dublin Fusiliers in the First World War and fought in Europe and at Gallipoli. In the 1920s he joined the British South Africa Company and moved to Ndola, Northern Rhodesia (Zambia) in central southern Africa. He transferred to Livingstone and was later posted to Fort Jameson (now Chipata) on the eastern border of what was then Nyasaland, now Malawi. This was an arduous journey at that time. It involved either a two-to three-week portered walk from the nearest railhead at Broken Hill (now Kabwe), or alternatively, the route he chose ... a passage by boat from the Indian Ocean, up the Zambezi and Shire rivers to Port Herald in Nyasaland, from where they travelled west via Lilongwe to Fort Jameson on bush tracks in a Model-T Ford and trailer.

Cuthbert had met his future bride on board ship from Durban to Southampton. She was on her way to the United States with her father to look at cattle, but romance intervened. They married in England and he took her back to live in Fort Jameson, where Robin's mother Rosemary was born. Robin has a charming photograph of his grandparents fording the Luangwa River with their Model-T Ford. Standing on the pontoon is his grandmother, wearing a long white dress and holding her baby daughter in her arms. Earlier this had been the principal slave and ivory trade route down both the Luangwa and Zambezi rivers to the Indian Ocean. The last Arab slave train passed through the Fort Jameson area in 1909, less than fifteen years before the arrival of Robin's grandfather.

Robin's grandmother was descended from the 1850 settlers of Natal – a group of Scottish families escaping the depression of 1848–51 to find a new life in Africa. Many of them became prominent, successful Natal families, including the Campbells who once owned Mala Mala.

Robin and his elder brother were born in South Africa, where his father John grew up. John Pope joined the Transvaal Scottish Regiment at the beginning of World War Two. Fighting in East Africa alongside other regiments, such as the King's African Rifles, they defeated the Italians and relieved Addis Ababa in April 1941, giving the Allies their first major victory of the war. John travelled north to fight in the western desert before transferring to the air force, and was flying in Yugoslavia when the war ended. Returning to South Africa he went to university, obtained a mining degree and married Rosemary Jenkins. While Robin and his brother were still small, John took the family to Northern Rhodesia, the country of his wife's birth, where they were blessed with two more sons. Their home was to be the Copperbelt in central Northern Rhodesia near the Congo border – a hive of activity, as copper was in great demand due to the post-war rebuilding of Europe. John worked as a mining engineer in Kitwe, Bancroft, and Broken Hill. A few years before they arrived, the skull of an early hominid, *Homo rhodesiensis*, had been discovered in a mine chamber in Broken Hill, causing much excitement. John ended his career at the Lusaka head office of Anglo American, which, after nationalisation, became the Zambia Consolidated Copper Mines.

Living on the Copper Belt in the 1950s and 1960s was great fun for the children; the town was surrounded by bush – paradise for little boys to explore, especially with frequent visits from their knowledgeable grandfather. However, it was their parents, with their great love for the bush and the country, who were the most important influences in shaping their passion for nature and the open spaces. John and Rosemary took their sons on many holidays in the Luangwa Valley and in Kafue National Park, where they stayed in self-catering government camps. They adored these holidays, which certainly set the tone for the future lives of the boys; two of Robin's brothers are still involved with wildlife in Zambia, while the youngest is in a similar line in Australia.

For Robin, going away to the strict regime of boarding school in Rhodesia (Zimbabwe) was a very alien experience. He simply could not understand half of the baffling rules that they enforced, especially the policy of folding his clothes exactly into one-foot square piles measured by a prefect. At first he felt like a square peg in a round hole, but eventually he conformed, worked hard and got into university. The first year of his higher education was spent at the University of Zambia in Lusaka, which he enjoyed, but it was 1971 and the mood of the time was very disruptive. The endless student meetings and marches in support of the various political events in the subcontinent were unsettling, making it hard to study, so he decided to transfer to the University of Natal in Pietermaritzburg in order to complete his degree in Geography and Zoology.

His great wish on returning to Zambia was to work for the Department of National Parks, but jobs in government departments for young white Zambians were not easy to get. However, as luck would have it, he had an introduction to Wildlife Conservation International, an American organisation that was attempting to turn the game reserve on the banks of the Zambezi River into a

Robin illustrating the size of the lion by the size of the print. Not long after, we came upon the lion and found Robin's drawing to be very accurate

national park. Robin was taken on to work for them as paymaster for the scouts. It was a very important project because a game reserve can be revoked by the stroke of a pen whereas a national park would require an act of parliament to close it and alter the land use. It was therefore of paramount importance to succeed and protect this special area. They were putting in systems and training scouts as rangers, but their efforts were eventually thwarted by the increasing intensity of the war across the

lads who were carrying a large net to fish in the river, I saw some vultures on the ground about three or four hundred yards away. I was walking with a scout and carrying our only weapon, a large stick. Thinking they must be at the end of a kill, I wanted to see what had been killed. When we had crossed the sandbank I suddenly realised that they were not on the ground but sitting on top of a ridge and as I approached they flew off. I thought to myself as I climbed the ridge that there would not be much left, how wrong I was! Peering over the top I confronted eight lionesses on a waterbuck. They growled and bounded off to my right.

"For some reason the game scout and I decided to go down and have a look at the kill; not really thinking very clearly we negotiated around a small lagoon to get there. While we were looking at the carcass I heard some strange noises coming from the riverbank beyond us, I thought maybe it was hippos fighting. As I turned to discuss this with the scout a huge lion charged from the bushes with an ear-splitting roar, his mane spread out and his tail rigid in the air, he came straight for us. The river was on my right and the lagoon on my left, the scout shouted 'Don't run!' I couldn't run back as that is where the lionesses had gone but I also had no intention of standing still! I ran into the lagoon and swam across as fast as I could go, the scout following me with the lion following both of us! Luckily we were the faster swimmers and had gone quite a long way away when he arrived on the bank, after shaking himself off, he decided to go back to the kill.

river in Rhodesia. Robin worked in this spectacular area opposite Mana Pools on the lower Zambezi for eighteen months. It was an exciting time for him; he learned a lot, not only from the scouts but also, and particularly, from the man in charge of the project – Erick Balson, formerly Wildlife Warden of Tanzania.

Robin has had many exciting moments through the years but here he recalls one early frightening experience while with Wildlife Conservation:

"The war in Rhodesia was intensifying during the time I spent on the Zambezi. Because of this we had to operate without weapons. All the wildlife officers had their guns taken away in case we were mistaken for Rhodesians or guerrilla fighters. We did a little fishing in the river to supplement rations for the scouts and to sustain ourselves. On one occasion while walking down to a sandbank with some of the

"It was a very close call, but we did learn a thing or two at the kill. We saw that the stomach and gall bladder of the waterbuck had been buried in the sand and the carcass dragged well away. This meant there must have been cubs nearby as these are parts of the body that would be bad for the cubs, hence removed from the animal before they came in to feed."

After eighteen months Wildlife Conservation International had to close down the project due to the increased military action across the river. Knowing that Robin was now out of work, his friends suggested that he apply for a job with Norman Carr Safaris and Wilderness Trails, based at Chibembe Camp in the South Luangwa National Park. This was both a hunting and photographic safari outfit, which was well known and operated in an area that Robin had often visited with his family. He joined them as a walking safari guide in 1976. Norman Carr was already the best-known and most highly respected man involved in wildlife and tourism. He worked tirelessly to improve the parks, introduce tourism and involve the local communities.

Both Norman Carr and the manager of Chibembe Camp, former Wildlife Department ranger and warden Phil Berry, inspired Robin to pursue the career of a walking safari guide. However, it was the superb wildlife scouts who really saw him through those turbulent and exciting early years. Norman had been in the King's African Rifles during the Second World War and had with him a most loyal group of ex-military scouts – superbly disciplined men who had experienced battle and were completely at home in the bush. They taught Robin everything they knew about tracking, self-sufficiency and adaptability, for which he is extremely grateful. Norman

had twenty-four professional hunters working for him at that time, all of whom had had to do a two-year apprenticeship before they could take out a client. They spent this time mainly walking in the bush, learning their skills from his excellent scouts – a regime that was strictly adhered to by Norman, giving Zambia an excellent reputation for good hunting.

Although he was not training to be a hunter, Robin was fortunate enough to participate in this exceptional training with the scouts and with Phil Berry, who was already an experienced safari guide. People coming on safari knew little about the bush or the names of the birds but Norman knew and insisted that anyone working for him was to learn them well and quickly. They had plenty of clients to satisfy, mostly British, for both photographic and hunting safaris.

In 1979, Robin was invited by some British clients to join them on a safari in Tanzania with Richard Bonham, in the Selous Game Reserve. Richard is another of Africa's great safari guides: he became famous for taking walking safaris supported by porters in the Selous Game Reserve and has two exceptional camps, one being Sand Rivers on the Rufiji River in the Selous Reserve in southern Tanzania; the other Ol Donyo Wuas in the Chyulu Hills in Kenya. Robin did not really wish to go as a guest, but longed to visit the area. In the event, one of Richard's guides had to back out, allowing Robin to drive the extra Land Rover on the safari, which he thoroughly enjoyed. The author Peter Matthiessen and the photographer Hugo von Lawick travelled with them to research a book which they later produced together, about Brian Nicholson and his experiences as a game ranger in East Africa.*

The Luangwa Valley was known as the Valley of the Elephants. There were an estimated 100 000 elephants,

---

* Peter Matthiessen, *Sand Rivers*, New York, Viking, 1981.

A bend in the Luangwa River

along with 6 000 rhino. Commercial poaching started in the mid-1970s and was a conservation disaster. Towards the end of the decade the Save the Rhino Trust, in which both Norman Carr and Phil Berry were involved, was formed to assist the National Parks Department in combating the monstrous poaching of these animals within the Luangwa Valley. It proved very difficult to halt; at the height of the killing it was estimated that twenty-seven elephants were being shot every day, and by the early 1990s, when poaching was eventually checked, there were almost no rhino left, and only 20 000 elephant.

During this period Norman Carr Safaris became Zambia Safaris and Wilderness Trails. Robin was asked to renovate and manage Nsefu Camp, a cluster of thatched rondavels that had been a self-catering government camp since the 1950s, and one he had visited as a child. It was by then very run down, but beautifully situated on a broad bend of the Luangwa River, and once renovated it became very popular, as it was in an excellent game area. In 1982, Robin was granted permission to open a tented fly camp, Tena Tena, twelve kilometres south of Nsefu as a satellite camp for walking safaris. It consisted of a circle of tents, one drum shower and a long-drop loo and provided a three-day optional walking safari from Nsefu for those guests interested in getting out into the bush. During the early days of these safaris Black rhino were still frequently seen.

At the end of 1985, Robin left Wilderness Trails and kept Tena Tena Camp, setting up his own company, Robin Pope Safaris. His was one of the first companies to open in the Luangwa after the government's nationalisation programme of the 1970s and early 1980s ended.

The logistics of running such a remote camp were formidable. A convoy would travel from Lusaka to Tena Tena at the beginning of the season with all the supplies, a long, tedious journey that was probably repeated at least once more during the season, depending on the cash-flow. Robin dreamt of having some land and a base at Mfuwe to ease his logistics problems. In fact, Robin's head has always been full of dreams and ideas, but, being so popular and therefore constantly busy with clients, he had little time to devote to them. He needed an energetic, dynamic person to turn them into reality.

Along came Jo

It was 1988 and Jo Holmes, head of the locations department of a film company, was living in Glasgow with her long-term boyfriend. Although life seemed perfect on the surface, for some reason she was less than satisfied, so when her sister was offered a catering job in Zambia, but couldn't take it and asked if she wanted it, Jo didn't hesitate. She knew immediately she must not let this opportunity pass her by.

Robin met her at Lusaka Airport and took her straight to the supermarket. She simply could not believe the lack of goods – it was a low time in Zambia's economy. She wailed that she could never cook any decent meals with the limited ingredients available, but Robin assured her she could. Once the vehicle was loaded with three months' supplies they took off like a couple of hillbillies on the long journey to Tena Tena. As they arrived, a hippo walked up the bank as if to greet her. Right away she felt at home, the glove fitted and within a month she had fallen head over heels in love with Robin. He kept his distance for a long while, convinced she had 'khaki

fever' and that it would soon wear off. She was a joyous addition to Tena Tena, bringing extra life and sparkle to the camp with her own brand of joie de vivre. Her laughter rang through the camp and her passion for dancing was incorporated into the evening activities. Guests arriving for a peaceful safari, many of them grey-haired old ladies who had not danced for years, found themselves joining in rock 'n' roll sessions on a sandbank in the Luangwa River, entered into the spirit of it and had a marvellous time. Life at Tena Tena took on a new vitality and Robin's feelings for Jo steadily grew.

Jo also learned about the bush, acquiring her guide's licence in 1990, frequently going out on game-drives with Robin as his 'spotter'. However, she spent steadily less time in the bush as she became more and more involved in running the business, and particularly in marketing Robin's safaris. Her first sortie into the world of travel was to Indaba, the African trade fair that takes place each year in South Africa. When she walked in she was asked if she was a 'seller' or a 'buyer' so she could be given the correct badge; uncertain, she told them she was there to persuade agents to send their clients to Zambia, so she was an exhibitor and received her yellow exhibitor's badge. She sat on the Air Zambia stand pulling everyone wearing a red delegate's badge over to her desk; she literally stood in the aisles and accosted them. Today it is the other way around; people line up to get an appointment with her!

As her role evolved and she became aware of how important it was to awaken the world to the qualities of Zambia as a tourist destination, Jo became a one-woman ambassador for Zambian tourism, travelling the world and spreading the word. She gathered the other tour operators around her, taking some of them with her on her travels, always supporting their products while selling her own. It is to her great credit that, although there are always jealousies in any business, no group of independent operators is as close to one another as are the Zambian companies.

Robin would discuss his dreams and plans with Jo, who then took them up and made them come true. "How lovely it would be," he said, "if everyone in the valley could get together and sing carols at Christmas on the bridge into the South Luangwa National Park." Jo passed the word around and from then on it has become an annual Christmas Eve tradition; carols are sung by candlelight for the guests at all the local lodges, their staff and anyone else who would like to join in.

Whenever Robin had an idea Jo would sell it, and then they had to work out how it should be implemented. Ever since he flew over the northern section of the park with the producer Cindy Buxton, when assisting her with a film she was making, he vowed he would come back and walk along the Mupamadzi River. On hearing this dream Jo decided to market walking safaris in this area and sold six of them for the following year. They then had to work out the logistics, buy the equipment, find the campsites and, most importantly, get a road made. This proved difficult; it took two years to complete one hundred kilometres of road that is used for only three and half months a year and has to be regraded at the beginning of every safari season. The rains and the black cotton soil make it impassable for half the year, so once the rains are over, Robin sends a team of twelve men to dig the gullies and clear the way for the grader to do its job. It's a mammoth task, but the joy of walking in such a remote place is a great reward.

Early morning at Tena Tena

Robin and Jo at Nkwali

Robin is the dreamer and perfectionist, Jo the architect. They are an incredible team, one of the best that Zambia has. In 1991, Mike Shirley-Bevan, a well-established tour operator in England, put together the Safari Guide Company, a group of the best guides in Africa at the time. The first meeting in 1990 was at Victoria Falls and Robin was chosen as the Zambian representative. The others were Søren Lindstrom, Jan van der Reep, David Foot, Richard Bonham, Charlie McConnell, Roland Purcell and John Stevens. The association, designed to help with marketing and to share joint problems, continued for eight years.

The love match

Robin still couldn't believe that Jo wasn't suffering from 'khaki fever', in spite of her becoming deeply involved in his business. After he had turned down two or three of her proposals, she mentioned that it would be difficult to remain in Zambia indefinitely if he did not really want to make a commitment. In 1991, they took a trip to America to see the whales at the Baja Peninsula, followed by a visit to Yellowstone National Park. At the famous waterfall in the park, which was frozen solid as it was midwinter, Robin asked Jo to become engaged to him. "Are you asking me to marry you or just to be engaged to you?" she said. "Well" he said, "I thought we would just try the engagement bit for a while, but I do want to marry you." He made her a ring of ice from the falls to pledge his love, but a long engagement was not for them. That year when they had a cancellation at Tena Tena they decided to use the time to get married.

The marriage service was held under the wide canopy of an ancient fig tree by Baka Baka lagoon. Hay bales were placed in rows for pews, a table with a white cloth under an arch crafted from elephant grass was the altar and a Roman Catholic priest from an up-country mission came to perform the service. He was a delightful man but a bit forgetful due to a bad knock on the head from a past accident, and required a little prompting during the service.

At one point he looked at Jo and said "What comes next?"

"It's time for the Lord's Prayer," Jo said.

"Of course, what language do you want it in?" he said, reeling off a string of African dialects.

"English will do," said Jo.

The party at Tena Tena went on all night, beating drums and throbbing music carried down the river and could be heard for miles. It simply didn't matter, because everyone within hearing distance was at the party. This was not only a joyous occasion for Robin and Jo and all their friends and families, but a blessing too for Zambia.

Robin's dream of having some land at Mfuwe, the hub of the Luangwa Valley, came true after years of negotiations. He had walked along the riverbank south of the bridge, searching for the finest piece of land, and found it on a beautiful sweep of the river, with huge, mature trees and magnificent views across to the national park. His permission to purchase arrived in 1991, although he had applied for the land in 1987. Nkwali is now his on a ninety-nine-year lease and supports, along with the attractive lodge, the administrative headquarters of Robin Pope Safaris and a newly built house for themselves. Their original two-bedroomed house by the river has become a special hideaway for anyone wanting peace and privacy for their stay in Zambia. The recent acquisition of Nsefu, now beautifully renovated without losing its traditional character, has added another dimension to Robin's safaris.

The local community also benefits in many ways from Jo's involvement. The government clinic in Mfuwe became inadequate for the ever-expanding population in the area. Jo has been on the clinic committee for many years and has helped raise money to enlarge it and improve conditions. She also runs a scheme that has brought in a doctor who is financially supported by the safari lodges. The doctor works mostly at the government clinic and takes care of guests at the lodges who become ill. It is vital for the community to benefit from tourism.

She has supported Kawaza School for fifteen years, not just financially but also with her approach to expanding the minds and skills of the pupils. Because the children live in and will probably work in a wildlife area, she is ensuring that they learn about conservation from a very early age. Art is another subject she has introduced; safari guests donated plenty of crayons and pencils but paper, a precious commodity, is not easily available in Mfuwe. When Jo first arrived at the school with a huge

stack of it from Lusaka and told them to start drawing, they would draw only on a small corner of the page in order to preserve the paper. It took six months to get them to use the whole page. Three years later, they entered an art competition in which they won first prize, and one twelve-year-old is showing considerable talent. Another educational tool – a video machine and television, powered by a battery linked to a solar panel outside by a rather Heath Robinson contraption of wires – keeps many little souls mesmerised. They sit on the floor in front of a black and white screen, gazing at wildlife programmes and children's stories. Among the older children the favourite game in the school is Scrabble! Fiercely competitive, they play individually or in teams. The government used to provide three teachers for 430 pupils, but Jo has persuaded them to provide five, and six more are paid for by Robin Pope Safaris. Having eleven teachers in a rural school in Zambia gives these children a rare advantage.

The Kawaza Village offers day trips for tourists who would like to see how the local community live; the visitors take lunch with them, visit the school and spend the night if they wish. All profit from the money earned in this way by the village goes to support twelve disabled residents and the orphanage. Robin and Jo feel very strongly that as much as possible should be put back into the community, not in cash handouts but in ways that benefit them all, improving their quality of life and aspirations for the future.

Robin plans to explore the escarpment, a place of ancient history, fossils and rare birds. This, along with his established trips to Kasanka and Lake Bangweulu, will give his devoted followers plenty of opportunity for variety. He also has a dream of taking safaris in the Sudan. The best season to visit Sudan would be during the rainy season in Zambia, and thus he could keep his business ticking over all year with new and interesting delights. Jo was conceived in the Sudan, which has always made her curious about the country and we know what happens when Jo fixes her attention on Robin's dreams.

The Luangwa Valley is truly one of Africa's greatest treasures. It has had some very dedicated people protecting it in the past and there is no shortage of young people in Zambia to continue this work. The wide, meandering river, with its pale, shifting sandbanks, grunting hippos and abundant bird life, is the main artery of the park. The place throbs with life and for me, having explored it with such an expert as Robin Pope was a special honour.

NORTH LUANGWA AND THE ZAMBEZI VALLEY

The safari community in Zambia is small and personal; their short season attracts people whose passion for the bush and wildlife creates a way of life rather than a hefty bank balance. Mainly Zambian-born, the majority of camp owners are first and foremost guides, who stamp their own personalities on their safari operations. Along with Robin Pope in the South Luangwa National Park, another exceptional guide is John Coppinger, who raises his guests' experience to dizzy heights with a bird's-eye view of animal behaviour on his microlight flights. There is also Rod Tether in North Luangwa and Grant Cummings in the Zambezi Valley, who guide in areas that complement South Luangwa. All their lives are interwoven with those of John and Robin in this small safari community.

A flight in John Coppinger's microlite

John Coppinger originally joined Wilderness Trails in 1984 for two years, working at Nsefu while Robin Pope was the manager. After Robin left to set up on his own, John and his wife Carol managed Nsefu for eight years, during which time (in 1990) he opened Mwaleshi, a camp in North Luangwa exclusively for walking safaris. The Wilderness Trails shareholders had felt it was not feasible to run such a remote camp for so few people, so when John left in 1995 to strike out on his own they allowed him to keep Mwaleshi. He built Tafika Camp in South Luangwa – a delightful place by the river with spacious, airy, reed and thatch rooms so typical of Zambia – and far more accessible for safaris than Mwaleshi, which he kept for those who wanted a bit more adventure.

North Luangwa is where we find Rod Tether and the Lower Zambezi is home to Grant Cummings; both these areas are a natural combination with South Luangwa for visitors to Zambia. Rod's passion for North Luangwa first began when he took mobile safaris there in 1994 and the lower Zambezi wormed its way into Grant's heart as a child on many fishing expeditions with his father.

ROD TETHER

Born in Uganda, Rod moved to Zambia with his family during the Idi Amin regime when he was only three. Growing up in Zambia meant family holidays spent in the bush as Rod's father, a geologist, was familiar with many of the remote areas of the country and was determined that his family should get to know as much of it as possible. Nsefu was a popular destination with the Tether family during Robin Pope's early management of the camp and being around Robin was a great inspiration to Rod. At seventeen, having finished his A' levels, Rod applied for a gap-year job at Chibembe Camp. Norman Carr had moved on to build Kapani Lodge at Mfuwe and Wilderness Trails, being very short-staffed at that time, took him on as a guide. Rod worked for the photographic side of Chibembe, which was still primarily a hunting camp. Three years at Southampton University in England studying politics and international relations did not sway him from his lifelong passion to live in the bush. The four-month summer breaks from university were spent back in Zambia working for Wilderness Trails, leading three-day walks. He obtained his guide's licence in 1990, the first year of formal examinations for guides in his country. Jo Pope, the first woman in Zambia to obtain the guide's licence, sat the exam with him. In 1994, Rod took a break from Africa to explore South America, returning to run tented mobile safaris for Wild Zambia Safaris in the remote areas of North Luangwa, Shiwa, Bangweulu and Kasanka. It was on these safaris that Rod became familiar with the beauty of North Luangwa, its wildness and its majesty. The journeys were thrilling, but because they were to places far away from civilisation the stress of the responsibility was great. Fortunately, nothing went seriously wrong, but if it had they could have been at least a day away from help.

Wild Zambia Safaris were based at Kapani near Mfuwe, the lodge built and owned by the legendary Norman Carr. Norman was the single-most important man in the safari and wildlife world of Zambia during the mid- to late 20th century. He introduced tourism to Northern Rhodesia and initiated walking safaris. As a member of the Game Department he helped create wildlife parks and also founded the Save the Rhino Trust and the Wildlife Society of Zambia. At one time he ran Chibembe Lodge, where many of Zambia's guides commenced their careers. His final years were spent at Kapani, overlooking a lovely oxbow lake, where he entertained his visitors with the stories and shared with them the wisdom he had acquired in his forty years in the bush. Kapani is a busy, happy lodge with tourists coming and going and visitors popping in for a chat, a great place for Rod to unwind after a strenuous mobile safari. It was there, during the last year of Norman's life, that Rod met and fell in love with Guz Thieme. She is a marvellous cook, who came back to Zambia, having left aged thirteen, to be the caterer at Kapani.

John Coppinger approached Rod to run Mwaleshi bush camp jointly with his resident guide, Bryan Jackson. It was a perfect step for Rod, as Guz went with him to Tafika, where she had been offered the position of caterer. They were extremely happy there, as it is not just a safari lodge but also the home of John and Carol and their two daughters, which gives visitors and employees that special feeling of being part of a family. Rod and Bryan shared the guiding at Tafika, taking it in turns to go up to Mwaleshi for the four-night walking safaris, Guz remaining in charge of the kitchen at Tafika.

The journey to Mwaleshi from Tafika was long and arduous, six hours over very bad roads through thick pockets of tsetse fly. Although the bonus was travelling through glorious forests of Cathedral mopane and marvelling at the scalding turquoise waters of the hot springs, it was a tiring journey. Clearly the destination would be more popular with an airstrip. Once permission was granted far more guests were tempted to Mwaleshi. Rod and Guz were delighted when they were sent to Mwaleshi to run the camp together.

The season in North Luangwa lasts about five months because the thick and sticky black cotton soil makes it impassable for vehicles in the wet season. The African staff are happy with these working arrangements and

Rod Tether and guests crossing the river to Mwaleshi Camp

enjoy being at home, as they traditionally farm in the wet season, growing crops for themselves and for market. Rod and Guz, needing to find alternate employment, spent their time away from safaris working in a ski resort in the Alps. Guz had already established herself as a chalet cook in the 'off season' when Rod took a job with the same resort.

After two seasons at Mwaleshi they felt it was time to create their own camp in the North Luangwa National Park. The park had only two tourist camps and the idea of a third was very welcome at the Parks Department when Rod submitted his application for Kutundala. Verbally, everyone agreed, but it took eight months for Rod to obtain the written permission required to get going, which was finally granted in April 2001. Many of their clients have come through Robin Pope Safaris and without Jo Pope's support it would have been a far more difficult start. Mwaleshi continues, as does one other camp, that belonging to Mark Harvey, grandson of Stewart Gore-Browne who built Shiwa Ngandu, a grand English manor house not too far from North Luangwa, in the 1920s.

Kutundala is across the park from Mwaleshi, reached by the one and only road that runs through the park. On arrival the vehicle is parked on the riverbank, where shoes are taken off and trousers rolled up in order to wade across the clear waters of the Mwaleshi River (too shallow for hippos) to the camp. The four delightful reed huts look onto the river and a giant Natal mahogany shades the dining area and the library containing Rod's collection of books on all aspects of Africa. This small, exclusive destination takes only six people at a time, the number that all guides choose as the maximum for bush walks.

Rod and Guz married in August 2002 in the chapel attached to Shiwa Ngandu. Their son Louis was born in

Wildebeest crossing the Mwaleshi River near Kutundala

2003 and lives with them in the bush at Kutundala. Their house is a replica of the guest cottages, except that instead of having an open-air view from the front, it has a barrier of chicken wire for protection as a lion could easily mistake the cry of a baby for that of a distressed bleating lamb! From her open-air kitchen Guz produces by far and away the best food I have ever eaten in the bush and she is at least seven hours' drive from the nearest shop. The kitchen is enclosed with a reed fence, the oven is a hole in the ground and a wood fire heats a hotplate on which mouth-watering delicacies are created. Rows of herbs, lettuce and other fresh vegetables grow in traditional clay pots, all overlooked by a monkey's skull attached to the reed fence. Skulls are traditionally placed in the vegetable patch to ward off theft.

Elephants wander through the camp, puku prance across the river and it is not uncommon while walking to get quite close to a herd of buffalo or even to find lions on a kill. The game-viewing is excellent, but it is the walking that attracted Rod to this park; he prefers to view the bush and its inhabitants on foot – the joy is being able to melt into the bush, to have the smells and sounds all around one every day and never hearing a car engine nor the drone of an aircraft; in fact, it is so far off the beaten track that not even contrails streak the sky. This is certainly his favourite area. He is the only person recording the wildlife in North Luangwa, having completed the identification of all the trees in the park for the Royal Botanical Garden at Kew, he is now compiling a bird list.

It was not always a place of peace and tranquillity. Some of the heaviest poaching in Zambia took place here. Thousands of Black rhino were slaughtered, the last one in 1984. Having exterminated the rhino, the

Rod and Louis under the mahogany tree

poachers turned to the elephants and, had it not been for an extremely effective anti-poaching unit, they would have probably gone the same way. Rod recalls the horror he felt at the age of seventeen at Chibembe, when the sound of gunfire meant finding eight or nine dead elephants every day.

The Frankfurt Zoological Society, which partly funded the anti-poaching unit run by Delia and Mark Owens, American conservationists who operated so successfully in the 1980s, is still involved today. The society doesn't manage the park – the Zambian government does that – but they do manage projects, the latest of which is very exciting: the reintroduction of Black rhino. They provide technical support such as vehicles, GPSs and fuel. Rod is thrilled they are there, as their presence, along with increased tourism, is generating new life in the park and has virtually eliminated poaching:

"Poaching would be very difficult to start up again; the lines of communication are broken, the local people have regular work and take great pride in their achievements. Working in a safari camp knowing you have a monthly wage to send home to your family is much easier than poaching. Carrying a backpack on walks and keeping the camp clean and tidy is certainly more pleasant than lugging tusks or dead animals over long distances.

"When Guz and I go to Lusaka leaving them in charge, nothing is locked up, all our possessions are right there in the park on the shelves. Not one item has ever gone missing. After seeing the petty pilfering that went on in the ski resorts I realise how lucky I am to be living in Zambia with staff that I trust implicitly. The Zambian employees who have so little wouldn't dream of touching anything that did not belong to them. If a guest sends a pair of trousers to the wash with money in the pocket it comes back to the guest."

As tourism increases, so do the jobs and Rod would welcome another camp in the area, as it is so vast. There is so much to see, not only the exciting bush walks from the camp, but in other areas such as walking to the top of the escarpment to picnic by pools and waterfalls or visits to the petrified forest and numerous fossil sites. Guz's father, also a geologist, loves the area. Together with a good friend, an Oxford professor, he has discovered many sites yielding mainly fossils of Dicynodonts – mammal-like reptiles that existed before the dinosaurs.

GRANT CUMMINGS

In contrast to Rod, Grant Cummings operates in the lush areas on the banks of the Zambezi River in the Lower Zambezi National Park; a magnificent addition to a safari in the Luangwa Valley.

Born and raised in Zambia, Grant's first brush with the wild was a bite from a tsetse fly when only three weeks old and one from a baboon when just over a year! Undeterred, Grant grew up spending many weekends exploring and fishing with his father, listening enthralled to tales of his years in Tanganyika (Tanzania), prospecting for diamonds in the bush. Grant's enthusiasm for game-spotting started when very young and has never diminished. As a child he always had his face pressed to the car window, searching – even when told by his mother that there was no possibility of seeing anything but a goat!

He took an Economics degree in the United States, returning each summer to accompany professional hunters in Kafue and Luangwa. After graduating, he thought his career path led down the hunting trail, so on completion of his two-year apprenticeship in 1989 he took hunting safaris in Luangwa, Kafue and Bangweulu Swamps. However, it was not long before he realised that he would much prefer to take photographic safaris and started combining them with his hunting trips.

Grant and his father had spent many happy hours fishing and walking along the Zambezi river, and always camping at their special spot on the bank. It was therefore the obvious site for his first small tented camp, and later his permanent tented lodge, Chiawa, for his photographic safaris. As the photographic side became busier, the hunting diminished, and stopped altogether in 1994.

Chiawa is a delightful camp, constantly visited by passing elephants that step carefully over the wooden railings as they walk into camp. Down the paths they go, never disturbing the stones that border them (buffalo kick the stones all over the place when they visit) take a branch of a tree and walk on. A wide, dry riverbed borders the camp and is used as a highway by all manner of animals coming down to drink. Grant likes nothing better than to walk around this area with his guests, mingling with the abundant wildlife.

He has now also opened Old Mondoro Bush Camp to complement Chiawa, a little further downriver in an area of vast flood plains and open woodland – ideal for walking and game-viewing.

His passion for the Zambezi National Park has never waned and his involvement with its care is intensive. He has been an honorary ranger since 1989 and has personally conducted numerous anti-poaching patrols in order to make the park habitable for wildlife and visitors alike. He is the chairman of Conservation Lower Zambezi, a non-governmental organisation protecting the wildlife and habitat of the area and providing logistical support for the Zambia Wildlife Authority's anti-poaching units. He recently started an environmental education programme for the local village communities to promote conservation awareness, raising US$500 000 in just over two years for this project. They also conduct aerial surveys and remove snares from lions, elephants, wild dogs and other species when necessary and have been extremely effective in dramatically reducing poaching in the Lower Zambezi. He spent many months compiling a comprehensive *Safari Guides Manual* for the Lower Zambezi National Park, which is now in use. He also implemented the Safari

Grant Cummings at Chiawa

Guide Evaluation and Examinations for the Lower Zambezi and is responsible for conducting practical and written exams for all aspiring walking guides. This is a breathtaking list of achievements for one man.

Grant's dedication to the safari industry in his particular area is phenomenal. The buzz of his motorboats may irritate Zimbabweans as they are forbidden in Mana Pools, but although they can disturb the peace it is a small price to pay for a park that so many can now visit in complete safety, thanks to his tireless efforts. Incidentally, I was interested to observe that when approached silently in canoes hippos sink, but when approached in a motorboat they just turn their heads and watch it go past.

In April 2004, Grant married Lynsey Kane in Scotland. Lynsey has been living at Chiawa where she is a great help to Grant, making all the guests feel totally at home with the skills she gained as a British Airways cabin attendant.

John Coppinger's two daughters are being brought up in the bush at Tafika, and now little Louis Tether is living at Kutundala. With a little luck, Grant and Lynsey will be able to add to the generation of bush babies that will grow up to help protect Zambia's priceless heritage.

EAST AFRICA

The conventional images of Africa come from
Tanzania and Kenya and have fired the imagination
since the earliest explorers to the modern day.
East Africa, also embracing Uganda,
has the richest diversity of animals in the world.

The conventional images of Africa come from Tanzania and Kenya and have fired the imagination since the earliest explorers to the modern day. East Africa, also embracing Uganda, has the richest diversity of animals in the world. This, along with the great variety of landscapes, from jungle to desert, open savannah, rolling hills and snow-capped mountains, has become every tourist's dream of Africa; and the East African guides are well aware of this heritage. This is where safaris began.* It is here that the early travellers' imagination was first captured by the immense and glorious landscapes and the vast numbers of animals that live there. Due to literature, films, paintings, and television there are few that are not familiar with them. A lifetime could be spent exploring from the Selous in southern Tanzania to Lake Turkana in far northwest Kenya.

The vast plains, the Ngorongoro crater, snow-capped Mount Kilimanjaro, soda lakes pink with flamingos, the Rift Valley and the tribes in their traditional vibrant adornments. The astonishing sight of the wildebeest migration, whether in southern Tanzania in January, collectively giving birth, or running the gauntlet of the crocodiles at river crossings when heading for the succulent new grass of the Masai Mara in Kenya, is a rare and wonderful spectacle. Along with a multitude of bleating wildebeest on the move is the graceful progress of giraffe across the plains, the elegant Maasai warriors striding out, their red *shukas* billowing behind them, forests of baobabs and the crystal-clear waters of Lake Tanganyika, form some of the images that visitors take home, generally finding that their safari far exceeds expectations.

Known as the 'cradle of mankind' the Rift Valley of East Africa is the site of numerous important fossil discoveries which are of interest to many visitors, and here it is important to have a guide who enjoys visiting the

On the road to Kibale Forest

* 'safari' itself is a Swahili word meaning 'journey'.

archaeological sites along with traditional safari areas. If the cultural side of East Africa is of special interest, choose a guide with particular knowledge of tribal life.

Uganda, owing to its higher rainfall, has a tropical luxuriance rare in the rest of East Africa. Jungles and forests provide habitats for numerous primates; the chimpanzee, our closest relative, can be found here, in Kibale Forest, as well as in Tanzania, along the shores of Lake Tanganyika. A visit to the habituated mountain gorillas in the Bwindi Impenetrable Forest National Park in southwest Uganda is a very special experience. There are others in the Virunga Mountains of neighbouring Rwanda. These magnificent and greatly endangered creatures (only seven hundred remain in the wild) need all the help and support they can get from us to ensure their survival.

In northern Uganda, the Murchison Falls National Park runs down to the edge of Lake Albert. So many people suffered and died in the 19th century to find this point

Wildebeest migration on the plains near Ndutu

where the waters of the Nile run out of the lake and travel thousands of miles to the Mediterranean. Nothing has changed. Fishermen ply the waters in their dugout canoes, Uganda cob, giraffe and elephant still quench their thirst at the water's edge and the mountains rise majestically beyond. This ancient landscape is just as it was when Burton and Speke finally arrived here in their quest for the source of the Nile. It makes you tingle at the thought!

The coastal areas of Kenya and Tanzania are among the loveliest in the world – deserted white sandy beaches for the purists, with coral reefs for snorkelling and diving, or the exotic aromas of eastern spices and the colourful culture of Lamu or the Stone Town in Zanzibar; for the more adventurous. East Africa certainly lives up to its promise.

Elephants crossing the Uaso Nyiro River in Shaba National Park

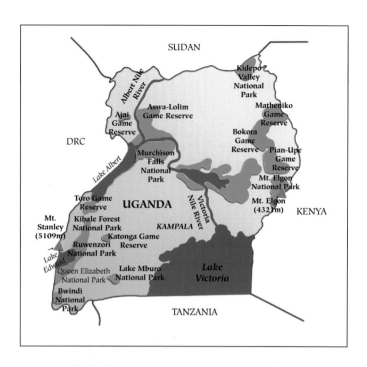

Young Mountain gorilla

The Murchison Falls – Uganda

A SAFARI TO SOIT ORGOSS IN NORTHERN TANZANIA

We left Ndutu Lodge at dawn, taking a packed breakfast and lunch for the journey across the Serengeti into the north-western section of the Loliondo Game Controlled area.

The immense undulating grasslands with their scattered herds of gazelle and zebra melted into the distant horizon; well-fed hyena waited by water holes, while stately giraffe ambled across the plain. It was a timeless scene, dry and dusty from the lack of rain, and there was no sign of the wildebeest migration. The year before we had been among thousands upon thousands of them, grazing on lush green grass on these same plains.

It was the time of year for the migratory birds to gather together in preparation for their flight back to North Africa, Europe and Asia. In the early morning, we drove through great flocks of Lesser kestrels stretching as far as the eye could see, flying or hovering over the grass, feeding and resting on the plains – a sight to remember when I see one hovering over a British motorway. A little later swooping European swallows surrounded our vehicle, catching the butterflies disturbed by our passing. Dicing with death, they darted in front of the vehicle, always avoiding collision and never once missing the tasty morsels they were after.

We breakfasted at the foot of the Gol Mountains before meeting Nigel's good friend Parkipumy Kaisoi, a Maasai whose *boma* is in this vicinity and whom I had met the year before. He wanted us to visit his *boma*, meet his new wife and see the hut she had just completed. Nigel had told him three months ago that we would be there on 21st March and there he was, waiting by Nasera, a huge granite boulder rising out of the plain. He jumped into the car and on the way to his *boma* he related the story of a recent rainmaking ceremony he had witnessed. The lack of rain was becoming critical. Ol Doinyo Lengai, the last remaining active volcano in northern Tanzania and god to the Maasai, required a sacrifice. Two hundred and seventy-two naked women, one of them a wife of Parkipumy, climbed to the top of the mountain taking with them thirty sheep. They slaughtered the sheep in an act of appeasement to Lengai, and remained up there for six days living off the meat of the sacrificed sheep. We all rather chuckled at the thought of this and asked him when the rain would come. He answered seriously, on the 24th! Amazingly, that was exactly what happened; we had massive storms on the night of 23rd March, continuing at intervals from then on. When we drove back through the same area on 26th March, the grass was already turning green. Rain in Africa is always a welcome miracle.

After visiting his *boma*, admiring his wife's newly built house and buying a few trinkets, we set off to have lunch at the 'Tree where man was born'. This huge ancient fig tree that stands alone, with hardly another tree or shrub in sight, naturally became a magnet for legends. The roots obviously found a crack in the hard pan over four hundred years ago and it just kept growing. There must have been other cracks in the pan, as it grows in a little gully where there are wells that give fresh water all year round.

Travelling on, we followed a rough track northwards until the plains gave way to rolling, wooded hills interspersed with granite kopjes, by which we knew we were entering the remote area of our destination. We turned off the road and drove overland, leaving all signs of civilisation and tourist routes far behind. By mid-afternoon we got our first glimpse of the jagged peaks of

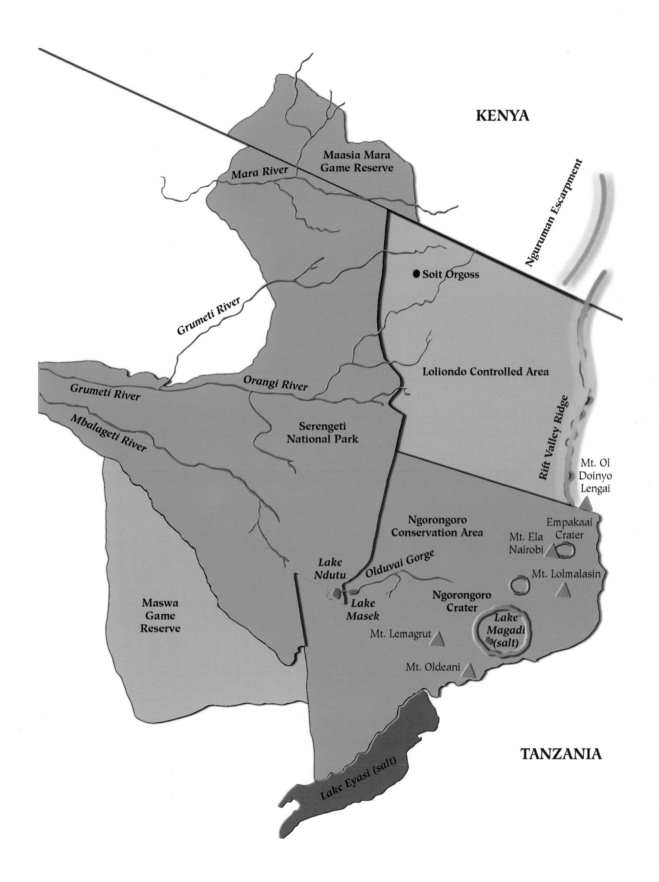

KENYA

Nguruman Escarpment

Maasia Mara
Game Reserve

Mara River

Grumeti River

Grumeti River

Orangi River

● Soit Orgoss

Loliondo Controlled Area

Mbalageti River

Serengeti
National Park

Rift Valley Ridge

Mt. Ol
Doinyo
Lengai

Ngorongoro
Conservation Area

Empakaai
Crater

Mt. Ela
Nairobi

Lake
Ndutu

Olduvai Gorge

Mt. Lolmalasin

Maswa
Game
Reserve

Lake
Masek

Ngorongoro
Crater

Lake
Magadi
(salt)

Mt. Lemagrut

Mt. Oldeani

Lake Eyasi (salt)

TANZANIA

Our camp at Soit Orgoss

Kipon, a Maasai warrior

downside for the visitor is, of course, that one may not photograph the people or their domestic animals. It takes considerable self-control, as there is nothing more appealing than the beautifully turned-out Maasai warriors roaming the land or delightful children tending new lambs and kids.

In 1989, Thad Peterson, one of three brothers born in Tanzania of American missionary parents, explored this area looking for new places to take his walking safaris. The Petersons' highly respected company, Dorobo Safaris, specialises in adventurous safaris in remote areas. Thad, who like all great guides radiates energy and charisma, persuaded the elders to allow him to use the area for his walking safaris, paying fees directly to the villages. Having agreed to this they in turn keep all their livestock out of Soit Orgoss during the season that Dorobo Safaris operate. Their cattle graze at Soit only in the dry season, which is also the hunting season. In Tanzania the people own the land, but the government owns the animals and in 1991, an Arab from Dubai paid the government for the hunting rights over this particular part of Loliondo. Luckily Dorobo Safaris were already established in the area and although requested repeatedly by the Arab to do so, the villagers would not ask them to leave. Being honourable people they stuck to their word. Conflict is avoided, as the photographic safaris do not take place here during July and August, the hunting season.

A few years ago Thad and the villagers discussed having one other operator, who would be able to use a vehicle combined with walking in the area, to increase their income. Thad asked Gibbs Farm Safaris (the firm Nigel worked with) if they would like to be that company. Of course they accepted!

Soit Orgoss on the horizon. Soit Orgoss (corridors of rock) is a secret, special place that is difficult to find on any map. Here the natural rhythm of the Maasai culture lives on in the traditional manner, untouched by mass tourism, and therefore happily devoid of roadside begging. The

Our campsite was set high up on a kopje with panoramic views, giving a sense of vastness and freedom. The kopjes are made up of massive boulders, some as large as a five-storey building, others balancing precariously upon one another resemble a natural Stonehenge. Due to the water retention in the kopjes the plant life is luxuriant and diverse. Huge fig trees grow in the cracks and crevices, their fat white roots travelling down the rock to find the soil, tall aloes, shrubs and exquisite tiny ferns tucked under the rocks all thrive happily together. The rocks are streaked with warm autumnal colours punctuated by swathes· of silver or yellow lichen. Breathtaking in the first glow of sunlight at dawn, they beg to be explored. The kopjes, which have many secret hiding places for leopards, are also home to klipspringers flouting gravity as they prance from rock to rock on their tiptoes. Baboons scale the rocks to their safe roosts where the youngsters, always playful, pull one another down by their tails, finding a foot- or hand-hold and scrambling up again in a death-defying Spiderman act.

Flat-topped acacias dot the golden grass that sweeps between each string of kopjes. Herds of sleek plains game graze on the nutritious grass: topi with their purple 'bruised' haunches, as well as hartebeest, Burchell's zebra, giraffe, dik-dik and impala. The impala rams are exceptionally large – apparently this is where trophy hunters came in the early twentieth century when they needed a good trophy-specimen for their collections! Buffalo and elephant and, of course, the cats also flourish here. However, all the animals are shy and skittish because of being hunted. One of the most astonishing sights was an enormous herd of eland. They rose out of a wooded gully as thick as the wildebeest

migration, more and more appearing until the herd covered the hillside ahead of us before disappearing over the crest. They were difficult to count but must have numbered over five hundred.

Each morning we walked for three or four hours, being met by the Land Rovers at a predetermined spot for

The Maasai are fine figures of men striding across the plains, tall and slim in their bright red *shukas*, fitting into the landscape as gracefully as strolling giraffe in harmony with nature

coffee or tea and a lift back to camp. After our afternoon siesta we usually went off to explore in the vehicles. Although there are plenty of animals in the area, this is not the place for portrait photography, but perfect for wildlife in their landscape. The prolific bird and animal life served merely to enhance the astounding vistas that opened up at each turn of our walks and drives. However, having had three days at Ndutu prior to our visit to Soit, everyone's aspirations to see good game had been satisfied. We had seen a lioness with tiny cubs, a very young baby elephant and its mother splashing near us in the water, two serval in a tree in the daylight, (the reluctant female having been chased to the top by an ardent male), Striped hyena, cheetah and leopard.

There was plenty of interesting animal behaviour. This is something one learns when travelling with a really good guide who takes the time to sit patiently, watching the scene unfolding. Nigel spotted a group of mongoose, which we detoured to see as they were running, then grouping, standing up on their hind legs to survey their

On the way back we found that Parkipumy's rain had brought out the blossom on the acacia trees along the winding road up to the Ngorongoro Crater

territory, rushing off again and behaving in a most agitated manner. It transpired that two jackals were trying to grab their babies, which they were protecting desperately while trying to get back to their den. In spite of their efforts the jackal did manage to grab one of the babies before the whole group disappeared into the safety of their underground burrow. Nigel had recently spent two weeks with a crew filming mongooses, but they never saw anything like that!

A member of Dorobo Safaris always accompanies Nigel's safaris to Soit Orgoss; it is their area and they know it well. Our guide was a splendid Tanzanian named Pallangyo, larger than life, with crinkly grey hair, infectious laugh and a great sense of humour that made him excellent company. We were well protected on our walks by Pallangyo with his rifle and our Maasai tracker with his spear and bow and arrows.

The lions roared below our kopje all night and twice we heard the rasping sound of a leopard in camp, so on the second morning Nigel decided we should find these noisy lions. Spotting two lionesses sitting on rocks high on the adjacent kopje, we crept round for a closer view while Nigel and our Maasai guide climbed a rock to find a path up to them. Needless to say the lions vanished, but Nigel and the guide had spotted what they thought was an old disused Ildorobo hunter's shelter. Climbing the slope with excited anticipation we looked up through the trees to see a man sitting high on a rock watching us. Wearing a well-worn brown coat over his *shuka* (toga-like garment worn by Maasai men), he was an old Ildorobo who did not melt into the undergrowth when he saw us, but waited to greet us because he recognised Pallangyo, whom he knows and trusts. It was not a disused shelter at all, but his home, and he was sitting on the rock making new arrows that were little works of art. Smooth and straight, they had perfect grooves to fit the bowstring, reinforced with sinew and feathers meticulously cut and inserted into the ends, with only the metal arrowheads yet to be fixed.

The old man, with rheumy eyes, a grizzled beard and a gentle smile, invited us into his home. A great flat overhanging rock formed the roof and branches of dense thorn bush leaned against it, creating a protective wall around the dwelling. Bunches of vulture feathers used for the arrows were attached to a pole propped outside the narrow entrance. We stepped in past the smouldering fire and looked around. The ceiling was about two metres high, and the room approximately six by four metres. On the left, two forked sticks held a thin straight branch on which hung curtains of buffalo meat. Bark and roots lay in heaps ready to be boiled and made into medicine or poison for the arrowheads, and a pile of skins on a layer of straw served as the bed. His possessions were few: the clothes he was wearing, his bow and arrows, a small knife, a big metal pot, with his only concession to modern life an old plastic water-bottle. This was no dark and dingy cave but a light and airy place, cosy with the smoky aroma of burnt wood and no flies. We all would have been delighted to stay there.

On our last morning, while the camp was being packed up, he sat on a rock nearby, watching and bidding us farewell. It was a rare and special privilege to meet an Ildorobo still living the traditional life of his ancestors and seldom seen by outsiders. We had spent much time contemplating the origins of man, visiting Oldupai Gorge, trying to envisage life thousands of years ago, but never dreaming we would actually meet a hunter-gatherer.

NIGEL PERKS

It is hard to imagine the cataclysmic explosion that must have taken place to create the vast bowl beneath us, when standing at the rim of the crater on a perfectly tranquil, cloudless morning. Nigel is explaining how the Serengeti were formed. We are in northern Tanzania at the edge of the Ngorongoro Crater, about eighteen kilometres (eleven miles) across and six hundred and ten metres deep (two thousand feet), it is the biggest of the numerous volcanoes in this area, similar in size to Mount Kilimanjaro. The ash and dust created by its explosion was blown east on the prevailing wind, joining the ash and dust from earlier volcanoes and filling the valleys as far as the eye can see, preserving all that lay beneath it and creating a fertile paradise for the plains game that now feed on it.

The road to the Serengeti winds down through a string of extinct volcanoes that fall away from the Ngorongoro Crater, so peaceful and green they give no intimation of the roaring infernos they once were. It was the ash from Mount Lemagrut, one of the older volcanoes on this route, that was instrumental in preserving the rich fossil beds in the gullies and gorges that have been slowly eroding in the valley on the way to the plains. The slopes are lightly wooded with flat-topped *Acacia tortilis* and the ground thickly carpeted with yellow and white flowers after the recent rains. Acacias are the favourite food of the giraffes that amble through the flowers as if in slow motion, nibbling at the tops of the trees.

This part of the world is Nigel's passion. He is a large man with a quick, infectious laugh and a gold tooth that glints in the sun; a New Zealander with the heart and soul of an African. He has the knack of making you feel that everything he sees is for the first time, creating a sense of discovery and wonder. He is such an excellent communicator that he sweeps up everyone in the drama of life and death on the Serengeti, both past and present.

As we explore the gorges with Nigel we learn that the volcanic activity preserved a tremendous number of fossils, giving a spectacular insight into life millions of years ago, not only human life but also the lives of the bizarre animals, long extinct, which once roamed these plains. *Pelorovis*, a bovine-like creature twice the size of a buffalo, with massive horns, an elephant with upturned tusks, a giant hippopotamus and many others. Relics and images of these creatures can be seen at the little museum situated at the visitors' centre at Oldupai Gorge, along with many other fossils unearthed in the gorge.

Oldupai Gorge has, of course been investigated extensively over many years, and is near Laetoli, where Mary Leakey, whom Nigel knew, found the famous footprints (of which a cast may be seen in the Oldupai museum) of the earliest known upright-walking hominid, *Australopithecus afarensis*. Mary Leakey's work was vital to our understanding and knowledge of human development and the extraordinary animals that lived here millions of years ago.

Nigel was taking a group of us to stay at a tented camp at Ol Karien Gorge in the Gol Mountains in order to take a trip across the Salei Plains to view the volcano Ol Doinyo Lengai from the top of the escarpment. We were exploring an idea for a television programme, which would involve climbing this volcano before it next erupted. This could be quite soon, as the salt crust inside the bowl of the volcano has risen to the top; it was about forty feet down ten years ago when Nigel last climbed it. Parkipumy was travelling with us, bubbling with excitement, as his *boma* is not in sight of Ol Doinyo

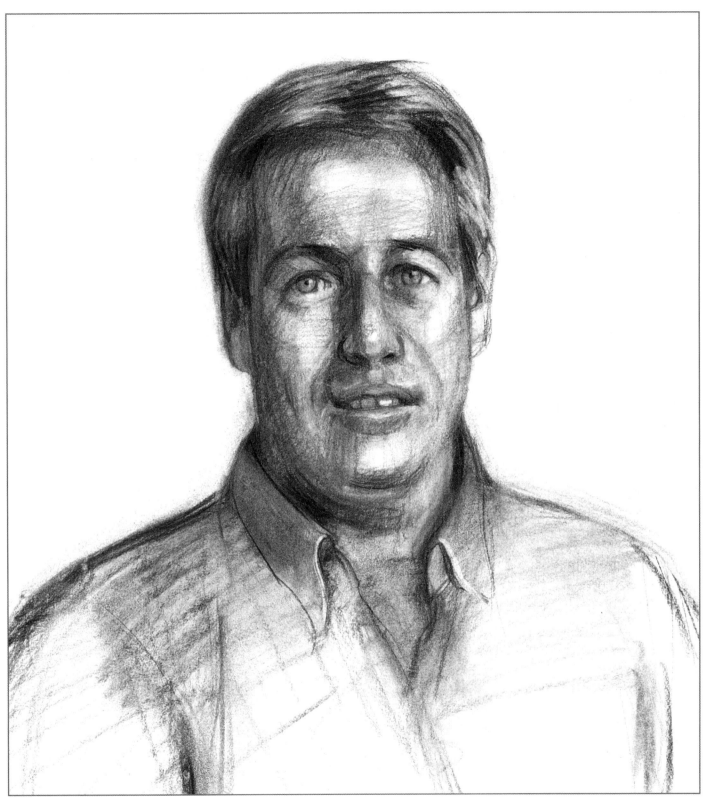

Nigel Perks

Lengai. When we all tumbled out of the cars at the first sight of the cone-shaped mountain on the horizon, Parkipumy stood on the rim of the valley gazing at the mountain. This is a very holy place to the Maasai and he spent a good fifteen minutes standing facing the mountain and chanting his invocation, which carried loud and clear across the valley.

The Gol Mountains in the Ngorongoro Conservation Area, right on the edge of the Rift Valley, are well populated with Maasai, but not with tourists. The fertile valleys and cool, high mountain slopes have been a favourite grazing area for their cattle probably since their arrival in East Africa, with Ol Karian Gorge and the Sanjan River being traditional sources of water during the dry season.

Entering Ol Karian Gorge through a fissure in the echoing, overhanging cliffs is like walking into a secret world. The first narrow pathway opens up into rock pools rimmed with huge boulders and gnarled trees, then contracts again into a narrow passageway through more towering granite walls. The top of the gorge is a favourite nesting place of Ruppell's griffon, hundreds of which may be seen rising on the thermals and circling in the blue sky above. A trickle of water ran down the gorge when we visited it, creating a little waterfall, splashing into a large bowl of transparent green quartz of startling beauty. The gorge is subject to flash floods after heavy rain in the mountains, when a wall of water roars through, carrying all before it. The Maasai lead their livestock deep into the gorge to drink at their ancient wells, the scene having a rather biblical flavour as the animals are herded up the narrow paths – boys whistling and shouting, the dust swirling around their red cloaks, cowbells tinkling, goats bleating and the women in blue robes bringing up the rear. The women collect the household water in containers that are put into straw panniers slung over the backs of donkeys.

The following day we drove across the Salei Plains to the very edge of the escarpment. Wildebeest, zebra and giraffe ambled through the carpet of white flowers that had appeared after the recent rains. It was a glorious journey that took all morning and ended at the rim of the rift valley. Everyone gasped at the spectacle before us; we seemed to be standing on the very edge of the world! The land drops steeply away for thousands of feet into the Great Rift Valley, an inhospitable furnace surrounded by the escarpment and mountains. Towering above us to our right was Ol Doinyo Lengai, the rivers of white ash flowing from its crater clearly visible. Way below, Lake Natron shimmered in the haze. This huge soda lake is the only regular breeding area of the Lesser flamingo in East Africa.

While we lunched in the shade of one of the few trees on the edge of the escarpment, Parkipumy was negotiating for us to visit a village perched on the edge, with Lengai as its backdrop. He returned with one of the village elders to collect us. Some of the *morans** stood in line to greet us at the entrance, very formally, with handshakes. Foreign visitors in this part of the world are seldom seen and all the people of the village had dressed up for the occasion. The women wore beaded head-dresses, large round beaded collars, necklaces, earrings and anklets, their clothing bright blue or red, nearly all of them had a baby on the hip or one on the way. The men were imposing figures in their bright red *shukas* with their hair pulled back in a band that held tight ringlets. The women dress the men's hair, forming ringlets from strands of wildebeest tails. It is then coloured with ochre and gathered in a loop at the back of the head. The men also wore colourful beaded necklaces and earrings.

152   * *moran:* young warrior.

The view of Lemagrut form Ndutu Lake

There was laughter and singing, and the men gave us a display of their extraordinary athletic jumping, when from a standing position they can jump as much as four feet in the air. The children were particularly excited, running around chattering away, many of them in English, as they attend a mission school and loved the opportunity to practise the language. There was much laughter and delight when they looked at themselves on the screen of a video camera.

Nigel's safaris are always full of surprises, and this visit, ostensibly to find porters for an Ol Doinyo Lengai climb, had been a highlight for us, and the conversation round the campfire that night was particularly animated.

Close to, the mountain looked daunting and fitness campaigns were planned before anyone felt they could climb it.

Nigel is happiest on the Serengeti in the early part of each year when 1,5 million wildebeest gather to give birth to more than 200 000 calves in just a few weeks; however, he is also drawn to the wilder and more remote areas of Tanzania.

As a young boy growing up in New Zealand Nigel had a strong yearning to see the world. He spent hours poring over brochures lifted from the local travel agency, plotting and planning his future. He was passionate about wildlife television programmes, especially those from the BBC, and

153

had read all David Attenborough's books. He would head up the rivers with a pair of binoculars, identifying birds and learning about the natural environment near his home. His father, a keen sportsman and marathon runner, instilled in his sons a love of the outdoors by taking them camping from a very early age. Nigel has gone the nature route and his brother Craig is the sportsman, a highly successful golfer on the American PGA circuit. He gained fame and fortune in August 2002 when he won the Players Championship, known as the 'fifth major'.

Nigel was unsure of what direction he would take until his Geography teacher spent a whole year teaching his class about Africa. From then on he was hooked and the focus of his obsession was the Serengeti – he just could not wait to get there. Once he had finished studying zoology at university, with $300 in his pocket he set off on his journey. His money got him to Australia, where he worked for six months to earn enough for the rest of the journey.

He and a friend travelled for eleven months overland through Asia towards England – Thailand, Malaysia, Nepal, India, Pakistan, Iran, Turkey, Jordan, Syria, back into Turkey and then to Greece. During this epic journey he made a new friend, a meeting that was to confirm the direction of his life. In a bar he chanced upon a fellow itinerant named Gary, who was driving a group of tourists to Kathmandu in an overland truck for a British-based tour company. They bumped into one another at least seven or eight times during their travels and became good friends. Gary had done seven overland trips from London to Johannesburg and Nigel pumped him for information on Africa. The last meeting ended with a cheerful "don't forget to look me up in England." After ten months his travelling companion left to go back

to New Zealand and by sheer coincidence Nigel arrived on Gary's doorstep in England just as he was about to depart for Tanzania. Gary was driving a group of eight people in two Land Rovers and his fellow driver had let him down. To Nigel's great joy he was offered the job – and grabbed it.

They spent twenty-two weeks travelling from London to Dar es Salaam on one of the most exciting journeys imaginable. It started with six weeks crossing the Sahara, climbing sand dunes, sleeping under the stars and learning how to survive the heat and dust. Their journey took them through Algeria, Morocco, the Cameroons and the Chad Republic into Zaire.

After two weeks' travelling up the Congo River with the vehicles on a boat, they headed off through the jungle on rudimentary roads that sometimes just disappeared into mud holes. On one occasion, after heavy rains, it took five days to travel twenty kilometres on a muddy road bogged down with more than a hundred other vehicles, also stuck in the mud. They all helped one another to get them through, pushing and hauling vehicles and being bitten all day by flies and all night by mosquitoes.

The great reward for all this was a visit to the mountain gorillas at Jumba in Zaire (DRC). Jumba had only just been opened up to visitors and there were no restrictions. They could sit in small groups of two or three with the gorillas all day. In Rwanda, where the gorillas had been a tourist attraction for some time, only one hour was permitted with them, as is now the case as well in Uganda.

Having reached Tanzania Nigel and Gary decided to stay and work together, driving visitors around Tanzania, Kenya and Uganda. Their clients were mainly backpackers between the ages of eighteen and twenty-five, mostly girls who were looking for fun and adventure and basically needing only to be driven around. Nigel and Gary took turns to take the trips, which lasted three weeks. Each vehicle pulled a trailer with the camping equipment and took four or five passengers, everyone helping with all aspects of camping. Somehow they always managed to pack one too few tents so someone had to share with the driver!

The group would roll across the plains singing and laughing, with the girls sunbathing topless on the roof of the vehicle. They did these trips for three years, following the wildebeest migration and visiting the gorillas in Zaire. Nigel went back to Juma many times until civil unrest made the visits too dangerous.

They explored all over East Africa with a freedom unknown today, and Nigel spent hours watching and learning about the animals and birds and finding exciting new areas – the best schooling any potential guide could have. He has never lost that first wonder he felt at the vastness and eternal beauty of the Serengeti.

Gibbs Farm

Nigel and Gary lived at the Kibo Hotel at the foot of Mount Kilimanjaro, from where they operated their safaris. Having British licence plates on their two vehicles allowed them free access over the borders and it took some time before the authorities caught up with their makeshift unlicensed activities. They were faced with two options; either pay the very large sum of money needed for foreigners to set up their own company, which they did not have, or set up with a local company. It was at this time that they met Margaret Gibb, owner of a coffee farm on the slopes of Ngorongoro, who wanted to set up a safari company based at Gibbs Farm where she had already built several guestrooms. She financed and supported their operation, which ran under her safari licence. In 1991, Gary broke up the partnership to set up on his own – it was a turbulent, unhappy time. Nigel remained loyal to Margaret and with immense hard work and dedication they turned Gibbs Farm Safaris into one of the most successful and respected companies in Tanzania.

Margaret, who was born in Tanzania, met her English husband Jim Gibb when he travelled overland to Africa after the war. He was headed for South Africa to start a new life, but at the bar in the New Stanley Hotel in Nairobi he heard of a coffee farm for sale on the slopes of Ngorongoro. He bought the badly neglected farm, revived it and married Margaret in 1959, and together they made a success of the coffee farm. Their house sat in an exquisite garden started by Margaret in 1960, with the coffee bushes spread out in the valley below them.

When the price of coffee hit rock bottom in the 1970s they decided to turn the farm into a guest lodge. They built guestrooms in the gardens overlooking the plantations from which the tourists could visit the surrounding areas, Lake Manyara and the Ngorongoro Crater. These original guestrooms are currently all being renovated twenty-first-century-style.

Jim died in 1977, but Margaret, who later remarried, stayed on all through the socialist era, when foreigners were leaving in droves and land was being nationalised. She and her farm survived and it remains a place of deep tranquillity and beauty. The rich soil produces an abundance of fruit and vegetables that supply the lodges and the safaris. Producing such a great quantity of food in an eight-acre garden has its problems. The area has to be very secure from animals, but there is nothing that will stop hungry elephants that have a penchant for strawberries! Guards have to sit by the patch all night banging on tin cans to keep the elephants away from the newly ripened berries.

The second lodge, in which Margaret has an interest, is Ndutu on the edge of the Serengeti. The co-owner is her good friend Aadje Geertsema, who also has an interest in Gibbs Farm. Aadje, while still very young, travelled from Holland to Tanzania with her father, a friend and advisor to Prince Bernhard, who was a keen hunter and conservationist, and the first president of the World Wildlife Fund. Africa did its familiar act of digging itself under Aadje's skin, causing her to return and live a large portion of her life in Tanzania. She started by working for George Dove, owner of Ndutu, a tented camp that George had set up as a tourist venue. There she first met Margaret Gibb, a friend of George's and frequent visitor to the camp. Aadje's role was that of a general assistant, but whenever she had some spare time she took out one of the old Land Rovers that belonged to the lodge and explored the bush.

During this time she made a very clever twenty-minute film about servals with a Super-8 movie camera, setting it to the music of Pink Floyd. It was a great hit and got her funding to do the first research on the serval. It took her four years, living alone on the floor of the Ngorongoro Crater. The cats were so shy and elusive that it took six months to write down her first data. Eventually she had some well-habituated serval and plenty of information on them. Her data was published in the *Netherlands Journal of Zoology* in 1985, after which she remained in Holland on a lecture tour, raising money for the Save the Rhino

Aadje Geertsema, owner of Ndutu Lodge

156

Foundation, before returning to Tanzania. Her heart has always been in Ndutu and when she learned that it was for sale she decided to buy it, together with Margaret Gibb, and run it herself.

Aadje and Margaret, both early starters in the modern tourist industry of Tanzania, were Nigel's mentors, giving a tremendous start to this enthusiast, who soaked up the knowledge. They were familiar with every nook and cranny of northern Tanzania and willingly passed on all their knowledge of the whereabouts of little-known places. However, they didn't make it too easy; they would describe a place, for example Ol Karian Gorge and, with a few vague clues, send him off alone to find it. The gorge is a most secret place; from the outside you would never know about the narrow twisting passages through the mountains, nor the ancient Maasai wells, though the circling vultures might give it away if one knew they nested on the high granite walls.

Nigel now runs the mobile tented safaris from Gibbs Farm. The safari staff are trained at Gibbs Farm where its kitchens, restaurant, bar and guestrooms provide the perfect opportunity for on-site training. They have the wonderful advantage of the farm supplying delicious homegrown produce, meat, fruit and vegetables, for both the lodges and the mobile safaris. It is a very convenient base and a lovely place for the clients to begin their stay in Tanzania.

It was early on in Nigel's association with Gibbs Farm that one of his wildest dreams came true – he met and drove David Attenborough into the Serengeti when the BBC was filming *The Trials of Life* series. Gibbs Farm often plays host to filmmakers and writers because of their reputation for excellence in both scenery and guiding.

Mary Leakey and the footprints

Margaret was a great friend of Mary Leakey, the famous palaeontologist who, having given up her camp at Oldupai when she returned to live in Nairobi, frequently stayed at Gibbs Farm on her visits to Tanzania. When Nigel joined Gibbs Farm, Mary Leakey was quite an old lady but still full of life. He often took her out on safari and tells the story of her last visit when he had the unique privilege of being with her when she uncovered the footprints for the very last time:

"I had the pleasure of knowing Mary and taking her on a couple of memorable safaris before she passed away a few years back. She was in her late seventies and early eighties when I knew her and was always incredibly energetic and enthusiastic and loved coming back to Tanzania. Each year we endeavoured to get her out to the Serengeti. Mary would often drive herself down from Nairobi to Gibbs Farm (eight hours) arriving like the living dead, but soon revived after a couple of large whiskies and a cigar, thrilled to be back and raring to go!

"A few months before Mary died she joined an expedition back to Laetoli to uncover and preserve the famous 3,6-million-year-old hominid footprints, which she had first discovered back in the 1970s. The footprints were made when three hominids walked through damp ash. They were then naturally preserved by continuous ash falls from the local volcanoes.

"It was probably the most significant archaeological discovery ever made, a huge

157

responsibility to Mary and her crew who documented them. When discovered the footprints had obviously survived 3,6 million years, but any further interference could destroy this most important site. Mary and her team re-covered the footprints so they would be protected from erosion and human interference.

Impala and Lilac-breasted roller at Nduto

"Imagine how she must have felt when they were first uncovered again? Had they sieved the returned soil enough to remove seeds so plant roots wouldn't crack the footprint trail? Had they left it as it was for future generations? Had anyone vandalised the site because she had made the world aware of it? Over a whisky the night before, we sat and talked about these issues.

"With a great deal of apprehension we visited the site the next day. To her obvious relief everything was in perfect condition, as we all knew they would be, because of the painstaking effort Mary and her crew had put in all those years ago. It was an incredible honour for me to be standing at this site with Mary Leakey and seeing the footprints for the first and last time.

"The footprints have been scientifically buried and there is no plan to ever open them to human eyes again!

"Mary died knowing that she had not only made some of the most momentous archaeological discoveries, but also had given the world an insight into our past.

"Her funeral happened exactly as she planned. Her coffin was placed on a huge bonfire overlooking the Rift Valley where she was cremated with all her family and close friends attending. She had requested that they finish off her whisky and cigars, which they did, throwing the butts into the fire in her honour."

Nigel spent years exploring and learning about the Serengeti and the surrounding areas, getting to know the people and becoming thoroughly familiar with this vast and beautiful land. He waited fifteen years to see his first leopard kill in the daytime; it came down from a tree using his vehicle to stalk a wildebeest, then kill it in front of them in broad daylight. Another very exciting moment was the first time cheetahs used one of his vehicles for a vantage point. He had very slowly approached a couple of cheetahs on the plains, stopping about twenty yard from them. One cheetah stood up, walked towards them, creating great excitement in the car as it was the first cheetah seen by his two American clients. The next moment it jumped up on the vehicle and they lay on the floor taking photographs while it sat on the roof with its tail hanging down into the car.

On a previous safari he had been watching a cheetah with three little cubs for a couple of days when he saw the mother take on a Grant's gazelle. The gazelle turned on the cheetah, flipped her over and stabbed her with his horns, killing her. Over the next few days they watched the cubs die. It was sad, but as he says, "it is survival of the fittest and the best genes. She should not have taken on a Grant's, but gone for a Thompson's gazelle with no horns."

One of his most startling moments was driving in Ruaha in the early morning when what looked like a stick across the road, but was in fact a Black mamba, suddenly reared up and hit the windscreen at eye level, a few inches from the open roof. It had been surprisingly fast, as it was a cold morning and snakes don't usually move fast in the cold. After dropping his guests off at the airstrip, he got back into camp where one of the staff told him there was a little snake in one of the store tents. He had seen it going in. Nigel lay down at the entrance to see if he could find it and was immediately confronted by a six-foot cobra sitting up waving in the air and ready to spit. The man had seen only the cobra's retreating tail so thought it was small. Nigel told him that he must take care of his 'little' snake himself. Two snakes in one day were enough!

He has journeyed all over Tanzania, walking in Katavi and Ruaha, both very large but little-visited reserves of great beauty and spectacular game. Katavi has buffalo herds of more than a thousand head on open plains reminiscent of the Serengeti. Ruaha has a rugged rocky landscape with forests of baobabs and a beautiful river. Walking is permitted in both parks: in Ruaha it is possible to look down on an eagle's nest from the top of a kopje. Mahale Mountains on Lake Tanganyika combines white sandy beaches and snorkelling in the gin-clear lake waters with trekking in a forest to observe chimpanzees going about their daily lives. Nigel has driven right across Tanzania from Lake Tanganyika. Near Lake Rukwa, along part of the old slave route, he came across long lines of mango trees growing from the pips of the fruit given to the slaves to eat a century ago. Sleeping under the stars, washing in crystal-clear, unmapped streams, following a compass and not knowing what would be over the hill nor where he would be that night, was truly a safari into the unknown.

As so often happens, visitors become attached to a particular guide, wanting him to accompany them on safari in other parts of Africa. This has certainly been true for Nigel. He loves to take his clients to new areas; it gives him the opportunity of meeting other guides with expert knowledge of their areas, as well as studying animal behaviour elsewhere. Nigel's observations on animal behaviour are fascinating and the differences in geographical ecologies have become one of his major interests.

Different behaviour

Nigel has observed animal behaviour that is far from the supposed norm; he has three stories that clearly illustrate his observations: First, cheetah behaviour in Ruaha National Park:

"The Serengeti is unique in Africa. The animals are so easy to see and study that the behaviour observed and studied on animals in the park is treated as normal behaviour everywhere and seldom questioned. Cheetahs are plentiful and we all know and have seen wonderful films of its speed and expertise when hunting. It is known as the fastest animal on earth. However, in Ruaha National Park, in southern Tanzania, there are just as many, if not more cheetahs, but they are seldom seen. The bush is thick and the grass long. As secretive as leopards and in complete contrast to the lightning sprint we are familiar with, they stalk their prey, get up close and pounce on it just as leopards do. This is very different from the studies done in the Serengeti."

His second story concerns wild dogs, which provide another good example of different behaviour in different habitats. Although no longer seen in the Serengeti, they would pursue their prey until it fell from exhaustion. On the open plains they could chase a wildebeest for over an hour. In more heavily wooded habitats, such as Botswana, the hunts are all over in a few minutes as they swiftly chase impala through the trees. In the late 1980s, before the wild dogs were wiped out by distemper and rabies caught from the Maasai dogs, Nigel had some of his best game-viewing. The packs were large, comprising twelve to fifteen adults and up to twenty pups. They were magnificent to watch. Once he spent five days with a group of guests, morning and evening watching one pack:

"We would be on the plains in the evening watching this pack take off, and they would go after big game, wildebeest or zebra. The lead dog would work out the strategy. He would pick an animal, causing chaos; there would be wildebeest running in every direction, dust whirling up, red in the evening sun. I would see the way it was going and race about five kilometres across the plain in order to get the action coming straight at us. The lead dog would race behind the beast for about ten minutes, the rest of the pack trotting along a straight line, when he was tired he backed off and another dog took up the chase and so on until the animal dropped and the kill took place. It was fantastically well organised teamwork."

His third story is about the perilous lives of lion cubs:

"One stunning evening at Ndutu's big marsh, in the glorious last light, we were lucky enough to be sitting watching and photographing two lionesses with three young cubs. A wonderful scene with very playful cubs, jumping on each other, tumbling, play fighting and generally being complete posers to my Land Rover full of very keen photographers.

"We left after a classic Serengeti sunset and decided to return in the morning to spend more time with this happy family! We arrived at the marsh the next morning at first light to a very different scenario. What had been the perfectly relaxed happy family the night before had turned into a very tense situation.

"Two unknown male lions were with the lionesses, one of the females had a fresh bite wound and one cub was missing. It did not look good for the remaining cubs as we assumed that these new males were in the process of taking over the pride, which generally means certain death to young cubs. Infanticide is something that occurs commonly with lions, but very few people ever witness it and even fewer have photographed it.

"We sat there in morbid anticipation, no one wanted to watch cubs being killed, but observing infanticide is scientifically important.

"The lioness with the missing cub was flirting constantly with one of the new males and eventually we watched as they mated every fifteen minutes for the next two hours. It's bizarre to watch such behaviour, but makes genetic sense as the male obviously wants to father his own offspring and by killing another male's cubs he brings the females back into oestrus. For the female, she hopefully will then be raising his genetically superior cubs!

"The other lioness still with her two cubs had moved away from the mating pair, but was incredibly nervous and never took her eyes off the other intruding male. He would edge towards her and she would move the cubs away. This went on for hours until it looked as if the lioness had just given up and walked her

cubsover to the male! Then it happened, we witnessed infanticide! The male picked up the cubs one by one and killed them with fatal bites to the head. It was shocking to watch as it had such inevitability about it! The male then proceeded to eat the cubs!

"The strange thing about what we had observed was that these two male lions were not huge, black-maned specimens, but young (maybe four years old) blond nomads that had literally just wandered into another pride's territory and taken up with the females. It was the middle of the wildebeest migration and there was such a huge abundance of food around that the pride was well spread out and the pride males were not spending any time with the females. This led to a totally opportunistic situation where the young blonds were successful.

"Over the next few weeks we returned to the marsh to see the progress, expecting to see the original pride males back with the pride and the blonds expelled. Amazingly, for two weeks we watched the two infanticide males mating constantly with the lionesses and a bonding occurring.

"It was an unforgettable experience and something we all found fascinating, but were astonished by the females' acceptance of the new males after the killing of their cubs – although it all make sense in the natural order of things."

Nigel spent many months in Ruaha National Park where he put up a tented camp for six weeks each year. It is a vast, wonderfully remote park, sparsely visited by people, but frequently by elephants. He tells the story of one such visit that took place over a few nights at the camp:

"Having a camp in Ruaha National Park in southern Tanzania was quite an expedition, supplies were difficult as Gibbs Farm's vegetable garden is a three-day drive north. All the camping equipment and dry supplies can be trucked in, but fresh vegetables and meat arrive on charter flights with our guests.

"Our camp was on the Ruaha River bank with a stunning amount of wildlife around camp day and night. Some of the highlights included a pack of wild dogs killing an impala fifty metres from camp in front of one of our guests' tents, leopard hunts, Sable and Roan antelope drinking, lion roars and endless elephant activity. Even elephant drinking from our shower buckets!

"Our first group had arrived and with them came baskets full of wonderful vegetables and fruit to last us the next five days. We had a delicious dinner and all went off to our tents anticipating our first night in camp.

"At about two o'clock I was awoken to the sounds of elephant wandering through camp and rolled over and went back to sleep thinking how wonderful it was to be back in Ruaha. A few moments later I awoke again to excited screaming from the kitchen tent. I raced over to see what all the commotion was about and witnessed one of the funniest things I'd seen in years. An elephant had broken into our store tent and was hoovering up all our valued vegetables. Silas, one of or cooks, was unimpressed and was tugging at one end of the tent as the elephant pulled at the other. A couple of our crew were picking up tent poles and trying to persuade the elephant to move on! The elephant (later named Fred) had no intention of moving off and it took us several minutes of abuse to get him on his way. During this entire hullabaloo Fred managed to trample most of our supplies and eat twenty avocados!

"Nothing further happened that night and in the morning we surveyed the vegetable damage and sent the crew off to Iringa (our closest market) to scrounge supplies so we could eat for the rest of the trip. The whole encounter was very odd as no one camps in the spot we use so there is no rubbish left around and over all the years we had been visiting Ruaha we had never had animals in camp looking for food.

"I chatted to the rangers about Fred and they told me that there was a young male that had be raiding the lodge's rubbish pit and had got very used to the taste of camp food – but surely this wasn't the same standard as our camp food? The rangers' description sounded very like our Fred.

"The crew arrived back with fresh supplies and we decided that it made a lot of sense to keep everything locked up in the back of our truck. That night Fred arrived again and this time broke a window to get at the supplies in our truck. Again our cooks yelled and screamed to try and scatter him. Eventually Fred disappeared leaving us a nice pile of dung full of avocado seeds!

"By now the park rangers had decided that Fred was a problem and thought the best solution was to scare him off by firing gunshots over his head. Not really what I wanted in camp, but there was nothing we could do. I warned my clients that they might hear a gunshot in the night. Night three and Fred was back, this time he was in for a surprise at the kitchen tent! Off went the shot and we were awoken to Fred charging off through the camp. I thought that would be the last of Fred as Ruaha elephants were severely poached in the '80s and always moved well away from guns. So came night four and at three o'clock when the gun went off again, I rushed out expecting to see Fred, but it was a herd of elephants charging through camp! I yelled at the ranger and asked what he thought he was doing.

'Oh,' he said, 'I thought you did not want any elephants in camp.'

"The whole thing was getting out of hand so I asked the ranger to leave. He replied, 'This is not possible, I am here for your clients' safety.' Night five came and again a gunshot! I hurried out of my tent to see a leopard charging through camp. It was wonderful, all these nocturnal sightings, but I had not any sleep for five nights, so when the ranger explained that he thought we did not want any animals in camp I sent him packing.

"Finally we got some sleep. Fred eventually came back, but was very well behaved and never attacked the camp again apart from once pushing over a small tree onto the kitchen tent."

Nigel, like all the guides, worked hard building a good business and an excellent reputation, but there were not many companions of his own age. Most of the guests were a lot older, so it was with great excitement that he set off one day to collect three clients from Kilimanjaro Airport, mother, father and daughter. At last, he thought, someone of my own age to chat to. The daughter turned out to be sixty-three, the mother eighty-four and father ninety!

However, light appeared at the end of the tunnel when Margaret asked him to pick up a friend's daughter who was coming out to work at Ndutu Lodge. Fiona Denton arrived to have six months off from intensive care nursing in London. At that time, Nigel tells me, there were about twenty white men to every white girl in Arusha, and he was thrilled to be the first to meet her. She was sent off to Ndutu to work pretty quickly as it was the busy season, and he was in and out of Ndutu with his clients. He slowly got to know her and when things quietened down they took a couple of safaris

Nigel, Fiona and Jake

The wildebeest migration at sunset

together. Over the next four years she would come out and work at Ndutu in the busy season and go back to London to nurse when it was quiet. Slowly she grew to adore the bush, and Nigel. But he certainly put her through many initiations, including climbing Nasera rock and Ol Doinyo Lengai. Her very first visit to a campsite was during the BBC filming of *The Trials of Life*, to meet David Attenborough on safari. Looking after a film crew is hard work; Nigel was up in the dark at five o'clock and with them all day. The plan at the end of the day was to film the moon coming up with zebras in front of it. It was the second day of the full moon, so it should have appeared just after sunset, but was nowhere to be seen. They waited until nine o'clock before someone suddenly realised there was an eclipse! All in all it had been an exhausting day. Nigel and Fiona were sleeping in a small A-frame tent with broken zips. At about eleven o'clock a lion started to roar right next to the tent, Fiona sat bolt upright, tried to wake Nigel, who grunted, turned over and said "Go back to sleep, it's only a lion."

For someone who lives in London, a lion roaring outside your bedroom is something particularly alien; she sat up all night terrified while the lions wandered around the camp. Eventually she got her own back. While on a marketing trip in America, they stayed in a flat at the back of a tour operator's office in New Orleans. At about midnight there was an awful racket in the street below them. Looking out of the window they saw a gang smashing windows and going on the rampage. It was Nigel's turn to be terrified. Being an urban girl, Fiona went straight back to sleep, not worrying about them at all. Nigel took a couple of Maasai spears off the office wall and stood by the door for the rest of the night, just in case.

They spent many hours in the bush together, camping, photographing and learning about wildlife and each other. He was lucky to find such a perfect soulmate, whom he married in 1993, setting up home at Gibbs Farm. Jake and Jessica were born while they lived there, but they eventually decided to live in New Zealand.

Nigel could not give up working on safaris; this is his passion, and life is always somehow filled with compromises. He now has one of the world's longest commutes – Auckland to Arusha. Lots of people say to Nigel, "How lucky you've been." "It's true," he says. "I have been lucky. But you also have to get out there and make your own luck."

RON BEATON

In a darkened cinema the audience sat on the edge of their seats holding their breath, watching in horror as a small boy walked across the lawn towards his house, tenderly carrying a tiny lion cub. Behind him the lioness, having discovered her missing cub, was accelerating through the bush towards the blissfully ignorant child. This was one of the heart-stopping moments in the film *Where No Vultures Fly*, released in 1953 and shot in Kenya with the help of Ron's father, then Warden of Nairobi National Park. The incident, though considerably dramatised for the screen, was based on a real story – Ron had done just that at the age of five. A lioness was keeping her small cubs not far from his house. While she went hunting Ron picked up one of the lion cubs, and took it home to his mother who nearly fainted when he walked into the kitchen with the little creature in his arms. After a sound beating from his father they took the cub out and placed it on the road. The lioness heard it mewing as she walked up the road with the other three cubs; she sniffed it, licked it and, miraculously, took it back.

Ron Beaton

The lioness used in the film was a pet called Iola, a beautiful animal that was eventually shot by a farmer who mistook her for a cattle killer. Quite a lot of people in Kenya brought up orphaned lions at that time. Ron's family had three lionesses as pets, and they ended up in a zoo when, quite frankly, they would have been better off being eaten by hyenas when they were cubs. Ron was never quite sure why he took the cub, maybe it was because lions had killed his Staffordshire terrier on the lawn outside their house and this was retaliation of a kind. He was, after all, only five years old.

Ron Beaton is a large man, with an easy, relaxed manner, generous smile and twinkling eyes. He has never lost his curiosity nor ceased to marvel at the magnificent country in which he has been so fortunate to live. This, along with his many years of experience, makes him a cosy and fascinating companion. For many years he owned and operated a delightful small bush lodge called Rekero just outside the Masai Mara National Park in Kenya. The lodge, along with a small but luxurious tented camp he owns on the Talek River in the Mara, expeditions to Lake Turkana in Northern Kenya and the Omo River in Ethiopia, offers his safari guests a unique and very exclusive wildlife experience. This is made all the more interesting by Ron's extensive experience, gleaned from a lifetime in the bush, along with his sense of fun and adventure.

Soon after the lion cub incident in Nairobi National Park Ron's parents separated. His mother married Tuffy Marshall, who worked for the Kenya Wildlife Department. His father, Ken Beaton, set off to make a new life for himself in Uganda. Growing up with both parents being involved in parks and wildlife naturally gave Ron an understanding of life in the bush. He spent every school holiday in Tsavo or with his father in Uganda, until his father died in 1954. Ron's mother and stepfather lived in Tsavo where his stepfather, Tuffy, was the head of Tsavo National Park. His *ayah* (nurse) was not a woman but a man, a Wakamba ex-poacher named Nduma. He had been caught poaching by Tuffy and given two choices, prison or looking after his son! Ron adored Nduma, who had him completely wrapped around his little finger, and would do anything for the old rogue, even stealing Tuffy's cigars for him. Although he was so young at the time, Nduma instilled in him a true empathy for wildlife and bush lore. Sadly, Ron was still quite young but away at school when Nduma died of malaria.

Children travel a long way to school in Africa and Ron was no exception. He was only six years old when he first went to boarding school, but for years, at the beginning of each term, he boarded the Mombasa-Nairobi train at two o'clock in the morning at Mtito Andei in Tsavo to attend a Catholic boys' school in Nairobi.

During the Second World War Ron's father, Ken Beaton, served in the King's African Rifles fighting in Abyssinia (Ethiopia). He returned to Kenya with Italian prisoners of war and bullion by a circuitous route down the Omo River to avoid the *shifta* (Somali bandits) who infested the country. They were merciless. In fact at the final capitulation of Gonda, the town had to be surrounded by British troops in order save the Italians from being slaughtered.

When the war ended, Ken, after many years spent working for Kenya Parks and Wildlife, was sent to Uganda as the first director of Uganda's national parks. He was a great hero to Ron, who adored those visits to Uganda. His father's brief from the governor was to set up two new designated parks, the Queen Elizabeth National

Park and Murchison Falls National Park, without upsetting the local people – not an easy feat, as there was plenty of opposition to relocation from the local people. Uganda was a protectorate, not a colony and as such the local Baganda people in Kampala decided all civil issues in the civil courts. These were the people that Ken had to deal with and they were fairly anti-British. He started by identifying the chief opponents and asking them to let him show them what he wanted to do. They all piled into

Ken Beaton and the then Princess Elizabeth at Murchisan Falls, Uganda.

a DC-3 to look at the area from the air. None had ever flown before; flying was a novelty for Englishmen in those days, let alone Ugandans, and the excitement was tremendous. Plied with food and drink, they were flown over the magnificent landscape being shown the proposed boundaries of what was to become the Queen Elizabeth Park. Their resistance melted away and the park plan was then passed quickly through parliament and gazetted.

Murchison Falls National Park in the north was much easier to set up, as it was remote and sparsely populated. The big draw is the Murchison Falls, where the Victoria Nile squeezes through a narrow opening in the rocks, creating a tremendously powerful spectacle. The journey up the Nile to see the falls is a spectacle in itself, as you glide through a multitude of animals and wonderful birds.

Ron had come up on a visit when his father was launching a brand-new boat on the Murchison River in order to take visitors to view the falls, and accompanied him on the trial cruise. Ken Beaton had been given the job of escorting Princess Elizabeth and the Duke of Edinburgh on safari during their visit to Uganda. This was the trip that ended so sadly for her with the death of King George VI while they were on a visit to Treetops in the Aberdares in Kenya after their Uganda safari. They were to be the first visitors on the river cruise.

Standing on the deck one morning with his recently arrived assistant, Frank Poppleton, Ken pointed to the shore saying, "Do you see all those crocodiles, son?" Ron could see nothing but the rocky shore, but on closer inspection, it became clear that the whole shore was literally carpeted in crocodiles. Frank, a real daredevil, wanted to do something completely crazy to impress Ken. Suddenly, with no warning to anyone, he leaped

overboard, splashing and kicking making a tremendous racket. As one, the monsters rose and plunged into the river; Frank swam swiftly through them all, climbing out on the bank to the sound of incredulous cheers from the boat. He believed – quite rightly as it turned out – that, because of the noise and sudden confusion he would be perfectly safe, but it was a heart-stopping moment for all on board. Frank eventually went on to become head of the Parks Department in Uganda.

Sadly Ron's time with his father was limited. After Ken's early death, Ron's stepfather Tuffy took over the role, but Ron has enduring memories of the happy times spent during his early years with his father.

In Tsavo, where he spent most of his holidays, Tuffy was opening up the park, which included road-building in Tsavo and the Chyulu Hills. At this time Tsavo had an abundance of Black rhinoceros and elephant but very little plains game, as thick bush is not their true habitat. The elephant population was estimated at forty-three thousand.

Hanging around the headquarters was not very exciting, but some activities had great allure – anti-poaching sorties for one. David Sheldrick living at Voi, co-ordinated all anti-poaching units in Tsavo. Simon Trevor, now a film producer, was then newly arrived from Zambia where he had been involved in game control, to be assistant warden to Tuffy. Simon would go out on these anti-poaching patrols with the rangers and his camera equipment. Ron remembers well how he was always filming something or other and that although filming was meant to be his hobby, it was really his main interest in life.

Ron decided to go on some of these trips, which horrified his mother as they were potentially dangerous, but that, of course, only intensified the pleasure. On one of the trips he awoke to find that hyenas had eaten his only pair of shoes in the night and for the rest of the trip he was barefoot, in the thorny *commiphora* scrub. The rangers were Borana and Somalis, excellent, fine-tuned bush men. After independence these men were disarmed and their jobs given to men from the ruling Kikuyu tribe. Unfortunately the Kikuyu at that time were not true bush men and thus no match for the Borana and Somalis who, having lost their livelihood, now turned their hand to poaching, their intimate knowledge of the bush making them perfect poachers. This was one of the biggest reasons for the success of poaching in Kenya, the new anti-poaching units being no match for these professionals. However, coups linger at the back of the minds of African leaders and to have an armed tribe that was not under their control must have seemed inadvisable.

Ron thoroughly enjoyed school, especially the sport, and although he did not see his parents from one holiday to the next, the parents of the boys who lived in and around Nairobi were very kind to the country boys, inviting them for outing Sundays and half-terms with their own sons. On one particular occasion Ron was supposed to go home for the day with a friend called Christopher, but for some reason, now forgotten, in the end went out with another friend instead. When they returned to school that evening, they found everyone in a dreadful state because Christopher had been kidnapped, killed and used in a Mau Mau earth-taking ceremony.

These were terrifying times for everyone. The whole Mau Mau rebellion was run on superstition and threats and even the most loyal employee could be dragged into it, and once the oath was sworn there was no turning back. White children were prime targets for some of the ceremonies. In this case, one of Christopher's parent's gardeners had taken the oath and had grabbed the child that afternoon when he wandered out on his own with his catapult.

Security at the school was tightened considerably after that. Barbed wire was placed around the perimeter of the school grounds, with machine-gun towers at intervals. The rules became extremely strict; no one was allowed out of bounds at all, and if a boy was caught out of bounds he was expelled immediately.

Ron and his friends were growing up and resented the prison-like environment, so the urge to escape was very strong. He tells of one illicit journey into town:

"A senior boy in the Young Farmers' Association had a 650 cc Thunderbird Tiger 110 motorbike, which I, along with my friend Martin Schofield (later to become Chief Conservator of Natal Parks Board in South Africa) decided to borrow to go into town to see if there was any action! On the way back, at about ten o'clock, we broke down, next to the graveyard, which made us feel decidedly creepy! Knowing how exceptionally wicked it was to sneak out of school, was this an omen? A few minutes after we had started pushing the motorbike back to school, headlights appeared in the distance. We rushed off the road hiding the bike behind a bush that only had room for myself and the bike, Martin jumped into the storm drain beside the road, crouching low, trying to keep hidden. The old Austin A40 that ground to a halt right across the road was full of our teachers, Catholic priests and brothers who having been to a party in town were all as drunk as skunks. As they tumbled out of the car, the sound of their voices was clearly heard on the night air singing, '...But for all that I found there I might as well be, Where the mountains of Mourne sweep down to the sea.'

"Only one alighted on the side of the car facing us, it was Father Paddy Noonan, our boxing coach. He wandered over to the culvert where Martin was hiding, picked up his cassock and peed on Martin who was crouching dead still in the dark. The teachers, having relieved themselves by the side of the road, climbed back in the car and took off down the road still singing of The Mountains of Mourne.

"Martin jumped up shaking himself like a dog and saying 'Christ that was close, did you see what happened?' I was doubled over laughing so hard I couldn't reply. We pushed the bike back to school, replaced it in the Young Farmers hut, climbed in through the windows and no one was the wiser, we thought. Three days later we were in the sparring ring together and Schofield had a bad habit of hitting with the inside of the gloves, which caught the attention of the coach. Father Paddy Noonan climbed in through the ropes and said in his Irish brogue: 'Schofield ye're rabbit punchin' again, and Schofield, by the way, have ye had a warm shower lately?' This was an old-fashioned, tough school where the boys only had daily cold showers; he just wanted us to know that he knew Schofield had been in the ditch."

When Ron left school his stepfather encouraged him away from safaris and hunting. He could see the writing on the wall for hunting and he was right, as it was soon to be banned in Kenya. Tuffy felt the future was in farming and sent him to England to study at Cirencester Agricultural College. He came back and very nearly went

straight into hunting as Jack Block interviewed him and offered him a job as an apprentice hunter with Ker and Downey in Botswana. He was swayed away from the Botswana offer because at the same time he was offered something else: a job buying and transporting cattle to a cattle station at the coast. He and a man called Johnny Antoni were employed to go up to the northern frontier to buy the cattle from the Somalis and then walk them down to the cattle station. Here they would be fattened up on the lush coastal grass before being sold on.

The lure was the coast. As a teenager Ron had been passionate about diving and spear fishing, at times spending six or seven hours in the water. He longed to get back to it and the job of looking after cattle for six months on the coast was too good to turn down. On the very first journey a group of Somali *shifta* carrying stolen British Bren guns attacked them and stole all the cattle. He and Johnny had only one .375 rifle and seven rounds of ammunition, so they prudently abandoned the cattle but, as luck would have it, got them back again within forty-eight hours. Ron reported the loss to the Stock Theft Unit and found that one of their officers was on holiday in Malindi with his plane. The officer searched for the cattle by air, found them and got them back, killing one of the *shifta* and recovering the Bren guns (which had been stolen from the Stock Theft Unit) in the process.

While waiting for the cattle to fatten up, Ron indulged in his passion for diving. The Mnarani Club asked him to lay the trotline, which is a line for yachts to moor on and needs to be secured on the sea-bed with weights. Diving was fairly primitive in the mid-1960s – there were no dive centres, the East African Oxygen Company supplied the bottles and Ron was self-taught. On one of his dives he came up too quickly, and was stricken with the bends (nitrogen narcosis). There were no decompression chambers anywhere on the coast and the nitrogen bubbles, having settled in rugby bruises on his body, caused excruciating pain. He had done three journeys north buying and transporting the cattle, luckily with no more trouble from the *shifta*, but after his bad diving experience he took the decision to move on.

This time he accepted a job opening a chemical plant, a job offer that got him into Tanzania, but did not last long. He met up with an old chap called Ben Pretorius, a professional hunter of Afrikaans origin and decided to join him. In spite of Tuffy's warnings, this was really the life he wished to pursue at that time. Ben's father, Major-General Pretorius, had been a dashing hero in the First World War. He had boarded the German cruiser *Königsberg* dressed as an Arab labourer to help the British remove the guns and scuttle the ship, which they succeeded in doing. His story is alleged to have been the inspiration for a similar story told in Wilbur Smith's *Shout at the Devil*, although there is a firm disclaimer at the beginning of the book

Ron and Ben were based at Moshi, near Kilimanjaro, and together they hunted all over Tanzania, but especially in South Masailand and down the Pangani River where Ron bought a beach house:

> "There was at that time an odd social thing about hunters in East Africa. There were the hunters of British origin, who had the finesse, charm and sophistication to entertain the rich clients who flocked out to Kenya, but many of whom knew very little about hunting, having difficulty even tracking an elephant and relying on local trackers to help them out. And then there were people like Ben, who had no etiquette at all, but was a truly fantastic hunter. He had a sixth sense in locating the game and predicting their movements, he understood about the habitats and how to use them to the hunters' best advantage. Ben's sister Elsie hunted in bare feet, and was one of only two women on the continent who had a hunter's licence."

Their happiness and success ended very abruptly when the Tanzanian economy came to a standstill and everything was nationalised by President Julius Nyerere. It became a very unpleasant place to live. Ron had many friends, one of whom was the head of Shell Oil, sent to prison or to concentration camps on very flimsy political grounds. Bands of TANU youths would walk the streets looking for women wearing trousers and gaoling any they found. Ron was nearly put in gaol himself for wearing shorts in the streets which they perceived a colonial, Ron suggested they take them off him, as he would be happy to walk through the streets naked but was afraid in might shock the Muslim women! Ron's house on the beach at Pangani was nationalised; one morning a number was painted on it and that was that.

The Tanzanian government decided one day that the borders were to be closed that very day. The parks were full of safari operators from Kenya, who lost everything they owned. They were allowed to return to Kenya with their guests, but all their equipment – tents, vehicles and aeroplanes – had to remain behind. It was in this climate that Ron returned to Kenya with his first wife Sally and their baby.

They travelled with another man he had hunted with, also of Afrikaans descent, named Robin Ulyate, with whom he formed a farming partnership. Robin married Janet, the daughter of Sir Michael Woods, founder of the Flying Doctor Service in East Africa. Their farm, growing mainly wheat, is situated about an hour's drive north of Rekero.

The land was leased from the Maasai and involved bush clearance. In the days before electric fencing, this meant culling a large number of buffalo and elephant; crop farming and large wildlife just don't mix. It was, of course, very detrimental to the wildlife, cutting off their ancient migration corridors and reducing their living areas. In 1974, when Ron first started farming, the wildlife was so prolific that this was never seen as a problem and the Masai Mara was a very different place. There were few camps and visitors. Governor's Camp had four tents and a manager who spent his time writing pornographic poetry, which had to be well hidden from his wife, but was shown to those he considered the right guests. It was another ten years before the park began to receive such a massive influx of tourists and lodges.

Once the farm was up and running it became apparent that it could not be run by two managers. In 1981, Ron had married for the second time. He and his wife Pauline moved into tourism and photographic safaris on the edge of the Masai Mara Reserve, but remain partners in the farm with the Ulyates.

Their life in tourism started off in an old farmhouse on a different site to the one they would use later. This wasn't a very satisfactory place because it could get cut off during the rains, and occasionally they had to swim their clients across to the house.

After a year they decided to move to the present location and built Rekero Guest House specifically for tourists. It began as a bit of fun and a hobby, though the timing was superb, coming soon after the release of the film *Out of Africa*, which stimulated a huge popular desire to go on safari in Kenya. He and Pauline did their own marketing and, through friends and guests, they acquired wonderful contacts all over the world.

Even so, some of the early years were tough going and they took in film crews to make ends meet. Four different productions have been filmed from there, including parts of David Attenborough's *The Private Life of Plants*. The BBC's *Big Cat Diaries* also did some of their filming from Rekero, especially when leopards were being filmed, as there are plenty in that area. As the general public has no access to the lodge it was easier for the film crews to operate there.

Eventually Ron and the Craig family, who own Lewa Downs, decided to join forces to make all their lives a bit easier. Will Craig, Chris Flatt and Ron were the instigators of this concept, which they called Bush Homes, comprising a collection of houses and lodges around Kenya, the only criterion being that the owners live there and personally host their guests. Each is independent of the others but all come under one umbrella for marketing and bookings, which Chris Flatt continues to run from Nairobi. They seem to have the formula just right, as the business has been a great success.

Ron's camps became so popular that very few film crews could be accommodated. The Rekero Cottages and the Rekero Tented Camp were filled with safari guests. The tented camp especially, being situated on the Talek River near its confluence with the Mara, and very close to the main crossing-point of the wildebeest migrations, is a real hot spot for game-viewing.

Ron continues his adventurous safaris in northern Kenya and into Ethiopia. This is an arid but spectacular area, where naked Turkana tribesmen still fish the jade waters of Lake Turkana with their cone-shaped nets. His original motivation for going up the Omo River in Ethiopia was to trace his fathers footsteps taken all those years ago with his Italian prisoners of war.

Ron times his expeditions into Ethiopia to coincide with some of the traditional ceremonies still practised by the tribes in this remote part of Africa, in particular that of bull-jumping, a rite in which youths pass into manhood by jumping and running across the backs of eight bulls.

The Talek River at Rekero Tented Camp

Koyaki Guide School

For some time now Ron has been training Maasai as safari guides. Having lived there so long, he knows them well and feels passionately that they should be more involved in all aspects of running the Masai Mara. He has been a prime mover in the creation of the guide school on the Koiyaki Group ranch adjoining the northern boundary of the reserve. Ron has been instrumental in securing funding and helping with his expertise to make it come about. Three hundred applicants came forward for fourteen places in the first intake! The plan is to be able to train and employ young Maasai men and women to guide at all the lodges in the Mara, especially important because visitors always want to know about the lives and customs of this colourful tribe. The guide school's emphasis will be on all aspects of guiding, along with learning good English for the vital communication skills required for social interaction with westerners. The students, of course, already have a deep understanding of animal behaviour and tracking before they enrol. Their teachers are highly respected guides from various countries who have reached the top of their profession, and I expect Garth Thompson's book, *A Guide's Guide to Guiding*, will be on the shelves. The trainee guides will obtain practical experience with guests at the in-house lodge participating in walks and game drives with them.

In order to concentrate on running Rekero Expeditions and setting up the guide school, Ron has sold his share of the business to his son Gerard, a fourth-generation Kenyan, along with his wife Rainee, a talented and successful artist, who are now running Rekero Tented Camp (the cottages have been closed down) with Jackson Looseyia, his Maasai partner and one of the special guides featured in this book . The Koiyaki Guide School will feature prominently in their safaris.

In March 2005, Gerard and Rainee's first child was born – Charlie – the fifth generation of Beatons in Kenya.

Gerard and Rainee Beaton

SAIGILU OLE LOOSEYIA (JACKSON)

Jackson Looseyia has become one of the best-known and most highly respected guides in Kenya and crosses the divide between traditional tribal life and the western world effortlessly. Many articles have been written about him in foreign newspapers and magazines including the *Sunday Times* and *Sunday Telegraph*, the *Boston Globe*, *Travel and Leisure* and several South African magazines. He is a tall, well-built man with an easy, graceful manner, natural charm and well-honed communication skills. Like all the top guides he has clients returning again and again to enjoy another safari with him. Not only do they have a very exciting and successful game viewing experience but they are also captivated by his tales of the cultural life of his people, which adds a wonderfully unusual dimension to any safari. In his current position as a partner and shareholder in Rekero with Gerard Beaton, he has travelled on marketing trips in South Africa, England and the United States.

Jackson's love of the bush and the wildlife suffuses his whole being. As we sat discussing his life story on a still warm afternoon by the Talek River, the stillness was broken by a flurry of bird chatter.

"Listen" he says, "they are having roll-call. Is everyone all right? I haven't seen Jane. Where's Mary?" The twittering continued for a few minutes and then they were gone. Many species apparently gather like this a few times every day to just check that all is well.

His attention was then taken by a small herd of elephant grazing on the long sweet grass so abundant in February. Elephants, he told me, are eighty per cent grazers and only twenty per cent browsers (leaf-eaters). Every single one of his senses was trained on his surroundings as he wove the story of his childhood, his life and dreams for the future. He remembers vividly the annual arrival of the wildebeest migration when he was at school. The migration was always a spectacle even though, since the area was more heavily forested then, it was not as large as it is today. It came right past his school, creating clouds of dust that could be seen for miles and causing the excited children to abandon their work to watch.

Jackson was born in the Mara; he and his sister were the sole survivors of five children born to an Ildorobo hunter-gatherer and a Maasai woman. His father, Selel ole Looseyia had been married before, but his wife had been unable to bear children, a harsh and sad thing for any woman, but particularly for Maasai women, as not only do they need to be cared for in their old age but their whole social structure revolves around child-bearing. So she was allowed to return to her own family, where her brother gave her one of his daughters to bring up as her own, her family assuming the responsibility for the care and dowry of this little girl. Selel then married Jackson's mother and she remained his only wife for life, although it was permitted to have more than one.

Prior to the 1930s, a large population of Maasai lived in the north with the Samburu, on the Laikipia Plateau and around Nairobi. Owing to pressure by the colonists on this fertile land for dairy and sheep farming, the Maasai were persuaded to move. The *laibon* (medicine man) approved the move and they came down south with their cattle in their own great migration. The men who walked to the Mara are now all dead, including Jackson's great-grandfather, who died in 2001, aged

Saigilu Ole Looseyia (Jackson)

about a hundred. The men who were babies on their mother's backs are still alive. Although some Maasai already lived in this area it was mostly inhabited by Ildorobo hunter-gatherers. The word *ildorobo*, occasionally with slight variations of spelling, means 'tsetse fly' or 'poor man who has no cattle'. It can also mean 'a village where bees live'.

The Mara was thickly forested and each Ildorobo family marked out its own territory for its bees, but the hunting was communal and could be done all over the land. They were incomparable beekeepers the hives were in hollowed-out branches placed in trees near to the abundant blossoms required for the honey. They knew which trees to use and when they would flower, and moved the hives accordingly. They were naturally very shy people, hiding in the forests and trying to continue to live as they had always lived, in spite of the arrival of the Maasai. They wore skins, even after the Maasai had switched to cloth *shukas*. They hunted with bows and arrows and were nomadic.

The rolling hills and thick forests of the Mara are very different from the terrain at Loliondo, where we came upon the Ildorobo house under a granite overhang. Here their ingenuity turned to termite mounds. The women would hollow out a large mound and light a fire inside to turn the earth brick hard. It was warm, cosy and watertight. The beauty of this functional nomadic architecture is that there is always another home waiting to be quickly made or re-inhabited in the next place. They knew the forests so well that when the first white traders came into the area looking for ivory, the Ilderobo only had to go and pick it up where the dead elephants lay. This was the beginning of trade for them, as they took a few goats for each tusk.

With so many new Maasai moving into the area and burning the forests to create pastures for their cattle, it was inevitable that the culture of the hunter-gathers would begin to disappear and that the tribes would intermix.

In the late 1940s, the Masai Mara Game Reserve was gazetted and hunting within its boundaries outlawed, although this was not the sort of news to reach a hunter-gatherer tribesman. Licensed hunting safaris took place along with game control outside the reserve, but Selel continued to hunt in his traditional grounds that were now out of bounds. He was caught and sent to prison for three years. Prison for a freewheeling soul like Selel, used to roaming at will, was extremely difficult. There he found a culture alien beyond imagination. Having learned this lesson, however, he did not heed it, but continued to hunt, was caught and spent another three years in prison. When the head warden of the area found him a third time, and he didn't run away, he asked him, "Why don't you run? Are you not afraid of me and another term in gaol?"

He answered, "No, I hunt to live, it is all I know, the only way I can feed my family. What else can I do?"

The man who caught Selel hunting illegally the third time was the colonial game warden of South Maasailand, Lyn Temple Boreham, who wisely decided to employ Selel rather than imprison him yet again. Known as Temple by the Maasai, this rather eccentric fellow was educated in England and Russia, his father having been in the diplomatic service. He was an imposing character, over two metres tall, physically powerful and popular with the Maasai. It was he who persuaded them to set land aside for the Masai Mara Reserve and was one of very few Caucasians to be given land by the Maasai. Jackson mentions his name with great reverence to this day.

Selel was now employed as a game ranger. Temple took away his bow and arrows, replaced the skins he wore with a shirt, shorts and long boots, which he found most uncomfortable, gave him a gun and taught him to shoot. Selel took to shooting with ease; anyone who can kill a buffalo with a bow and arrow has little problem learning how to use a gun. Of course he was thrilled as he could now feed his family legally. Being a ranger meant being involved with game control, game control meant culling animals outside the park that interfered with farming and villages, which included very many elephants and lions. Considering how aggressively this policy was carried out it is quite amazing that so much game still lives outside the parks. Temple never regretted his decision, as Selel was a superb tracker – so good, in fact, that he was also employed tracking Mau Mau fighters in the 1950s.

Jackson was brought up strictly in the traditional manner of his people. Maasai children learn at an early age to be responsible for their animals, so Jackson tended the goats and the sheep as a small boy and the cattle when a little older. The elders know every single animal they own, by name. Even if there are five hundred sheep they will know which one is missing, which have had lambs and which are not well. In times of plenty the herds stay close to home but when drought persists the animals are taken far away to better grazing near the water in the established Maasai wells. When this happens *layonis** are sent along with the morans to help care for the animals and to act as runners to come home and report how they are doing. About once a month an elder might come out and inspect the animals, but with enough trustworthy sons this is usually unnecessary. They live on maize meal porridge and the occasional goat or sheep, usually one that had succumbed to illness or old age. However, they are allowed to slaughter a goat if all their maize meal is finished. It is always a joyful moment when the message comes that the rains have arrived and they can go home to their families.

Jackson attended the local mission school, but continued his responsibility for the goats and sheep, tending them each evening. In the flock were male twin goats that had been castrated and were a closely bonded pair that never parted. One evening on returning from school he noticed at once that one of the twins was wandering around alone; there was no sign of the other. He sought out the small boys who had been herding them during the day and asked where it was; they vaguely muttered something about a leopard. Jackson noticed guilt written all over the face of one of the boys and asked to see his knife and found it smelt of meat.

View over the Mara

The boy insisted they had killed a gazelle and eaten it, but there was no evidence of any extra meat for the family so this was patently untrue.

"I smell goat on your knife," he said.

The boy was defiant but obviously scared. Jackson, having searched for the truth thus far, now decided it was time to seek his father's advice on how to proceed. After careful contemplation, Selel decided to speak to the boy's father, but as they approached the man's hut it was apparent that they were walking into a family dispute. The boy's older brother was cowering in the back of the hut, begging for mercy and asking forgiveness; he had killed the goat and sworn the boy to silence. Such action necessitates retribution and the fine was very heavy – two goats and eight calves to Jackson's family. His detective work had truly paid off, though sadly not for the remaining lonely goat.

Maasai do not traditionally grow crops; surrounded by cattle and goats their natural diet is mostly meat. It is hung in strips on the fences to dry out, making portable protein.

It was stewed and roasted and soup was made with the bones, but the greatest delicacy of all was the buffalo tongue. So prized was this portion that the custom of one of the tribes who hunted with dogs and spears was to cut out the tongue, and present it to the first man who had speared the animal. The Ilderobo were very careful killers; mothers and young were never touched, for conservation of the herds was paramount. An old buffalo bull was popular; although his flesh was tough there was a lot of it, along with large amounts of marrow in his bones and a lot of fat around his kidneys, excellent for soup. One of their greatest annual treats was Jackson's mother's speciality, buffalo hooves. These she split and stored on the ceiling of her hut, where they rotted, dried and were smoked for about two months. She then boiled them for a day and a half, by which time they were so tender they could suck the meat out of the bones.

All the rituals of a young man growing up in the Maasai culture were observed. Jackson had to experience the ennobling passage to warrior status by submitting courageously to having his two lower front teeth removed (cut out by his grandfather) and to the rite of circumcision. For Selel the old traditions lingered on and he made sure that his son learned self-sufficiency in the bush and the art of hunting with a bow and arrow. Western culture was encroaching rapidly upon them and Selel's plan was for his son to be a good warrior and join the army, as he felt that this would be an excellent career. Jackson reluctantly went along with this, but he never really wanted to be a warrior or a soldier.

Young Maasai boys are aware of all that will be expected of them as time goes on and Jackson and his friends were no exception. As little boys playing together in the fields and knowing there is so much to learn they had started teaching themselves about the poisons. First they poisoned ticks to see how long they took to die, then mice and other small creatures, as it was essential to understand how the poison worked. They then practised with little bows and arrows dipped in the poison, shooting lizards and birds and porcupines, until finally one day they shot their first large mammal, a Thompson's gazelle.

Selel decided the time had come to take his son, now in his teens, out into the bush with a bow and arrow to teach him to stalk and kill successfully. To kill a giraffe you had to creep up on it very slowly, getting close enough to shoot the poisoned arrow into the animal of your choice at the first try. When Jackson's arrow hit, the startled animal would jump and look around but, seeing nothing, would continue browsing. The poison took about half an hour to work. Jackson lay still in the grass keeping an eye on the giraffe until it moved off to browse a little further away; he then climbed up a tree to watch and wait. Once it fell he had to get to it very quickly and cover it completely with branches to hide it from the vultures until it could be butchered. Giraffe meat remains his favourite to this day.

His other three tasks were to kill a buffalo, a lion and an impala. The buffalo was dispatched without too much trouble, but he was very unsure about stalking and killing a lion. The prospect filled him with terror, and he hoped his father would not realise just how afraid he was. They spent most of the day together stalking a lion until finally they got within sight of it. Once again, it called for shooting from close quarters. His father stayed back and made him approach quietly and carefully upwind so as to not to alert the lion and to get a clean shot. With only his bow and arrow he was aware of 'chills in his legs' and a thumping heart as he crept closer and closer. Just as he felt sure his end had come the wind shifted suddenly, the lion got a whiff of him and Selel and streaked away as fast as he could, to Jackson's great relief!

However, the most prestigious animal to learn to kill was an impala. Impala are so nervous and acutely sensitive to all that goes on around them that they are about the most difficult animal to stalk – it is said that even their hairs have eyes. If you hunt them successfully you are considered a great hunter. Jackson manage this feat and, even though the lion got away, he gained the respect he sought.

Ron Beaton at his nearby lodge, Rekero, had a group that wished to visit a Maasai village and he sought Temple's advice on which one to visit. Temple suggested Selel's village and, because Jackson had a smattering of English, he was asked to show the guests around. The visitors were to learn this was a place of mixed cultures as their tour took them through one of the houses before learning how the bees were cared for and how the cows were milked. Full-blooded Maasai never keep bees or grow anything, but in Jackson's village they had a small vegetable patch.

Selel took Ron to show him certain aspects of his hives and in doing so, the disturbance caused a few angry bees to sting poor Ron, not Selel, as apparently because they knew him they never stung him. The bees were usually quite docile but became very aggressive at mating time, when the hives were full of larvae. Then the drones fly from the hives in a swarm, high up into the air, trying to mate with the queen, then down in a tight ball, nearly hitting the ground before bursting like a skyrocket, dispersing up into the air, only to form again. At this time everyone, even Selel, stayed well clear until they had settled down into their family units once more.

Ron had been extremely impressed with Jackson's expertise when showing the group around the village and felt he had great potential as a guide. He invited Jackson to stay at Rekero in order to perfect his English and to learn all the Latin and English names of the trees and plants he knew so well. This was the very beginning of his guide training. As a young man he had watched the safari industry burgeon, observing the guides and trackers and longing to be one himself. However, he knew no one who could help and was told he would have to go to Nairobi, where the travel companies had their offices, to find work. He had no intention of going there as he had heard chilling tales of what happens to you in the city, so he stayed and continued his traditional life in the village. His meeting with Ron was a dream come true.

Over the years he perfected all the skills required to be a top safari guide – perfect English, western table manners, polite conversation around the table as well as all the practical skills of driving and motor repairs. His love of the bush was there from boyhood and, having tracked and hunted, he already had great bush skills. He and Ron's son Gerard became firm friends and one feels that he is truly a part of the Beaton family.

Tribal tradition was such that Jackson was expected to marry young and quickly produce sons to help with the cattle. Over the years his mother had produced no less than eleven suitable girls from Maasai families but none was right for him. He didn't want to marry young as his plan was to work in the safari industry and to have time to keep learning his trade. It was a few years later, when he was already working for Ron Beaton, that he met the girl who was to become his wife.

They met at a church social at Jackson's church. These were merry occasions, filled with enthusiastic discussions

Jackson in the Mara

always game for a party; the other, though charming, was more reserved and shy. The quiet girl, who worked as a clerk in a small local company, watched Jackson having fun with her friend, all the while knowing in her heart that it was her he would marry. Eventually her friend took off with an older man and moved away. Jackson continued his friendship with the quiet girl, their relationship blossomed and he was extremely elated when she agreed to marry him.

This story is a clear indication how quickly the Maasai living in multi-racial areas had taken on western values and habits – the fact that he could choose his own wife and progress in a career of his choice was a great leap forward in personal freedom.

As his bride had not been picked out at birth for him, the first thing that had to be done was the formal introduction to each other's families. Once this has gone well and the dowry decided, it is custom for the church elders to have a talk with them and only with their approval can the engagement be announced. Jackson's life and experiences had moved so far away from his tribal upbringing that it was essential that he and his future wife spend a lot of time discussing how their life would evolve. He was in one way moving away from the traditional Maasai life, although still living as a traditional Maasai in his home. His education had opened his eyes to knowledge denied his ancestors and some of his contemporaries. Managing a life between the two cultures calls for a very fine balancing act. For example, he has learned that circumcision for girls serves absolutely no purpose at all (it was believed that uncircumcised girls were infertile, in spite of the fact that they regularly became pregnant). His daughters will not have to suffer this cruel procedure, his main concern being that the girls make friends with

and plenty of singing. At one of these church socials he spotted two attractive girls and introduced himself. One of the girls – who were housemates – was full of fun and similarly educated children and don't get swayed by other girls whose parents are not as enlightened as their own.

His son, on the other hand, will have to go through the agony and suffering that all Maasai boys have to go through, including having two of his teeth cut out. This, Jackson knows, will make a man of him. Nothing that life throws at him will ever be quite as difficult as it would have been had he not courageously faced the traditional initiation into manhood. Jackson will have only one wife; although Maasai culture still allows him more than one, he does not wish to have more. He is very strict about Maasai inheritance laws; his son is his sole heir as he was his father's sole heir.

Jackson has been managing and guiding at the Rekero Tented Camp on the Talek River, right in the path of the annual migration. His future plans include running a camp in Shaba along with Gerard Beaton and James Robertson. I hope this plan will come to fruition as this is a beautiful and very under-used park.

He will also assist in the new Koyaki Guide School, in which Ron Beaton is involved. He plans to take as many of his guests as possible for a night or two in the visitor's lodge to experience walking in a wilderness area. These young people, the students, already know the land, the river crossings, the secret places and the traditional cultures; they just have to learn how to communicate them to visitors and how to make the tourist's brief visit to their land one of joy, knowledge and understanding. A Maasai guide can bring a whole new meaning to a discussion of local culture through being able to say 'we' instead of 'they'. It is Ron Beaton's and Jackson's plan for every tourist vehicle in the Mara to have a Maasai guide, either driving or accompanying the driver.

CALVIN COTTAR

While sinking into a hot canvas bathtub, I can't help but marvel at the scene before me. A scattering of flat-topped acacia trees on a grassy slope that melts into riverine forest, beyond which the vast plains of the Masai Mara stretch to the distant purple hills where vultures gracefully circle. As I take in this timeless scene, I wonder if the late Queen Elizabeth, the Queen Mother, then Duchess of York, had enjoyed the same view from her canvas tub in 1924, when on safari with Bud Cottar, son of Chas. In those days everyone on a luxury safari had the opportunity to indulge in a hot bath; bucket showers were not used until much later. Now in the 21st century Calvin, Chas Cottar's great-grandson, born two weeks after Kenya's independence, has come full circle and reintroduced this blissful treat in his own safari business: Cottar's Classic Safaris.

Calvin is tall and handsome, and in his battered brown safari hat resembles a character that has stepped out of a western movie. He is quietly spoken and has a calm sense of authority in the bush and is very aware of his inheritance. His beautiful camp is situated on a rise overlooking the Masai Mara and styled to evoke the camps used by his great-grandfather in the 1920s. From there and from his father's bush home, Bushtops, he takes walking safaris for those with an adventurous spirit. Either way it is a soul-restoring experinece.

Teddy Roosevelt wrote a book in 1909 called *Game Trails in Africa*, all about his safari the year before. When Chas Cottar read this book at home in Oklahoma, his imagination was so fired up that he went off to Africa to see if all that Teddy Roosevelt had said was true. It certainly was, he spent three months there, fell in love with the place

Calvin Cottar

and went back to America where he gathered up his wife, six daughters and three sons – Mike, Bud and Ted – and returned to East Africa in 1912. He spent the rest of his life there becoming one of the top safari guides in Africa. Together with his sons he mainly hunted but also took photographic safaris, advertising them as early as the 1920s. They were also the first safari outfitters to use vehicles on safari and the first to film the animals, making a colour feature film called *Africa Speaks* in 1928. Chas was an adventurer and risk-taker, whose action-packed life ended abruptly while filming a charging rhinoceros!

Calvin's father, Glen, was unlike his own father, Mike, in that he was not a showman in the mould of his father, uncles and grandfather. However, he was similar in that he was an explorer and a serious hunter who was very popular for his care and expertise. His clients knew that with him, while they would not shoot a lot of game, what they did shoot would be the best. He spent hours picking out the best animal, not choosing the best out of only a hundred buffalo, but more like three thousand!

His adventuring took him far afield; he opened up Katavi and hunted in Rukwa with Jack Bousfield and the tracks they made in those remote areas are the ones still in use today. He was in the first group of East African hunters to go to Botswana. This was virgin territory; southern Africa did not have the same hunting ethos that East Africa had, and the area was ripe for the picking. In the 1950s and early '60s tourism had not yet discovered the Okavango Delta, givng the East African hunters a field day. Glen was one of the first people to venture into areas that are all so familiar to tourists today. He discovered the Selinda Spillway, which was overflowing with water and teeming with game. He told of huge herds of animals that stood looking at them fearlessly. In those times the game was indeed fearless, as they had never seen vehicles or people, rather like penguins in the Antarctic. Photographic safaris really only started in earnest in the 1970s, around the time the hunting areas came under strict control. Some of the hunters stayed to hunt while others started photographic safaris, as this was a place of breathtaking beauty which, once the secret was out, they knew everyone would want to see for themselves. Glen, however, returned to East Africa, as he was first and foremost a Kenyan. Back home he continued to hunt, but started to combine these trips with photographic safaris, as he was quick to see the potential of non-hunting safaris. In 1964, he built the very first dedicated tourist camp in Tsavo. It was at the time of the 40 000 elephants and 10 000 Black rhinos and, by 1975, only eleven years later, most of the big game in Tsavo had disappeared through drought and poaching. Deciding it was time to move, Glen sold his camp and built another just outside the Masai Mara at Sianna Springs. When all hunting in Kenya was banned in 1977, he was well set up to service the tourist industry.

Calvin was born in Nairobi where his mother Pat was what was known as a 'safari widow', living in Nairobi with her daughter and son and keeping the logistics of the safaris going. The family would visit the Tsavo camp from time to time and one of Calvin's earliest memories is of a rhino chasing and whacking their car.

When Calvin was thirteen he went to stay in a hunting camp on his own with his father, who felt he was then old enough stay in camp helping the staff and not being a worry to anyone. His father taught him how to drive and how to use a rifle, but his father's trackers and gun bearers taught him about everything else – the bush, animal behaviour and tracking.

One of Glen's hunting campsites was not far from where Calvin has his camp today – a lovely place with big trees and a sparkling stream called Oloibor Miotoni (the River of the Martial Eagles), where Glen taught Calvin to shoot with a heavy-calibre rifle. He was a natural shot: after an afternoon of target practice into a tree, he bagged his first antelope the following morning.

Calvin spent most of his teenage years at the Mara camp. At age fifteen he was taking guests out on game drives, which gave him a very early introduction to guiding. At eighteen, having finished school, he set off to find out what the outside world was like. He went to America to explore his Cottar roots, though there are no more Cottars in America. The last one, Tom Cottar, was sheriff of Red Bluff in northern California. The Cottars are related to the Waltons, an extensive American family that boasts several thousand at its reunions. Calvin met up with his sister in Colorado, where they had both been

offered a job in a restaurant belonging to Nancy van Loon, a family friend. His last two months in America were spent skiing and, once he had blown all his money on skiing and especially the après-skiing, he left for home. He had gone to see if the grass was greener, and found it wasn't.

At the time when Calvin returned from America, Glen was running Cottar's Camp at Sianna Springs in the Masai Mara. It was a large camp with twenty rooms, about to be increased to thirty. They didn't see eye to eye over this at all. Glen was anxious that Calvin should take over Cottar's Camp, but his heart was set on running a small, exclusive camp, with no more than six tents. Glen believed that only big camps made money and stubbornly refused to change. Calvin, equally stubborn, left to join Robin Hurt to hunt in Tanzania. Calvin did not have a close relationship with his father, who had been away for long periods while Calvin was a child. This, combined with fact that Glen's own father died when he was a child, leaving him with no paternal role model, left little room for understanding between father and son.

At about the same time (1985) a Maasai friend of Glen's came to tell him that a Kikuyu man wanted to farm in the valley where Bushtops, the Cottar family bush home, is now situated. It is a beautiful valley, very close to the Mara, and the only place Glen had ever seen Roan antelope on that side of the Mara. He felt it would be dreadful to have a farm so close to the Park and decided to take over the area himself. He paid the Maasai more than the Kikuyu farmer had offered and built Bushtops, taking apart an old house he had had at his original camp and rebuilding it on the new site. It remains a special place for the family; Glen always loved it and his ashes are scattered there.

The years spent working for Robin Hurt were some of Calvin's happiest. Hunting is a young man's adventure; he had no responsibilities, was fearless and thoroughly enjoyed shooting and exploring. Hunting is in his blood; it's what his family has always done, but he no longer hunts. Like many young men, he grew out of it. He also became disillusioned with the way hunting was run in Tanzania, so he began to look for an alternative life in the bush. Back in Kenya he became involved in wildlife management. He worked as a consultant for the Kenya Wildlife Service in a programme devised to help farmers manage wildlife, but it was not very successful or satisfactory. At that point, encouraged by his father, Calvin went back into the safari business. Being in wild remote areas, he realised – waking each day with a feeling of excited anticipation as to what the day might bring and how he would open its splendours to visitors – was the only life he wanted to live.

The lessons he had learned when hunting were very useful for the many walking safaris he takes these days, but one, in particular, has been invaluable, as he relates in the following story:

The wounded buffalo

"One of my most frightening moments was on a hunting safari with a client who had come to shoot a buffalo. We found the one we wanted, a very big old guy, in a thicket ahead of us. When shooting a buffalo the gun rests on a tripod of sticks held with a rubber band in front of us. I had slung my gun over my shoulder in order to use both hands to secure the sticks, telling my client to be ready to shoot it in the heart when it smelled us, which should take about ten seconds. As I was lowering the gun from my shoulder and with absolutely no warning, the buffalo charged straight for us, wild with explosive anger. The client pointed his gun at this advancing juggernaut, which was moving like a bullet from hell, and shot it between the eyes ten metres from where we stood. The massive creature collapsed, its nose scraping the ground, eyes bloodshot and bulging, and lay dead five metres from us. It was an incredible shot, if he had hit it anywhere else it would not have died as he only had a .375, which is a small gun.

"I think I would have been able to shoot it but I will never be certain, and it taught me one of the biggest lessons of my life. You can only assume so much of wild animals. Normally a buffalo will stop, look and sniff the air, before running away. But they are like people; their behaviour is not always predictable. Whether it is lion, elephant or buffalo, ninety-nine times out of a hundred you can guess what they will do, but it is that one time that they will get you.

"The reason that this buffalo had been so charged up was because he had a stump stuck in his hoof, between his toes, causing a painful, suppurating sore. His leg was very swollen and he was in agony. He would have killed someone, whether it was a honey hunter or a game warden just checking the area; he was going to strike at someone, who most likely would have been completely defenceless. We were glad we had killed him.

"Now when I walk, particularly in bush country where you can't see, I always carry a loaded gun. It is far more reliable as you don't let up on safety. You are constantly aware of where the gun is pointed and what support there might be from the bush and trees around you. I realised that the time it takes to load the gun and be ready to shoot could cost a life."

The Cottar family count among their friends many well-known people who have been on safari with them: one in particular is Peter Beard, the photographer, artist and author. He was on safari with Calvin when an elephant attacked him; the following is Calvin's account of that incident, when having his gun ready would not have helped.

Peter Beard and the elephant drama

"Peter, an old family friend, had been staying at my camp with me for three days' filming. On the fourth day we planned, that fateful morning, to drive to the waterfall. On the way we saw a nice herd of elephants and decided to stop and film them. They were about forty metres away from us on the top of a slope, at the bottom of which is a large termite mound. Peter and I stood on the mound while being filmed, after which we started to walk back to the car. The cameramen were ahead of us.

"I said, 'Peter those elephants are so calm, let's stay and watch and walk a bit with them.' Peter was in a bit of a dream world that morning, not really into the elephants, more in tune with his own feelings, but went along with it nevertheless!

"By now the elephants were at the top of the slope, about one hundred and fifty metres from us, moving slowly away. The wind was coming from them to us and we were walking parallel with them.

"Suddenly from the back of the herd an elephant gave a mock charge. We immediately started to walk away from them, not running but stepping up our pace. She was a young cow, probably in her first pregnancy; the size of the wound Peter was to receive, as seen later, indicated the size of her tusks and her age. All of a sudden she lost the plot. Her ears went back and she charged down upon us. We ran for our lives, a very long distance, but you can never outrun an elephant. I turned and looked at her, she was practically on top of me. Peter suddenly veered off to the left. He is an amazing man; although sixty years old, he was terrifically strong! The elephant saw a quicker and easier target than me and went for Peter. I turned and saw him on the ground with the elephant about to pierce him with her tusk.

"I tore to the car; the driver was in a state of paralysed fear with his hand stuck on the horn. I pulled him out and drove to Peter who was now surrounded by six or seven cows that had come down to see what was happening. They were walking around him in a circle and I was sure he lay dead in the middle of them. The car driving up scared them all away. As I jumped out of the car, up popped Peter's head, 'Shit, Curly,' he said. 'It looks like my screwin' days are all over, man!' Notorious for his womanising, these were the first words out of his mouth.

"The tusk had pierced his thigh missing both the artery and the bone, but the broad part of the elephant's head, at the top of her trunk, had crushed his pelvis. And it was certainly crushed; when we moved him we could hear the shattered bones crunching. From the radio we always carry I called AMREF (the East African flying doctor service, one of the finest in the world) and got him into the vehicle while he bellowed with pain, cracking jokes in between the bellows! It took an hour to get to Keekerok, the nearest lodge and airstrip, as we were deep in the bush and the roads were quite rough. At Keekerok we at last were able to obtain some morphine for him. The plane arrived half an hour later and we left for Nairobi. On the stretcher going into the hospital his heart stopped. They revived it with electric charges and kept him in the hospital for about seven weeks until he was stable enough to fly to New York. Once in New York his broken bones were replaced with titanium to hold up his pelvis. When I last visited him, there were two gorgeous Russian models with him, one on each knee! He is an incredible guy. Ever commercial, he used the story and the publicity to sell more pictures at even greater prices."

Accidents like that are very rare in the bush, but as we know, wild animals can be unpredictable. Experiencing the adrenaline rush in close encounters with these animals in the wild, especially when walking, is probably the reason that people find Africa so exciting. However, Peter Beard has told Calvin his African days are over.

During the time Glen and Calvin were discussing Calvin's future, Glen became terminally ill with cancer. There was no longer a camp for Calvin to run, as Cottar's Camp at Sianna Springs had been sold. Together they planned to run mobile safaris as they had been run in the 1920s by Chas Cottar and later his sons. During this time father and son became much closer, with the excitement of creating a new and unusual form of mobile safari. Back in the 1920s and '30s the safari tents were white, elegantly furnished and large, the camp staff dressed in long, white robes with red fezzes and sashes and many little luxuries were provided. After Glen died in 1996, Calvin went to work on the re-creation of the 1920s' safari style and went into business running mobiles.

I went on one of these safaris with a group of friends and witnessed at first hand just what was involved. The safari was superb and we were royally looked after: I had

The Shaba campsite

never slept in such comfort in a tent. It all went very smoothly and professionally; the staff was immaculate and friendly, the food excellent and the drink flowed. We dined on fine china, drank from crystal glasses and were surrounded with well-researched memorabilia that decorated the sleeping and mess tents.

The day we moved camp I watched as all this was packed up into wooden crates to travel on two large Bedford trucks, six hundred kilometres over some of the worst roads in the world. We spent two days at Bushtops while this took place, before flying direct to Shaba National Park, which was to be the next campsite. On arrival an old-fashioned, wooden-bodied car was at the strip to pick us up, taking us to the campsite, which had been Joy Adamson's (of *Born Free* fame) last home.

And there it was like magic – lunch and a view to die for, all set up and ready for us under magnificent spreading acacia trees as if it had been waiting for days. It seemed flawless and everyone had one of the best safaris they could have had, fantastic game viewing, excellent guiding and the most luxurious camps imaginable

Before his father died, Calvin had met and married an Australian girl of exceptional beauty, an ex-Miss Australia. They had a son, Danny, but the marriage was not successful. Meanwhile Calvin was starting up his new mobile business, buying the equipment and marketing the concept. It was a very ambitious undertaking and his wife made an excellent contribution designing the tent interiors, but his personal life was distracting and causing him to feel great anxiety.

The mobile safaris all ran extremely well, with happy satisfied guests. However, behind the scenes all was not well and the next two years proved to be more difficult than he could ever have imagined. Every journey they took between camps saw more and more of their precious items broken and replacing them was a drain on the finances. Meanwhile Calvin's heartbreaking situation with his wife was taking its toll. A brief reconciliation, which had not been successful, produced a second son, Jasper. His manager was plagued with personal problems too, and no one was keeping an eye on the ball.

Enter Louise

It was around this time that he met Louise, who was to become his wife. She was running the United Nations World Food Programme in Mogadishu, Somalia. At a time when Calvin was probably at his lowest ebb, he found a sympathetic and intelligent ear. She is young and lovely, but a no-nonsense girl, forthright and outspoken, and Calvin's lifesaver.

She worked in Somalia for four years organising the distribution of famine relief to the refugee camps deep inside the country. It was a very frustrating task, as by the time their trucks arrived at the camps the food was badly depleted. Being transported by United Nations trucks and personnel from the docks made it very vulnerable. The white trucks and blue berets were seen as soft targets; they had no mandate to shoot and wholesale theft was taking place. The lorries would be stopped and the drivers had to stand by helplessly as people – mainly children – swarmed all over them, taking whatever they wanted. Warlords orchestrated the thieving and the food was sold on. It was a situation that was deeply worrying for the people running the programme.

Louise gave this a lot of thought and came up with an idea that she took to the directors of the programme, who occupy offices in Nairobi and are definitely not out in the field. They didn't like her idea, thinking it might backfire if the press got hold of it, but she continued to exert pressure on them until finally they told her to go ahead and try it, but that they would not take responsibility for it.

The following is Louise's brief explanation of her plan to protect her food and get it to the refugee camps. It was an audacious strategy and it worked:

"Seeing that Somali traders were importing their own high-value food items, such as sugar, without loss from theft, I developed a system whereby the Somali importers provided to the UN a bond equal to the full value of the UN food and the cost of transport. These importers would arrive in my office with the cash, sometimes as much as a quarter of a million US dollars! The dollar bills would tumble onto my desk, out of pockets, from up their sleeves and down their trousers. The importers would then collect the food from ports such as Momabasa, ship it in and transport it by road to the destinations required by the WFP. The food travelled from the port in their vehicles with their own tough Somali guards. If it arrived and I could see and verify that it was distributed without loss, the importers would be reimbursed their bond and given a margin on top. Such was the success of this method of transportation of food that it is now being used in several other insecure countries."

Calvin and Louise in the 1920s' camp

Louise, the only white woman on the WFP, showed remarkable courage, travelling throughout the country. She had to be present at the docks and at the point of distribution, as these high-value cargoes were particularly at risk from criminal gangs when landing in ports in a lawless country where anything goes. She was shot at and only just avoided being kidnapped; because they couldn't find her they took her colleague instead. Food is big business everywhere! Her scheme was an outstanding success, for which I hope the directors gave her full credit.

Louise is a strong and clever woman who, once she and Calvin decided to pursue a life together, would invest in and be part of his business. This was the point at which she looked at the figures and had a dreadful shock because of the rate at which the company had lost money.

Hard reality had to be faced. Staff were trimmed and economies made, but marketing was increased. It was clear that they could not go on operating mobile safaris, as the running costs were too high. The mobiles were stopped and the permanent camp idea put into place. They kept the format and built the 1920s-style camp at Olentoroto on the edge of the Masai Mara, with flush loos and showers (canvas bathtubs on request), still with the white tents and four-poster beds and comfortable sofas, but with much more space. The added luxury of a massage during the siesta is much appreciated by many guests.

It has been incredibly hard work, but is a great success story. They are building a house for themselves above the 1920s camp; a home for his boys and their two little girls. Calvin's happiness with Louise shines through everything.

Calvin's plans for the future

The Cottars have initiated the Maasai Development and Wildlife Conservation Trust, whose long-term objective is 'to ensure the continued co-existence of the wildlife and people of the eastern Mara area in the long-term through the development of a sustainable system for land use and management'.

Calvin's camp is situated in the eastern part of the Mara, very close to the Tanzanian border. It is an area in which the family has operated safaris for many years, making them well known to the local Maasai community. The area is called Olderikesi Group Ranch and is eight hundred square kilometres with a population of about four thousand Maasai.

It is Calvin's fervent wish to maintain this pristine wilderness area by working with the community, improving their standard of living by increasing revenue. Taking a leaf out of Botswana's philosophy of high-cost, low-density tourism, he wants this area to operate in a similar manner. Much of the Masai Mara is swamped with vehicles and large lodges, but the eastern part, where he operates, has far fewer tourist facilities. Calvin's 1920s camp, along with one other upmarket mobile tented safari company that has the use of a campsite in the area, are the only operators here at this time. He is passionate about keeping it this way and his plans have the full approval of the park warden.

Instead of yet another large lodge, he has located five sites and plans to build one house on each site. These would produce revenue for the community in fees and jobs, and benefit them in many ways, including medical, educational and in animal husbandry. Dams would be built in areas where the cattle traditionally graze when water is present, to lessen cattle impact on the park in the dry season.

His idea of private houses, bush homes for those who prefer to holiday in the bush rather than at the beach, is unique. He would oversee first the building and then the maintenance and care of the houses, providing staff and guides. A guide school is part of the overall plan, thus increasing the involvement of the local community in tourism.

To own a house overlooking the Masai Mara, one of the most beautiful and abundant landscapes in the world, must appeal to anyone who aspires to 'have a farm in Africa', but without the hassle.

Calvin looking towards Olentoroto

Namibia has a landscape as old as time; a spectacular desert of dusty-brown,
rocky mountains streaked with hues of purple, pink and gold, surrounded by shifting sand
dunes ranging from white to rusty red. The treacherous, icy sea thunders onto the beaches that are
extensions of the desert controlling the climate for at least fifty kilometres inland.

Namibia has a landscape as old as time; a spectacular desert of dusty-brown, rocky mountains streaked with hues of purple, pink and gold, surrounded by shifting sand dunes ranging from white to rusty red. It is as if the forests and the grasslands have been peeled away to expose the bare bones of Africa, making the great upheavals that took place when the earth was formed look as fresh and clear as if it had all happened yesterday. The Namib Desert stretches the entire length of the coastal area from Angola to South Africa and inland for about one hundred and fifty kilometres. This is the most beautiful and interesting part of Namibia; the names themselves evoke a sense of excitement: Damaraland, Kaokoveld, Sossusvlei, the Omaruru, Khumib and Hoanib rivers and, of course, the Skeleton Coast.

Once called the Kaokoveld Coast, it was renamed when so many shipwrecks and bones, animal and human, were found strewn on the shore. The treacherous, icy sea thunders onto the beaches that are extensions of the desert and home to thousands of Cape fur seals. Each night the cold air above the Atlantic Ocean (kept this way by the Benguela Current from the Antarctic) meets the hot inland air, creating a fog that creeps over the land, sometimes as far as fifty kilometres inland, bringing life-giving moisture for the desert creatures.

The fact that such a variety of wildlife lives in this arid area is extraordinary and makes the Namib unique, as no other desert of this size carries anything like the number of animals that survive here. There are desert-adapted elephants, which never destroy their source of food, oryx and springbok, ostrich, Black-backed jackal, Spotted hyena, lion and giraffe. Certainly they are nearly all found in very small numbers outside Etosha National Park, but with only two perennial rivers in Namibia, situated at either end of the country, it is remarkable that they manage to find enough to eat and drink at all, especially considering how much water elephants need. Hidden in nooks and crannies are a surprising number of little oases formed from freshwater springs, and some of the rivers retain water from rainstorms for quite a long time, but the elephants have had to learn to use less.

The solitude and sense of peace one feels in this landscape is beyond compare. The breathtaking beauty of the colours and sculptured shapes of the sand dunes never cease to please or surprise. If you scoop a little sand from a pink-flushed dune and look at it through a magnifying glass (binoculars the wrong way work as well) you will think you are holding a cluster of diamonds and rubies rather than particles of garnet and quartz. It is my theory that the extraordinary glowing quality of the light is caused by the reflection from the myriad particles of sand, allowing even the novice photographer to produce spectacular pictures. The sharply outlined red dunes and rocky mountains against cobalt-blue skies; the spectacular vistas punctuated occasionally by a pair of finely etched oryx on golden sand, also help!

It all looks untouched, with no sign of human interference, and the care that is taken to keep parts of the Namib Desert in pristine condition is admirable. There are large, well-managed national parks and programmes for reintroducing Black rhino, terribly depleted by poaching, into their old Kaokoveld habitat. Etosha, the best known of all the parks, has permanent waterholes, insuring a greater abundance of animals. A whole day spent at one of them will, without a doubt, give anyone exceptionally rewarding game-viewing.

The guides in this part of Africa have extended their knowledge to include geology and desert habitats. Some are real experts, who raise the experience you have in this magnificent country to the highest level, such as Jan and Susie van de Reep at Huab Lodge, Chris Bakkes with Wilderness Safaris and the Schoeman family.

BERTUS AND ANDRÉ SCHOEMAN

Sitting on the bank of the Kunene River, which marks the border between Namibia and Angola, we picked garnets out of the rocks with our fingernails as we listened, enthralled, to André's tale of the coastal elephants. A small herd had lived peacefully by the edge of the sea prior to the Angolan war, when they disappeared.

André's plan to return elephants to the mouth of the Kunene was to fly them to the coast suspended from a specially constructed mega-microlight. The Schoeman family have operated in Namibia for twenty-five years and are highly respected for their innovative ideas regarding the care and protection of this splendid land known as the Kaokoveld.

This was the last morning of our fascinating journey with André that had begun four days earlier with a dawn flight from Windhoek to the legendary orange dunes of Sossusvlei. As we flew south, the scattered farmsteads near the town were soon left behind and the seemingly empty land rolled away into the distant haze. One of the most unexpected aspects of Namibia is the kaleidoscope of earth colours: beneath us the straw-coloured grass growing on silver sand turned, as if by the stroke of a paintbrush, to pale ochre on deep red earth as a series of hills came into view. The landscape was dotted with clumps of dark-green trees and 'fairy circles' – large, perfectly round areas of bare earth, rimmed with thick tufts of grass.

We climbed the orange dunes of Sossusvlei before flying over them for nearly an hour – a rolling sea of rusty red dunes which gave way to the newer, creamy dunes of the coast, where we landed on firm gravel next to a beach for our picnic lunch. The ruin of an abandoned prospector's house stood in the sand nearby. What must once have been a shed had disintegrated, leaving the rusty chassis of a 1920s' truck proudly facing the elements since being abandoned many decades ago.

The sculptured backbone of a whale lay amongst lesser bones of seals scattered on the beach and a little family of jackals who had made their den in the foundations of the old house were very startled by our arrival.

We walked on many beaches on the Namibian coast next to the icy, roaring sea, watching the Cape fur seals surf and dive through the waves with grace and ease. This Skeleton Coast shoreline is littered with not only a variety of bones but also the flotsam and jetsam of countless shipwrecks, victims of the treacherous

A flush of green grass after a rare rain storm

201

Bertus Schoeman

André Schoeman

Lunch on the wing with André

Benguela Current. For centuries the strong cross-currents, high winds, fog and shifting sand banks have been a nightmare for the navigators of sailing ships and once grounded, they had little chance of survival in the barren dunes and blistering heat.

How blissful it would have been for shipwrecked sailors had they only had André or Bertus to guide them to freshwater springs not far inland! The Schoemans know of these springs, ancient sources of water that create tiny pools hidden in folds of granite that were once used by the Strandlopers* or San people. When the Schoemans find a pool they then explore all the areas nearby to collect more information on the San. Their explorations have led them to hidden caves, sometimes containing rock paintings. This sort of information has been collated by the Schoemans for many years, so it is wonderful to travel with them and to learn all the geological and historical details that they so happily share with their guests.

At first glance, what seems a barren desert in reality hums with life. Every morning the fog rolls off the icy sea onto the hot dry land bringing life-giving moisture to the lizards, geckos, gerbils and snakes that inhabit it. One could spend days just studying the differences in desert creatures' methods of drinking; sidewinder adders lick the droplets off their bodies, while little Tenebrionid beetles obtain moisture by standing on their heads, allowing the condensation to run down their legs and bodies into their mouths.

Under the expert guidance of André or Bertus eyes are opened onto a world undreamed of. Their knowledge fires the imagination and fills one with awe. There are rocks so ancient that they formed the landscape of Gondwanaland, well before South America split from Africa. Unimaginable upheavals caused what was once the muddy bed of a lake to stand up vertically, stretching hundreds of feet up into the air, the ripples still clearly visible on the surface. The flight over the Ugab River Valley revealed the incredible rock formations on the summits, mile upon mile of furrows undulating neatly into the distance as if scraped by bulldozers. We stopped in far-flung places where only God and the Schoemans can see a landing strip, exploring wild coastal areas or remote rocky valleys. A timescale of two thousand million years is hard to grasp, but it was an astounding geography lesson. As Bertus brought the formation of the earth to life, the layers of time became clearly visible and especially exciting.

We had seen animals that manage to eke out a living by finding nourishment in dry grasses and detritus known as 'desert meusli' that is blown in on the east wind and caught on scrub and dry twigs. Gemsbok (oryx), springbok and ostrich all manage on very little water, but most extraordinary are the desert elephants, picking and choosing branches of trees along a dry river

204   * literally 'beachwalkers' or 'beachcombers': ancient peoples who lived on whatever they could find on the shore.

bed; having learned to preserve their food source, they never push them over as they do where trees are abundant in other parts of Africa.

During our safari, André was involved in a community problem at Purros that directly related to the community involvement in conservation. The Himba, a traditionally nomadic tribe are gradually becoming settled in certain areas for extended periods. Their children have to go to school as directed by law. That, and the influx of tourism, has altered some Himba's struggle for survival. They still live and dress traditionally, but their diet has changed. They now eat maize meal sold to them by travelling traders, along with sugar and other modern delights such as Coca-Cola. Money, unknown in the past, has become a requirement. The week before we arrived two male lions, living in the vicinity of Purros on the edge of the Skeleton Coast Park, had killed the Himba's only bull (having already killed seven cows), so they were understandably irate. The natural inclination of the Himba was to track down and kill the lions. André was due at a meeting a few days later when this issue was to be discussed. Our little group had visited the Himba settlement that morning, spending money on some of the craft items they had for sale, such as baskets, beads, carved palm nuts and other items they make themselves. Although we had not spent very much money in our terms, it was nevertheless enough for them to buy at least two more bulls if they wished. André was there to discuss this point with them: if the wildlife is all killed, then what incentive do the overseas visitors have in coming into the area? In this way, they are being encouraged to protect and understand the value of their wildlife, but old habits die hard. The animals in the Skeleton Coast have been greatly depleted. Twenty-five

years ago lion tracks were commonplace on the beaches. The final outcome to this crisis was that André replaced the bull with one from his farm and made an agreement with the tribe that they graze their cattle away from the lion's territory.

Our journey had brought us to the Kunene River, a wide green expanse of water flowing swiftly to the Atlantic Ocean between rocky banks and the desert beyond, a marvellous sight in this thirsty land. The Himba people on both sides of the river water their cattle here. Baboons scamper on the rocky cliff faces and some of the largest crocodiles on earth bask in the sun or lie in the shallow waters by the bank. While quenching our thirst with fruit juice and looking for garnets we sat listening to André make plans for the future. We were all deeply sad that in an hour or two we would be flying home.

The Schoeman family have had some rough times, but their stoicism and hard work has seen them through. Bertus, André, Leon, Marie and Henk Schoeman – their ages range from mid-thirties to mid-forties – are all involved in the operation of Skeleton Coast Safaris, the company their father Louw started in 1977. André and Bertus are the two brothers that I know; Henk has now obtained his commercial pilot's licence and now joins his brothers on some of the safaris. Their beautiful sister, Marie, was until recently in charge of the marketing and Bertus's wife, Helga, a pilot and guide, accompanies her husband on many of his safaris and has been influential in their development.

When I first visited Namibia, probably in common with many others, I had very little or no interest in geology. However, after a four-day trip on a fly-in safari with Bertus or André in northwest Namibia you will come away electrified by the splendour of the creation of our planet. For it is here you can really see the bones of the earth, untouched by humanity. Due to the stable weather pattern and lack of water over a large proportion of this country, the crops, settlements and forests that hide these bare bones on most of the rest of the earth's surface have here been unable to grow.

The Skeleton Coast Park was created in 1971; Louw Schoeman had been instrumental in helping create it and in 1977, safari companies were asked to apply for a licence to operate in the park; only one was to be granted the concession.

Only one applied – Louw Schoeman. He had explored the area intensively when prospecting as a young man and had realised the potential it had to thrill and fascinate. His competitors were much amused at his application, thinking he had lost his marbles. They were mistaken, as Louw gave his clients undreamed-of excitement and adventure in a new and pristine environment for sixteen years. On safari with Louw, grown men whooped with joy as they slid down the roaring dunes, marvelling at the white prehistoric 'castles' in a narrow canyon at Hoarusib (only ten thousand years old, these castles are towering structures of solidified sand that look as if they were dripped from a giant's tablespoon). They rode on the roofs of the Land Rovers swooping up and down the steep dunes; they collected agates and tried to grasp the age of *Welwitshchia mirabilis* (prehistoric, low-growing plants that look like aloes but are related to the pine tree, and some of them are over 1 000 years old). And in the evening they settled under the *Omumborumbonga* tree with a long cool beer, watching a tame genet scamper along the branches whilst peering down at the visitors with great curiosity. Louw would tell them the *Omumborumbonga* is a leadwood tree, sacred to the Herero tribe who believe it is their ancestor; one of so many snippets of information in Louw's desert treasure-chest.

The world soon realised that Louw had an area quite unique. Human nature being as it is, it became much coveted. However, every five years he had to re-apply to be re-granted the concession. Other operators for a time held off out of respect for what he was doing, but after fifteen years the government decided to alter the way the concession was handled. While the ministers were planning their new strategy he was granted the concession for just one year. The following year it was granted for ten years (1993 to 2003) to the only other applicant, Olympia Reizen, a German company with no known track record of tourist activities in Namibia. It broke Louw's heart. They had not complied with the requirement that the applicant should have extensive knowledge of the Namib, the park and adjoining areas; he felt it would cease to be managed in the careful manner that is required for such a fragile and delicate environment. He decided to take the case to court, but unfortunately died of a heart attack before the case was heard. In the end the Namibian cabinet granted the concession to Olympia Reizen. Skeleton Coast Safaris' application to operate in other parts of the park was turned down. This is well documented in Amy Schoeman's book *Skeleton Coast*, published by Southern Book Publishers (Pty) Ltd.

It was a very sad ending for a man who had a unique vision to put Namibia on the world tourist map.

Once Olympia Reizen had the concession, unfounded rumours flew around as to what they were going 'to do'; one such rumour was that they were going to build an enormous hotel, another that they were going to use it

Himba woman

The road from Kunene Camp unusually carpeted in flowers

for the disposal of nuclear waste! In fact, nothing happened; the area was virtually unvisited, with little revenue for the Namibian government. Needing to find another source of income from the park, it then allowed Wilderness Safaris to operate under the Olympia Reizen licence. Wilderness Safaris is a company with a strong ethical and ecological culture and the result has been a beautiful camp, successfully bringing the park's wonders to many visitors.

Louw's sons took up the challenge to keep their operation going. Although they no longer had access to some of the unusual sites inside the Skeleton Coast National Park, the places they visit are all spectacular and deeply interesting. One of their prime areas is Purros, where they have, as Louw had before them, worked very closely with the community. Olympia Reizen had tried to get that concession too, with generous proposals to the local community. The tribe had a three-day *indaba* (meeting) over the issue. Their conclusion was that they considered Louw their father; now that he had died, the boys were orphans and it was not in their culture to abandon their children. Today, the Schoemans work in a successful partnership with the local community in Purros.

André and Bertus reveal the beauty and the secrets of the Namib to us so skilfully because they have lived with it all their lives. Their knowledge and expertise started when they played as toddlers on the remote, desolate beaches of the Kaokoveld Coast. Their father had prospected the area long before any tourist had ever heard of it. Louw started out as an attorney and one of his clients had mineral rights in the desert. He became a director of his client's company and finally left law to prospect and seek his fortune in Namibia's mineral-rich ground, looking for precious and semi-precious stones. While prospecting along the coast he marvelled at the mystical beauty of the land and gradually altered his focus of interest. A couple working for Louw's company lived in a hut at Cape Frio doing research; they took their leave for a month in December and Louw decided to move his family into their hut for their Christmas break. Bertus, the eldest, remembers his first plane ride at the age of six, when they went to inspect the hut and meet the researchers.

The family spent every Christmas holiday after that in the researchers' hut until the centre closed down when Bertus was fifteen. The research station was originally based at Cape Frio but later moved to Möwe Bay. While Louw explored this empty and wild environment, the children played. Wearing their cowboy outfits they played cowboys and crooks in the dunes. They were submariners in the boiler of the *Dunedin Star* wreck when it washed up on the beach looking exactly like a submarine; cricket and rounders were played with palm-nuts and wreckage debris; and the old derelict mine and its equipment were perfect for *Star Wars*. Their favourite game of all, though, was aquaplaning behind the Land Rover. A long rope was attached from the car to a piece of wreckage, the children taking it in turns to hold onto the wreckage and skimming over the waves while being pulled behind the Land Rover as it raced around the bay. Most of the wreckage on the beach was the remains of a wooden sailing ship and while digging around they came upon broken pieces of blue and white china. This was identified in England through the museum in Windhoek as Kerman porcelain, an imitation of Chinese porcelain used on sailing ships around 1665. Later on, as the boys grew older, they helped their father with his work.

Marie's early memories are of endlessly cleaning fish at Rocky Point and going on expeditions to collect drinking water at Orupembe, a day's drive there and back from Cape Frio.

Their mother was passionate about collecting interesting stones and Marie recalls helping her find exquisite examples for her collection.

Maureen, Louw's first wife and mother to all five children, died in 1979 and is buried close to the old Sarusas Camp in the Skeleton Coast Park. Louw married Amy Cosburn a year later and she was instrumental in helping Louw set up his business. Amy is extremely knowledgeable about the area and, as I have already mentioned, wrote a definitive book on the Skeleton Coast and illustrated it with her own excellent photographs.

The children, naturally instilled with deep knowledge of this special area, never really wanted to go away from it, but higher education had to happen. Before leaving for university, Bertus spent a year helping his father, who had become more interested in showing people the Namib and exploring the possibility of building a travel business within the Skeleton Coast Park than in prospecting. He had created a camp in the abandoned Sarusas mine buildings, which is where Bertus lived while waiting for his father to fly in with guests. Bertus had not yet obtained his pilot's licence, but of course he could drive, as all the

Schoeman children had been driving since they could reach the pedals. When the first group of guests – eight women from South Africa – arrived, Louw took four of them in one Land Rover and the teenage Bertus took the others. So began a most impressive career.

Both Bertus and André went to Stellenbosch University in South Africa, Bertus to read Geology and André to take a degree in Business Administration and Marketing. André's entrance to university was postponed for seven years while he flew for the South African Air Force. He started out in jet fighters, but later transferred to helicopters, becoming involved in search-and-rescue operations in Angola during the Namibian war. Bertus says he had wonderful teachers. Those teachers were equally lucky in their pupil, not just for his eagerness to learn but also for his access to some of the most interesting geological features in the world. The whole class visited the Skeleton Coast for one of their field trips.

Louw created his first campsite, inland on the Khumib River near the Sarusas Fountain, a freshwater spring. The

Helga and Bertus

Khumib is a mostly dry riverbed, but occasionally it floods dramatically when heavy rains occur inland. This is where the *Omumborumbonga* tree is situated. It is not a large tree by most standards, but impressive to find in a desert. With its spreading, gnarled branches it made a perfect spot for Louw to set up his bar.

Finding that the drive to and from Khumib Camp and Cape Frio made for rather a long day, Louw set up a delightful beach camp in order to visit the coast, the wrecks and the seals. The beds were in snug little wooden huts nestling in the dunes. On the beach, facing the sea, stood a gaily striped mess-tent, from which one could watch the sun setting over the crashing waves. Dinner entertainment included pretty little ginger gerbils, residents of the dunes, hopping about the floor looking for crumbs. The camp had a dreamlike quality; being lulled to sleep, warm and cosy in a wooden hut by the roaring ocean, it was easy to picture those early sailing ships dipping and rolling as they struggled in the swirling spray.

The Schoemans set up a third camp in the park and, lastly, a camp outside the park, on the Kunene River bordering Angola. With these four camps they had the perfect format for showing their guests the intricate ecology of this intriguing area. Although their camps are no longer within the park boundaries they are all in appealing places. However, very little time is spent in camp, as everyone is far too busy exploring the surroundings. Sometimes it is an effort to get people back into the planes to make camp before dark! Each morning brings excited anticipation of what wonders will unfold that day as one is greeted with the smiling face of Bertus or André calling "knock, knock" outside your tent with a piping hot cup of tea or coffee. Few people are quite as knowledgeable as these sons of Louw; their enthusiasm, sense of adventure and continuing awe in their surroundings is infectious and, I have to say, addictive.

Both Bertus and André give their guests a memorable safari; but each is different in character. André is jolly and easy-going with a quick smile, rosy cheeks and twinkling eyes above his bushy moustache. He instantly sweeps you up in the magnitude of the landscape with his great energy and enthusiasm. He has been married for quite a while and has a bevy of children. He farms in his spare time!

Bertus, though one is always aware of his passion for the area, is a quieter, more reticent man; never ruffled, and the one with the greater geological knowledge. The more his guests show interest, the more he opens up

with fascinating insights. Bertus married much later than André, to Helga who is now part of the team. An extovert, she sparkles with fun and laughter as her enthusastic comments fill the air waves making her a perfect balance with Bertus on larger safaris where two planes are required. They clearly adore each other.

In fact, flying with the Schoemans is one of the most exhilarating parts of the safari. When they fly very low, sometimes between towering granite walls, you feel you can almost touch the tufts of grass beneath you as you watch a startled springbok darting off. The pilot of a Boeing 747 once remarked that they were flying at the height he normally sat at when taxiing down the runway.

View of Angola from the Kunene River Camp

At other times they fly higher up in order for their guests to appreciate the immensity of this ancient landscape with its intricate network of craters, mountains and dunes spread out beneath. They are both superb pilots. André became the South African champion for precision and rally flying while at university, and was sent to England for an international competition at Sywell in Northamptonshire, where he came fourth out of one hundred and fifty competitors.

Being on a Skeleton Coast safari is an exhilarating experience for the whole family. Sliding down dunes, exploring caves, examining skeletal remains of whales and seals, hoping to find a human bone here and there, and picking up semi-precious stones are experiences way beyond the wildest dreams of most children. But the thrill of it all is allowing them to sit up front in the plane, being shown how it flies and being given the chance to hold the dual controls for a moment to get the understanding of how it works, heady stuff for anyone! Even adults can be lucky enough to be included in this experience. Flying from the coast to Etosha I sat next to Bertus, who showed me how to hold the plane steady while quite high up in the air. Watching the horizon and the wings was very exciting, but best of all, he helped me to bring it down to circle the lodge near the strip where we were to land and disembark. Concentrating with all my might, I thought I was doing quite well, when he quietly said,

"Susie, if you don't pull back on the controls we will hit the ground!"

I abruptly yanked back the control column and in doing so discovered why so many people love to fly. The plane banked steeply upwards, my stomach and soul soaring. It was one of the most unexpectedly rapturous feelings I had ever had. Bertus then took over (no doubt he had been in control all the time) and with my hands on the dual controls I could then feel the plane landing and, frankly, it took about twenty-four hours for me to come back to earth. However, I am sure the two ashen-faced Belgians in the seats behind us were very relieved to see the back of me.

The Schoemans' fame has spread the world over and their visitors' book must read like a Who's Who of the western world. But in the early days their holidays were not always very well sold, probably because most travel agents hadn't done their research and had no idea how it all worked. André remembers their first group of Italian guests, neither spoke a word of each other's language and the visitors did not quite understand how the day would unfold:

"At breakfast, I watched bemused as all the food on the table disappeared into little rucksacks that they donned before stepping into the vehicles. Obviously worried as to when the next meal would come they were taking precautions against hunger. The first time I stopped to show them something they all alighted and immediately took off in different directions returning after about an hour. Oh well, I thought, if this is what they want to do, I will just have to let them. The same thing happened the next time that I stopped the vehicle. This time they skidded down the steep banks of a ravine and as I sat on the top watching them, I could see a large gemsbok coming round the bend, clearly on a mission to get through the ravine. He caught sight of the group of humans

About to descend

and stopped, he must have been escaping a predator, for he certainly did not want to go back. As he circled uncertainly the Italians suddenly saw him, for a few seconds they stood looking at one another then the antelope lowered his head shaking his massive horns from side to side in a threatening manner and walked forward. Startled, they shinned up the rocky cliff as fast as their legs could carry them, never again leaving the vehicle on their own. They settled down after that and having devised a method of communication, started to learn about the interesting features of the area and ended up having an extremely happy safari."

Leon, who has an uncanny likeness to Louw, takes care of the multitude of vintage Land Rovers that they use, building and rebuilding these wonderful workhorses. The new computerised variety would not last five minutes in this environment, nor could they be rebuilt on the spot. Astonishingly, they just leave these vehicles dotted about the desert, standing next to an almost invisible airstrip, keys in the ignition, ready for the next arrivals. However, it is so empty and remote, there is no one there to steal anything.

Bertus enjoys nothing more than exploring unknown places, where no man has trod before. His excited anticipation as to what he might find is contagious and the thrill his guests get out of actually going where no one else has ever been spurs him on.

André still longs to get elephants back on the beach at the mouth of the Kunene. The twelve elephants that once frequented the area often crossed the river into Angola; André, when patrolling the border during the Namibian war would herd them back with his helicopter, afraid they would somehow get caught in crossfire. In 1992 these twelve elephants disappeared completely. One cow and her calf joined the Hoarusib elephants near Purros and one died of wounds inflicted by AK-47 bullets. The other nine just went missing. Louw and Sir John Aspinall, the millionaire who ran a private zoo in England and used the profits from his casinos to protect wild animals, had often speculated on how to relocate elephants back into the area once stability returned. John Aspinall was a good friend of the Schoemans and had been very involved in the protection of the desert elephants and it was he who designed the mega-microlight aircraft that would have the capabilities to transport an elephant; he and Louw both felt it was perfectly feasible if the elephant were sedated and flown in at night. In spite of the support that, with the death of John Aspinall, has now sadly disappeared, André would still dearly love to see it happen, and maybe one day his wish will come true. He and his youngest brother Henk recently went on a trip to Angola where he spotted elephant dung and tracks from the air in Angola's Iona Park, which links with the Skeleton Coast Park. They are planning to go and get samples for DNA testing to see if by any chance they are the original Kunene elephants.

André takes one or two riding safaris each year, sleeping under the stars and exploring dry riverbeds that run down to the sea. These safaris provide access to hidden places that can be reached in no other way. It is also possible to travel with André or Bertus for ten days or more, discovering Namibia from the South African border and into the Iona National Park in Angola. There they explore marine fossil beds, a hidden oasis behind a huge rock arch which is home to flamingos and a multitude of exotic

Seals surrounding a wreck on the Skeleton Coast

birds. A visit to the Baia dos Tigres (Bay of Tigers) reveals dune cliffs the colour of tiger stripes and inland *Welwitschia mirabilis* twice the size of those in Namibia. (There can however be problems obtaining visas for Angola.) Both brothers continue to explore new areas, creating fresh excitement as they alter their safaris. No two are ever quite the same – a compelling reason to return again and again.

INTO THE FUTURE

What began many years ago as a wild and daring adventure
has become a serious profession with a deep understanding
of its responsibility for the protection of the environment.
Its professionalism and understanding must go on if there is to
be a future for safaris and wildlife in Africa.

Hope and opportunity

I write here of my own personal hopes and wishes for the timeless beauty of the African bush, its animals and its people. My feelings and thoughts come simply from observation and chats over the years around many campfires.

Safari guides are anything but 'devil-may-care' people, but they do have a tremendous sense of fun and adventure that liberates their guests, dispels their inhibitions and induces joy from the world around them. They cannot reproduce a magnificent wildlife television programme, but what they do give has far greater personal value – the excitement of observing animal behaviour in the wild, learning to recognise a leopard's grunt in the night or identifying a bird the second time you hear it. Overcoming fear, shedding material worries, thinking laterally about the universe and creation, all these things can be a life-changing experience. They produce this with expert knowledge, courage, excellent organisational skills, a strong sense of theatre and a controlled temperament. In the course of interviewing the guides I have included in this book, the future of safaris and the Africa we all know and love often crops up in discussions. Most of them are tremendously optimistic, especially the younger and more recently trained guides, but a nagging worry lingers for the future of the wildlife and wilderness areas that have given many people so much pleasure.

The word is spreading that specialist guides give their guests a remarkable experience. They create a market of return clients unparalleled in most other long-haul holiday destinations. A safari can open a multitude of windows on the world, with intriguing views never dreamed of, but the visitor needs to be led in the right direction. There is plenty of fun to be had, along with drama and pathos, tenderness and terror unfolding in the wild every day, if only one can take the time to sit still and observe with an expert.

There is a world-wide realisation that something must be done to protect and preserve these precious wilderness areas. The people optimistic about the future are those on the ground in Africa, trying to do something about it. In my experience, those that shrug their shoulders and say, "Africa is doomed" are most likely to be sitting around a dinner table in England. Perhaps one day they too will change their attitude. Often we seem to be on a path of destruction, but this has been noticed, and there are some very dedicated people trying to help. Isn't it imperative to make an effort for future generations?

These days many more young men and women are training to become guides, and guides of all races should be welcomed. It is heartening to note the huge increase in interest among the indigenous people of the popular safari countries in becoming guides. This is of paramount importance, not only because their livelihood is so often intermingled with game reserves and conservation areas but also because they are the people to whom their governments will listen when they put forward the case for the protection of their natural heritage. It is more difficult for white guides, however many generations of forefathers they have in Africa, to gain the same attention. I firmly believe, however, that there should always be a place for good guides, whatever their nationality or colour; passion and knowledge should be the priority.

The Buffalo-thorn

I once had an experience that graphically illustrates the need for local culture to be explained by the people who know it best: I arrived at a lodge in South Africa in time for the evening game drive. There were five of us – a couple who had already had two nights at the lodge and two other tour operators who had arrived with me. Our guide, a jolly Zulu called Zacharias, had been looking after this couple and it was their last evening. They had not seen any elephants during their visit and were desperate to do so; Zacharias set out determined to find them. After about an hour his radio crackled and another guide contacted him to say he had located a small family of elephants, resulting in the two of them talking a great deal on their radios. It was dark by the time we caught up with the second car and the herd had disappeared into a thicket. The second vehicle was positioned behind the thicket on the other side of the elephants, and between them they tried moving the elephants out of the thicket, flashing their spotlights on the animals who were frightened and trumpeting angrily. It was appalling behaviour, but at least the guests did get a glimpse of elephants before their departure.

The following morning the three of us met over a cup of coffee and set off on our game drive with little confidence; but we had a surprise in store. We had driven with Zacharias for about an hour, birding and enjoying the early morning light, when he stopped by a Buffalo-thorn tree (*Ziziphus mucronata*). This tree has supernatural qualities, both religious and medicinal, and has vicious double thorns that hook inwards and outwards causing great difficulty if you happen to get caught on them. We settled ourselves under the thorn tree, our backs warmed by the rising sun, gazing on the green hills fading to purple in the distant haze. Zacharias spoke of the importance of the Buffalo-thorn, illustrating it with the story of his father's death and his mother's grief.

His father, who had been working on the mines outside Johannesburg for some time, had got into trouble over money. This led to a drunken brawl outside a bar, a knife was pulled and his father fell in the street, fatally wounded. When this sad news came back to the family his mother was inconsolable, heartbroken that she had been unable to bury him in his homeland. Zacharias had never visited Johannesburg, but decided he would take the train and go there in order to help his mother in her misery. Before leaving he broke a branch off the Buffalo-thorn, wrapped it in a sturdy cloth and set off for the nearest station. With the branch cradled on his lap, he sat up all night on a wooden bench in a crowded third-class carriage. On arrival in Johannesburg he faced another long journey, this time in a bus, to the mine. From the records of his father's death he managed to find the bar and the exact spot where his father had died. It was here that Zacharias unwrapped his Buffalo-thorn branch and carefully laid it on the ground, saying a prayer to his ancestors. In this way his father's restless spirit was caught on the thorns, which he rewrapped and carried back on the train to his home. His mother, overjoyed, buried the branch that held the spirit of her husband next to her house, where he now rests in peace.

The amaZulu are great storytellers, they spin them out with colourful embellishments. This was no exception and we were all enchanted, as it was so gently and beautifully told. I wouldn't for all the world have missed that morning, gaining an understanding of Zulu beliefs and customs told with such sensitivity by a man who had shown scant sensitivity towards the elephants the night before. Better training on game drives is all that is required to instil respect for the wildlife.

Rural people and animals are traditionally linked together in the wilderness, where they have lived in harmony for thousands of years. Today, with the dramatic increase in human population, the conflict is all too obvious. The pressure on land is relentless and unless they see another source of income those dazzling plains might be teeming, not with wild animals, but with combine harvesters. Can we not find a way to empower the people most affected to protect their heritage and to gain from it?

Guides are of great importance in the grand scheme of things; the better trained and more widespread they are, the more enlightened the world will become. Many intelligent, forward-thinking safari guides all over East and southern Africa are working towards this goal. A safari is an excellent contact between the wilderness and visitors from the outside world; opening their eyes to the splendours of the wild and making them conscious of the need for conservation.

What are the answers?

It is vital that wilderness areas throughout the world, and especially in Africa, are not destroyed, as they have been in so many other parts of the world, by greed and ignorance. There is most definitely an increased awareness of conservation worldwide; ten years ago Chicago would not have dimmed its lights for migrating birds in the spring and the autumn. Today it does. Prior to the skyscrapers of Chicago participating in this programme, birds migrating at night navigating by the stars and the moon would become disoriented by the lights of the tall buildings, dying in their hundreds as they flew into the plate glass windows. This is only one example of many acts of public awareness and concern for the natural rhythms of nature.

Huge areas of contiguous land are required to preserve the wilderness. The larger the area the less 'management' is required; nature manages far more efficiently than man ever has; man tends to blunder in and destroy the very thing he thinks he is preserving. I think the most sinister idea that has crept into environmental management in recent years is the concept of 'sustainable utilisation of land', in other words, in order to survive, it must make money; this often means meddling with nature and most assuredly, killing.

Elephants are a prime example; Map Ives has noted in his monitoring of the Chobe elephant population that they have a key role in natural environmental management. Their particular brand of 'farming' is clear in Botswana, where they systematically crop the mopane forests. Acres of trees are broken down to about five or six feet (two metres) in height while clumps of tall seed-bearing trees are left standing as the seedpods are a gourmet delight for elephants, and this in turn assures re-generation. In the dry season, these stark black stumps look most forlorn in the gray dusty landscape, however, come the first rains when they burst into leaf, the baby elephants that have been suckling during the dry months reach the fresh green leaves with ease. In an ever-changing landscape they share this nourishing crop with browsing antelopes, thus opening up areas to species that have been hard pushed to survive in them in the past.

There is a move afoot to cull elephants in Botswana. If this happens it could mean a serious setback for tourism in a country which has been seen as having the most responsible and successful government in Africa, and whose second-most important industry is tourism. I can't see how the plan can possibly help the elephants, although what do you do if there are 'too many elephants'? Then again, how would you know? I fear it could mean reaping profit from a 'natural' resource: skin, meat and ivory. Elephant culling is often promoted by those with their own agenda and with little understanding of the immense contribution the elephants make to the bush. Elephants have a complex social structure, which has already been discussed in this book, and one of the most important factors for elephants is their matriarchal memory. The drought in Botswana in 2003 was devastating in Savuti and Chobe, an habitual north-eastern range for elephants. There was such a shortage of water that some elephant families were walking to the Okavango Delta to drink. Travelling through the night when it was cool and resting during the heat of the day it took them three days to get to the water. Even though the weak and vulnerable were dying the families that knew where to go were the ones with matriarchal memory from the last drought. One of the babies from each family on the latest journeys to the Delta will in time become a matriarch herself. It will be her memory that will lead her family to the water during a future drought. It may be forty years on, but the memory will never fade. Culling could shatter this eternal gift; even though the plan is to wipe out whole families, it is a difficult and cruel process.

Both Map Ives and Michael Lorentz have spent many years observing the structure and pattern of elephant families and the dependence upon them of the animals and environment in which they live. Their knowledge is considerable and it is a subject on which both could speak for many hours, and the following is their combined view:

"As Africa's human population expands, its natural habitat and biodiversity become ever more pressured, with human conflict the inevitable result. As habitat shrinks, many 'keynote species' such as elephant, that function naturally as ecological engineers, are deemed the villains and not the victims of habitat destruction. The result is a heating up of the 'culling debate' once again.

"In addition to the purely ecological argument, it is also necessary to take heed of the social and emotional impact that culling has on the elephant population. Elephants are highly complex, sentient beings with a lifespan similar to our own. Their society is structured around a tightly knit family unit with the accumulated wisdom of the matriarch and her sisterhood of elders being the fabric that weaves the lives of the herd together. They are animals who, like the great apes, whales and dolphins, share a high degree of emotional intelligence with us. All of those who have worked closely with elephants will testify to this deep intelligence and family bonding. It is obvious that mass slaughter of members of this society will have an enormous and traumatic effect on the population as a whole.

"With the jury still out on the environmental imperative to cull, and in light of the unacceptable social and emotional impact, would it be anything less than morally irresponsible to advocate culling?"

Hand in hand

Ultimately the animal numbers must be allowed to recover after the devastation inflicted on them by our ancestors over the last one hundred and fifty years. Trophy hunting is still common throughout Africa, but there is hope that it will one day be banned completely. Botswana has one of the most responsible wildlife policies in Africa and has recently banned lion hunting due to lack of control, a depleted gene pool and an increase in bribery and corruption. Unfortunately, powerful foreign politicians and hunters – who should know better – try to put pressure on the Botswana government to lift the ban. On the other hand Botswana has recently lifted its moratorium on elephant hunting

and regular visitors to Botswana will have noticed that the gentle giants they used to see are often now aggressive and nervous. This is clearly an impact of renewed hunting pressure. With luck, trophy hunting will die out with the older generation. Intelligent younger people do not appear to have quite the same macho need to kill.

Like so much in this day and age of fast food and instant gratification, old-fashioned hunting ethics are definitely hard to find. There are of course a notable handful of ethical professional hunters, Ivan Carter being one of them, who still strive to hunt in such a way as to cause minimum impact and who reinvest the proceeds in conservation. However, there are few hunters who want to stalk their quarry for three or four weeks as they used to. Minimum effort, maximum impact and back on a flight home is more the norm these days.

As an example, in 2002 in Tanzania, twenty thousand hunting licences were issued to residents alone. Each licence represents one animal to which many more would have been added. A lot of extra killing is done under the 'legal' banner. It is not uncommon for a licence to kill one leopard in a particular area and in another used to kill many more. In addition there are the licences issued to foreign hunters. How long can the animals survive?

The counter-argument in Tanzania is that vast tracts of land have been saved from farming development because of hunting, though most likely the tsetse fly (Africa's saviour) alone would remain a deterrent to human habitation. One day, I am sure, Tanzania will open up these areas for photographic safaris, benefiting local communities with jobs in the tourism industry – with the income being used for schools and clinics. Hunting often means wealth beyond belief for a tiny minority; non-consuming tourism means a richer life for all.

Of course local people have traditionally killed many animals to feed their families – but with expanding populations this too has an impact. I once visited the farm of Richard Peek in the Matobo Hills of Zimbabwe. He farmed eland commercially. Eland are large, heavy antelopes that produce excellent meat and, being natural to the African habitat, unlike cattle, they do not destroy the land. His farm was a paradise of lush pastures so unlike the surrounding areas of *dongas* and thorn scrub caused by overgrazing of cattle and goats. Would it not be possible for innovative farmers all over Africa to copy this idea? Although nature provides significant climatic changes, bad land management can speed up the process; for example the Romans' five-hundred-year occupation of North Africa significantly helped wipe out the fertile land that existed before their empire spread from Europe. Things moved more slowly then, and unless something is done, and quickly, it will take far less than five hundred years to destroy the remaining wilderness areas today. The true value to our planet is to allow large tracts of land to remain unmolested by man for the generations to come – they should not have to justify themselves financially. Our forefathers did not truly understand this, but we do, and it is up to all of us to protect our planet and halt the mindless destruction that is so prevalent. Are we capable of doing this?

Partnerships

Plans for private concessions in Kenya are being set up with increased momentum. Ian Craig of Lewa Downs has initiated extremely successful community projects on the Laikipia Plateau, in which tourist lodges are built, owned and run by the Laikipiak Maasai. Ian and the Maasai elders have put in safeguards to make sure the funds are correctly managed, something that was lacking in an earlier experiment. Il Ngwesi was the first of the new projects and winner of many awards, including the Equator Initiative Award from the United Nations Development Fund. Tassia, the newest lodge, is on Lekurruki, also part of the Il Ngwesi group ranch.

Namunyak Wildlife Conservation Trust, a Samburu project in an equally beautiful area near the Matthews Range north of Lewa, has been Ian's mission since the early 1990s. With funding from his Norwegian friend Halvor Alstrup he employed anti-poaching personnel and, once the poaching was under control, the Trust was set up, the lodge built and vehicles provided. Ian and Piers Bastard, two of Ker and Downey's senior guides, have forged a partnership that will give security to the project. Ker and Downey have made a fifteen-year commitment to bring their guests to the lodge in exchange for the exclusive right to do so.

These large regions known as group ranches have ensured a substantial amount of land for the regeneration of wildlife – sorely needed after decades of poaching. Ian estimates that, with the animals' normal birthrate, and sound management of cattle and finances, it will take about twenty years to complete.

The Honourable Francis Ole Kaparo, Speaker of the Kenya National Assembly, has been closely involved throughout the development of the community initiatives, working alongside Tusk Trust that has been instrumental in much of the funding.

Partnerships with local people are on the increase, especially in Botswana, South Africa and Zimbabwe, a vital condition for the continuation of safari businesses. Countless intelligent and forward-thinking people are beginning to realise how quickly the wilderness is disappearing and how precarious are many of the most beautiful and seemingly timeless environments. They create or join conservation projects, often helping with isolated pockets of wildlife or wilderness areas where there is a particular problem. Of course, every little bit helps, but the noblest vision of all is the Peace Parks Foundation, started in South Africa by Anton Rupert.

Transfrontier or Peace Parks

Although fraught with political obstacles, the idea is to link national parks through as much of Africa as possible, in what will be known as 'Transfrontier Conservation Areas' or, more commonly, 'Peace Parks'. Ancient corridors will be reopened, along which the animals will be safe to migrate, to breed and thrive with no encroachment from farming or hunting. It's a grand and ambitious idea, which needs to be supported by all conservation groups and governments. And it need not just be national parks, but could include private concessions, such as the group ranches in Kenya, which could surely link up without losing their own identity and personal incomes?

The first and most successful project so far is the Kgalagadi Transfrontier Park, which straddles the borders of South Africa and Botswana. The second is the removal of the fencing on the Mozambican border of the Kruger Park, linking it with the Limpopo National Park. Together with Gonarezhou in Zimbabwe and four areas that adjoin these great parks, a vast expanse of land, to be known as the Great Limpopo Transfrontier Park, will

be created. In a country such as war-ravaged Mozambique this involves far more than just removing fences. Not only do many species need to be reintroduced into the areas where poaching by soldiers decimated the wildlife, but rangers must be trained to care for the park and, most importantly, the local people must be taught the benefits of protecting the animals. The Peace Parks Foundation will be in charge of the difficult job of administering these requirements.

Thirdly, work is being done on a most ambitious project called the Four Corners Park. This is the area where four countries meet at Kazungula on the Chobe River – Namibia, Botswana, Zambia and Zimbabwe. The land under review encompasses Hwange National Park, the Victoria Falls National Park, Kazuma Pan National Park and Matetsi Safari Area in Zimbabwe; the Kafue National Park in Zambia; the land from Chobe to the Okavango Delta in northern Botswana; and, eventually, the Kaudom National Park in Namibia on Botswana's western border and the creation of a new park in the eastern Caprivi. The plan is eventually to include south-eastern Angola once the land is made safe from landmines. This is the traditional migration route for elephants and, when it is once again open, should relieve population pressure on the land in northern Botswana.

This is an immense piece of land and a very ambitious plan, being worked on tirelessly by dedicated people. All five countries have signed an agreement to allow preliminary studies. Such a vast area will have a massive impact on the economies of all five countries, with local people benefiting greatly from job creation and the influx of foreign exchange. It will mean some sacrifices, as villages and farms will have to be moved, but the benefit to wildlife and communities will be immeasurable.

Map Ives believes he will see this happen in his lifetime! He also dreams of Botswana being linked with Kenya, and is sure it will happen, though probably not in his lifetime. The creation of Peace Parks is a bold and grand plan – it has to be, in order to work. Is it not possible for mankind to rise to nobility in the 21st century and rescue the last remaining wilderness areas from destruction?

Guide training all over East and southern Africa is becoming increasingly popular as the demanding public become more aware of what it wants from a safari. Short courses also exist for people not involved in the tourist industry, but who wish to gain more understanding of the natural world.

What began many years ago as a wild and daring adventure has become a serious profession with a deep understanding of its responsibility for the protection of the environment. Its professionalism and understanding must continue if there is to be a future for safaris and wildlife in Africa.

ONX AND HOWARD

These two young men epitomise the future. Exceptional safari guides from vastly different backgrounds, they share the passion and drive to protect the wildlife for which they both care so deeply, by becoming actively involved in programmes to educate both the indigenous people and the more sophisticated western visitors they meet. They have independent spirits and a sense of joy in all that surrounds them in their chosen vocation – both crucial to the success of a safari guide.

Onkgaotse Manga (Onx)

Known as Onx, was born in Maun, on the edge of the Okavango Delta, in 1975. He grew up and went to school in this bustling little town, whose main purpose was to service the safari industry. His introduction to the spectacular beauty of the Delta was on short visits with his mother to see his father, who worked for the Tsetse Fly Control Department, whenever they were working within easy distance of Maun. The seed was sown, and he knew he had to be involved with wildlife, but was uncertain of which direction to take.

Onkgaotse Manga

His early passion found expression in starting a wildlife club at school. Through the local Wildlife Department he arranged for guest lecturers to come to the school and the club members in turn volunteered their time at weekends to clean up Lechwe Park, a small wildlife park outside Maun belonging to the Maun Wildlife School.

Knowing he wanted to work with nature in some capacity and having completed his Cambridge O' levels he discussed his options with his father, who suggested he join an anti-poaching unit. However, he had rather mixed feelings about hunting; although he abhorred trophy hunting he nevertheless understood that a man with a hungry family might have to kill for the pot, so this was something he did not relish getting involved in. Another option was guiding, which had far greater appeal. He enrolled at the Wildlife School near Maun, where he discovered that the knowledge he had already gained, from the wildlife club and from devouring all the books he could find on the subject, far outstripped most of the other students; for example he knew the local and botanical names of all the trees before he joined. He was their star pupil.

On completion of the course he joined the Desert and Delta Safari Company for his apprenticeship and was based at Savuti Safari Lodge – the old Lloyd's Camp, renamed when it was acquired by Desert and Delta. While in Savuti, and together with the camp manger, he tested his theory of 'elephant pruning' in the mopane forests exactly as Map Ives had recently done. He loves pointing this out to visitors as it indicates yet again the clear evidence of animal intelligence.

Desert and Delta would have liked him to stay when his apprenticeship was completed but he felt he would still be considered an apprentice, and decided to move on when Orient Express Safaris offered him a job. Now their top guide, he travels between the three camps, Khwai River Lodge, Savute Elephant Camp and Eagle Island Lodge (Xaxaba), entertaining and educating their guests.

His serious, dedicated side is ever present, and his mentor has been Pete Hancock, an ex-lecturer at the Wildlife School and a member of Endangered Wildlife Trust (EWT). Pete left the school to work as an independent nature consultant for community development and the lodges, but was quickly approached by Endangered Species to become co-ordinator of Birdlife Botswana – part of EWT. Knowing that Onx would be interested, Pete enrolled him to assist in the Crane Project. His initiation was to participate in a workshop in the Kafue Park in Zambia, organised by a very experienced South African group. At the end of this he became a full working member whose task is to monitor Wattled cranes in the Khwai area of the Moremi National Park. Each day he is up before dawn to take his guests on their game drive, returning to camp for brunch. Once his guests are happily surveying the world from the hammocks on their tent decks, he is out again taking GPS co-ordinates of new nest sites and recording the behaviour of the birds and the troubles they face. These reports go via Pete Hancock to the EWT. Cranes do have huge problems. There are four pairs in the Khwai area but only one chick has hatched in four years of monitoring. One of the common causes of breeding failure is predation of the eggs, particularly by pythons. But another serious cause is the threatened habitat. Onx has a key role in community awareness, spending time educating the communities, particularly in the Jao Flats and Xaxaba areas. He talks to the *mekoro* polers and guides individually, making them understand the importance of the cranes in the eco-system and engaging them to help in their preservation. Until this project began, no one realised the importance of not burning the grass during May to August when they breed. Slowly he is getting the message through.

Onx is truly fulfilled in his role as guide and protector:

"I don't consider this a job, it is a lifestyle. As long as I love it I will always do it. I don't see myself happy doing anything else. I believe as long as there are people like Pete Hancock there is hope. If I had to sacrifice my job I would definitely teach in the remote community areas to open the minds of the young. If I could, I would take off three months to do full-time monitoring and educating. If I could do that I would make sure they would never burn again at the wrong time of year, but always in November, just before the rains when it can really benefit the grazing for livestock and not destroy the nests of the cranes. As it is I am volunteering to go to Namibia for Save the Rhino Trust during my next leave. Again this involves community education and will extend my knowledge. I love doing voluntary work, I see it as a way of giving something back to Nature. After all, I have had so much."

Howard Saunders

Howie is an Australian who visited East Africa at the age of seventeen on a safari with his parents. Completely enthralled by all he saw he went home vowing that he would make his life Africa. Born in Sydney in 1972, he grew up with his time divided between life in the city and his parent's farm north of Sydney. All their holidays were geared to outdoor activities and these, together with the time he spent on the farm created his love of the bush. He would catch snakes with his father, learn the names of the birds and sleep out under the stars. His parents knew he would enjoy Africa when they took him on safari and how right they were. On his return he taught himself to speak fluent Swahili and read everything he could on East Africa. At university he did a business course that included International Relations, specifically on developing countries, and returned to Kenya the moment he finished university in 1994, at the age of twenty-one. On his arrival back in Nairobi he found his Swahili was too pure to be understood in Kenya. It would have been fine in Tanzania or Zanzibar, but the Kenyans use a slightly different version, which he soon picked up.

Soon after his arrival he was offered an apprenticeship with a company called Natural Selection owned by a New Zealander, who probably felt a kinship with a fellow antipodean. They focused on mountain gorillas, taking four-wheel-drive safaris through northern Tanzania to Lake Victoria and into Uganda's south-western corner, home of the mountain gorillas. He learned about the management of mobile-tented safaris and, after the first one, took the safaris himself. Later he acquired his own vehicle and freelanced until 1999, when he was invited to join Ker and Downey, the old and highly respected safari company. A year and half after joining he became the first Australian to be invited to be a full partner. Ker and Downey have a mentorship programme, where new young guides are attached to older, experienced ones. Howard's mentor was Alan Earnshaw, the chairman of the company. Under Alan he learned how they liked

Howard with orphaned gorilla – Uganda

safaris to be run, how to do the marketing and about the vital aspects of conservation.

Being on safari and in remote wilderness areas is when Howard is at his happiest, but he takes conservation very seriously. He is a member of the Kenya Professional Safari Guides Association and a Director of Campfire Conservation in Kenya. He is involved in educating the Maasai elders who run the Masai Mara, helping them to look forward and to understand the importance of independent revenue collection, vital for the benefit of the whole community, not just a few individuals. Many Maasai see farming as an alternative source of revenue, as up to now they have had few benefits from tourism – a situation that has to change. The revenue from the Masai

Mara National Park is worth approximately US$8 million, a very substantial sum of money, and should deter them from mechanised farming. The collection and distribution of the money, along with independent management, is the subject of an ongoing project in which Howard is involved, as well as helping Ron Beaton and Jackson Looseyia with the Koyaki Guide School. He is delighted that Ker and Downey have a partnership in Namunyak and takes as many of guests as possible to visit the park. Everyone realises the importance of involvement in community projects that protect wilderness areas for safari visitors.

However, some of his most exciting moments have been in Uganda, where the Ugandans welcome people to their country to help with their budding safari industry. He is currently working on a programme to train Ugandan safari guides and takes as many safaris to that country as he can. It is not only about gorillas and chimpanzees. There is a multitude of exciting places to visit and sights to see in this beautiful country, as I discovered when travelling with him on a visit to Uganda and Rwanda.

Howard is engaged to Steffie Dloniak, an American scientist who has spent the last three years studying hyenas in Kenya and is about to embark on an ambitious project to study the lion population as a whole in the Masai Mara. Their joint contribution to the wildlife experience is exceptional.

Howard is thrilled that his dream has come true – that he is working, laughing, playing and living in East Africa as he dreamt he would when he was seventeen. He puts his heart and soul into all he does and feels a special responsibility for the future:

"To be involved in securing a future for the great charismatic creatures of the East African wilderness is surely to conserve far more than just the animals themselves. It will enable future generations to experience those sights, which have been part of the human visage since our ancestors first strode across the cradle of mankind. East Africa is the home of much of the story of how humans evolved, from the great apes of the rainforests to those evocative savannahs lined with flat-topped acacia trees. Conserving this environment should be a matter of pride and deep importance to all those who have ever visited. Having been moved to follow a life out here in this wilderness, I believe it is crucial that we, the younger generation of

professional safari guides, become the ambassadors for this unique resource. It is up to us to pass on the treasures of Africa to others around the world in a way that inspires them to see the value of what we have here."

I believe that Howard speaks for all the young professional guides in both East and southern Africa. Onx and Howard are so alike, brothers under the skin. Together they give us faith that there is goodness, strength and the will to battle against the odds to do the right thing to the best of their ability.

ACKNOWLEDGEMENTS

I am indebted to so many people for their help in producing this book and my deepest thanks go to all who encouraged and believed I could do it. Firstly, I thank my daughter Jessica Hoffman for her sensitive and superb portraits of the twelve guides profiled. I greatly admire her ability to make each of these active men sit still for four hours while she created not only an excellent likeness but also the essence of their personalities.

I am eternally grateful to all the guides who opened up their hearts and put their trust in me relating their life stories. I have done my utmost to do them justice. Ralph Bousfield, Michael Lorentz, Garth Thompson, Benson Siyawareva, Ivan Carter, Robin Pope, Nigel Perks, Ron Beaton, Saigilu Ole Looseyia (Jackson), Calvin Cottar and the Schoeman brothers, Bertus and André. A special thanks goes to Garth Thompson for getting me started and for being so certain I was capable of writing a book.

My thanks to Yvonne Short and Tony Adams who spent hours relating stories of the early days at Londolozi, (many unrepeatable) and of course to three special guides who were there in their youth and are still great forces in the safari industry today, Mike Myers, Lex Hes and Map Ives. They too, trusted me with their personal stories.

I thank Mothupi Morutha for his enthralling life story, told so freely and candidly and hope he continues for a long time to fascinate safari visitors with his tales around the campfire.

My thanks also go to Grant Cummings, Rod Tether and John Coppinger, three superb safari guides who run their own camps in Zambia. Grateful thanks go to Onkgaotse Manga, known as Onx, and Howard Saunders, both of whom have impressed me with their outlook and positive vision for the future.

Enormous thanks go to all who have facilitated my visits to Africa starting with the excellent travel arrangements of Charlie Harper and his team, particularly Louisa Verney at Cazenove and Loyd Safaris. In Africa my thanks go to Catherine Raphaely of Uncharted Africa, Chris Flatt of Bush Homes, Wilderness Safaris, with a special thanks to Colin Bell for all his help since 1988, Orient Express, Gibbs Farm Safaris, Skeleton Coast Safaris, Jo Pope of Robin Pope Safaris, CCAfrica, Cottar's Safaris, Bushmad Safaris, Passage to Africa, Elephant Back Safaris, Aadge Geertesma at Ndutu Lodge and Peter Sandenberg of Okavango Tours and Safaris.

I would also like to thank all those who have shared with me some of their own experiences on safari, in particular Jan Astell, Trina McMullen, Fiona Ramsay and Carolyn Elwes. Thanks also go to Louise Cottar for her fascinating insight into working with the United Nations Feeding Scheme in Somalia.

I thank Henrietta Loyd for years of support; we entered the safari travel business together, our special friendship is forged by shared experiences and filled with understanding and memories. Thanks go to David and Nicky Rattray for their constant encouragement and invaluable advice, and my Washington based friend Tamara Lloyd for her skilful editing help while on a visit to England.

A special thanks to the team at Jacana. They have done a superb job especially Chris Cocks, Kerrin Cocks and Shawn Paikin. I am deeply indebted to Val Thomas who was the first to read my finished manuscript, believed in it, and introduced me to Jacana.

My family have been truly supportive, particularly my sister Jessica Craig who teaches English in New Zealand, correcting my grammar by e-mail. Last but never least is my beloved husband Dick and children Dominic and Olivia who have supported and encouraged me every step of the way. They have read the stories, always with good grace, commented and given positive criticism.

But it is the guides who are the heroes and I thank them all from the bottom of my heart for the joy they have given me and for opening my mind and eyes while exploring so many remote and beautiful corners of Africa.

The photographs that were given to me for inclusion are:

- Mike Myers and Tutan Sithole taken by Mike on a time release, page 24
- Lex Hes and pet parrot Spike: provided by Lex Hes, page 25
- Mike Myers in genet skin: Lex Hes, page 27
- Map Ives conditioning safari hat: Catha Nix, page 28
- Lex Hes – 'the Mother' leopard, page 31
- Robin and Jo Pope: Simon Cousins, page 125
- Grant Cummings at Chiawa: Francois d'Elbeé, page 134
- Ken Beaton with the then Princess Elizabeth: provided by Ron Beaton, page 169
- Howard Saunders: Stephanie Dloniak, page 226

May many follow in their footprints.

*If anyone wishes to donate to the community projects
in East Africa, please visit www.tusk.org for details.*